best of the best
cook's essentials®
cookbook

best of the best
cook's essentials®
cookbook

Gwen McKee
and
Bob Warden

QUAIL RIDGE PRESS
Preserving America's Food Heritage

Library of Congress Cataloging-in-Publication Data

McKee, Gwen.
   Best of the best Cook's Essentials cookbook / Gwen McKee and Bob Warden
     p. cm.
   Includes index.
   ISBN-13: 978-1-893062-92-4
   ISBN-10: 1-893062-92-9
   1. Cookery. I. Warden, Bob. II. Title.
   TX714.M3838 2006
    641.5--dc22   2006010690

All cooks essentials® product images are courtesy of QVC®.
Photos courtesy of Gwen McKee, Barbara Moseley, and Bob Warden.
Illustrated by Kent Whitaker. Design by Cynthia Clark. Printed in Canada.

First edition

QUAIL RIDGE PRESS
P. O. Box 123 • Brandon, MS 39043
e-mail: info@quailridge.com • www.quailridge.com

Contents

Gwen's preface

I don't remember the first time I met Bob Warden, because it seems at QVC, we have always been side by side . . . one of us on air, the other waiting to go on, sharing a taste, a hug, always checking out each other's newest product. Truly Bob has introduced many wonderful cook's essentials products over the years . . . my kitchen is full of them. I am an avid fan, realizing the durability, dependability, and easy clean-up that helps me to prepare recipes efficiently and successfully.

Bob and I have a lot in common in that we are perfectionists, take pride in what we do, and share a sincere desire to bring to the QVC audience the very best we are capable of, feeling that if someone gets our product, they will be happy they did. We both feel that the preparing of good food is an art form that should have delicious rewards. Anybody can do it with good tools and a little guidance—namely good cookware and dependable cookbooks. So, though we had mentioned it to each other on numerous occasions, the day came when we both knew it was time to put the best cookware and the best recipes in the same pot! The marriage of BEST OF THE BEST and cook's essentials just seemed a natural.

Gwen and Barbara take time to smell the daffodils outside Studio Park.

Like Bob, I am surrounded by capable, talented people, who are truly good cooks. Most significant among these is my best friend and partner, Barbara Moseley, who has literally been around the country with me searching for great recipes for 24 years! Our assistant Terresa Ray adeptly edits, organizes, and puts everything in its proper place. We have a great tester/ taster team, the captain of which is Melinda Burnham, who gets so excited about testing recipes! Sheila Simmons, Holly Hardy, Dana Walker, Cyndi Clark, and Lisa Flynt are also official testers and tasters, with numerous other family members and friends added to the mix. But unlike Bob's team, none of us are chefs. We are home cooks who strive to make recipes so friendly and easy to understand, that anybody in any home kitchen can make a delicious dish every time. The chef on my team is my food stylist at QVC, Bobbi Cappelli, who, along with her daughter, Holli, makes our dishes come to life for the camera. I sincerely thank everyone who shared their best recipes and best efforts in helping to make this fun project come to life.

Whether you are whipping up a quick supper, planning a party, or creating a special dinner, we hope this book will enhance the process, and that you will enjoy this collaborative *Best of the Best Cook's Essentials Cookbook* as much as we have enjoyed bringing it to you.

Always my best,
Gwen McKee

Bob's preface

One of the first times I was on air with cook's essentials, I watched Gwen McKee showing one of her BEST OF THE BEST cookbooks. I was invited to be one of the tasters, and I was blown away by how good all of the recipes tasted. Gwen gave me a copy of the book and every recipe was simple and easy. From that moment on I knew that if cook's essentials became successful, I wanted to do a *Best of the Best Cook's Essentials Cookbook* with Gwen and Barbara. As the idea evolved over the years, we decided that this book should be more than just a great recipe book from Gwen and Bob. We wanted to include the "best of the best" from the entire cook's essentials on-air team.

Meredith Laurence of Technique contributed her professional bests and favorites. Jenny Repko, Carole Haffey, and Lisa Brady, recently added to the cook's essentials team, also contributed their favorite family recipes. Gwen and I both work with a great team of QVC food stylists—professional chefs—who do lots of work to make our food look great when we go on air. They also shared their personal favorite recipes in this book. Eric Theiss, who works tirelessly behind the scenes to make sure every cook's essentials product is of the highest quality and that it gets to QVC's warehouse on time, is also a professional chef who contributed some really great recipes.

Once we started work on the book, we knew that we wanted each and every recipe to be easy to prepare, and easy to select the best products to prepare them in. We designed a unique index (page 267) that helps you find recipes that use many of the cook's essentials products you may already have in your kitchen. In addition, every recipe has photos that suggest the best equipment to use in preparing the recipe. Simple . . . easy . . . the best recipes from the two teams . . . and the best cook's essentials products to prepare them with—that's the *Best of the Best Cook's Essentials Cookbook.*

We have had fun creating this book for you. We know you are going to enjoy using it as a resource for years to come.

Bob Warden

Introduction

This cookbook has several extra features designed especially for cook's essentials owners. Every recipe in this cookbook shows in the sidebar the cook's essentials products that we recommend for preparing the recipe. These recommendations are deliberately generic. For example, any 2- or 3-quart saucepan could be made of any fabrication—steel, hard anodized, etc. That is why we don't offer a specific item number. If we recommend a small electric appliance, for instance a blender or deep fryer, most any will work. Most often there are many other cook's essentials products that you could use just as easily as those shown in sidebars. Use our recommended products if you own them, or mix and match similar products that you may have in your kitchen. If you would like to order a specific cook's essentials product, go to www.qvc.com or call 1-800-345-1515.

Some recipes have editor's extras, provided by Gwen and Barbara. You will also find comments from Meredith and me in the sidebars. Both the editor's extras and the sidebar comments are given to provide the reader with extra information.

Bob Warden

beverages and appetizers

Achieve kitchen success as you easily blend your ingredients and mix up some tasty creations your family will crave. Blenders can be used for milkshakes and other drinks, as well as for chopping small amounts of foods such as bread crumbs and herbs, or making dips, soups, purées, and sauces.

electric
stockpot

OPTION:
tea kettle

Tupper's Famous
Spiced Tea

Tupper England is Quail Ridge Press' "Best" artist, and a dear friend. She is also a wonderful cook. Try her famous tea . . . it's great!

4 quarts water
6 regular tea bags
2 teaspoons whole cloves
2 cinnamon sticks

2 cups sugar
2 cups pineapple juice
¾ cup lemon juice

Bring water to a boil in an 8-quart electric stockpot. Turn to low end of SIMMER; add tea bags, cloves, and cinnamon sticks. Cover and steep 15 minutes. Remove bags, cloves, and cinnamon sticks with slotted spoon. Add remaining ingredients. Serves 20–24.

You may also let cool, then refrigerate, for serving at a later time. Reheat as needed. Freezes well, too.

Option: Boil water in a tea kettle; pour over tea bags and spices in stockpot. Proceed as above.

Yummy Pudding Smoothie

smoothie maker

3 cups milk
**1 (3-ounce) package
    chocolate instant pudding
    mix**

1½–2 cups vanilla ice cream
**Whipped cream or topping
    (optional)**

Pour milk in smoothie maker or blender; add pudding mix and blend 5 seconds. Add ice cream, and blend 30 seconds more. Serve immediately or refrigerate to serve later (may need to add a little more milk, as it will thicken). Add a dollop of whipped cream, if desired. Serves 4.

Peanut Butter Sandwich
Cookie Milk Shake

blender

Blender and smoothie maker are interchangeable for these two recipes.

Great after-school treat for the kids . . . and grown-ups, too.

**8 peanut butter sandwich
    cookies**
2 cups vanilla ice cream

1 cup milk
¼ cup chocolate syrup

Break cookies into small pieces; put into blender or smoothie maker. Add remaining ingredients; cover and blend one minute on high speed. Serves 4.

Baked Three-Cheese Artichoke Dip

1 small onion, quartered
1 clove garlic
1 (15-ounce) jar artichoke bruschetta spread, drained, or 1 (14-ounce) can marinated artichokes, well drained, finely chopped
1 cup grated Monterey Jack cheese
1 cup grated fresh Parmesan cheese
1 cup grated Cheddar cheese
1 cup mayonnaise
1 (7-ounce) can chopped black olives
1 teaspoon Greek seasoning
1 teaspoon Tabasco
1 tablespoon Worcestershire
1 round sourdough French bread

food processor

Chop onion and garlic in a food processor. Combine in a bowl with remaining ingredients, except bread. Cut slice off top of bread to make a "lid." Hollow out center of bread, leaving a 1-inch shell. Reserve bread pieces for dipping. Spoon dip into bread shell, then put "lid" back on bread; wrap in foil. Bake at 350° for 30–45 minutes.

Option: This can also be made without the bread. Bake in a 2-quart baking dish and serve with chips or Melba toast.

ALTERNATE:
mini food processor
Want to make a smaller amount? The mini food processor works great for halving this recipe.

OPTION:
stoneware baking dish

It all starts with an idea. Assistant buyer, Noelle Mayer, goes over new cookbook proposals with Gwen.

mixer

mini everyday
pans

Warm Crab and Artichoke Dip

Guests like this dip so much, you may want to double the recipe.

2 ounces cream cheese, room temperature
½ cup mayonnaise
Salt and pepper to taste
¾ cup (about 4 ounces) crabmeat, well drained
¼ cup plus 2 tablespoons grated Parmesan cheese, divided
3 tablespoons chopped, marinated artichoke hearts

2 tablespoons sliced green onion
2 tablespoons diced red bell pepper
2 tablespoons diced celery
1 tablespoon finely chopped fresh Italian parsley
1½ teaspoons sherry wine vinegar
½ teaspoon Tabasco
Toasted baguette slices

Preheat oven to 400°. Beat cream cheese in mixer until smooth. Add mayonnaise; beat until just blended. Season with salt and pepper. Using spatula, fold in crabmeat, ¼ cup Parmesan, artichoke hearts, green onion, bell pepper, celery, parsley, vinegar, and Tabasco.

Transfer crab mixture to mini everyday pans or soufflé dish. Top with remaining Parmesan. Bake until crab mixture is warm and cheese melts, about 15 minutes. Serve immediately with toasted baguette slices. Makes about 1½ cups.

Missy's Black Bean Party Dip

2 cups grated Cheddar
   cheese
2 cups grated Monterey Jack
   cheese, 1 cup reserved
1 (4-ounce) can chopped
   black olives, drained
1 (15-ounce) can white
   kernel corn, drained

1 (15-ounce) can black beans,
   drained
1 (10-ounce) can Ro-Tel
   tomatoes, drained
½ (8-ounce) jar salsa
1 cup sour cream

casserole

Combine all ingredients (except reserved cheese) in bowl; put into greased 3-quart casserole and heat 15 minutes at 350°, covered. Put reserved Monterey Jack cheese on top and heat another 15 minutes uncovered. Serve with Tostitos, corn chips, or anything crunchy. Fix a pitcher of margaritas and enjoy!

ALTERNATE:
stoneware
casseroles

Spinach Dip with Feta, Lemon, and Oregano

This dip can be made ahead and kept in the refrigerator for up to 24 hours.

1 (10-ounce) package frozen
   chopped spinach, thawed
   and squeezed dry
½ cup sour cream
½ cup mayonnaise
½ cup packed fresh parsley
   leaves
2 tablespoons chopped fresh
   oregano

½ cup crumbled feta cheese
1 tablespoon fresh lemon juice
1 teaspoon grated lemon zest
3 medium scallions, thinly
   sliced
¼ teaspoon Tabasco
Salt and pepper to taste

food processor

Combine all ingredients in a food processor until well combined. Transfer to a mixing bowl with lid and refrigerate until flavors have blended, at least 1 hour. Makes about 2½ cups. Good served with Pita Treats (page 22) or any crusty bread or chips.

Editor's Extra: It is critical that you squeeze as much moisture as possible from the thawed spinach. And if you substitute dry for fresh parsley and oregano, use ¼ as much.

mixing bowl

mixing bowl

OPTION:
kohaishu knife

Chopping ingredients with the kohaishu knife makes this a snap.

blender

ALTERNATE:
mini food processor

Hoagie Dip

My girlfriends love this. I actually get tired of always making it, but they all rant and rave if I don't bring it to our "girls night out" functions. —Jenny Repko

¼ **pound Genoa salami, chopped**
¼ **pound bologna, chopped**
¼ **pound capicola, chopped**
¼ **pound American cheese, cut into small pieces**
1 **onion, chopped**
1 **tomato, seeded and chopped**
½ **cup shredded lettuce**
Pepper to taste
2 **teaspoons Italian seasoning**
1 **cup mayonnaise**

Mix all ingredients in mixing bowl. Serve with slices of small party breads.

Editor's Extra: Capicola is a thinly sliced Italian lunch meat similar to ham or salami.

My Little Chickadee Dip

Even kids love this dip! And it's so good for them.

¼ **cup almonds**
1 **garlic clove**
1 **(16-ounce) can garbanzo beans (chickpeas), drained (reserve liquid)**
1 **tablespoon lemon juice**
1 **tablespoon olive oil**
2 **teaspoons cumin**
½ **teaspoon salt**
½ **teaspoon pepper**

Grind almonds in blender or food processor for 10 seconds. Add garlic and blend another 10 seconds. Add remaining ingredients and blend till smooth. Serve with Pita Treats (page 22) or anything crunchy.

Ranch Cheese Spread

We use this as an appetizer at our catering business. Our guests always rave about it and I love to share the recipe with them. —Jenny Repko

1 (8-ounce) package cream cheese, softened
½ cup mayonnaise
1 packet ranch salad dressing mix

½ cup milk
1 (8-ounce) package shredded Cheddar cheese

In mixer, beat cream cheese until smooth. Add mayonnaise, dressing mix, and milk. Beat on low speed. Scrape sides of bowl and beat in shredded Cheddar cheese. Refrigerate for several hours. Serve with crackers, bagel chips, pretzels, or veggie slices.

mixer

Pizzazzy Pimento Cheese

No matter what you spread this on—celery, carrots, peppers, crackers, chips, bread, toast—it's delicious!

⅔ cup mayonnaise
4 ounces cream cheese, softened
3 cloves garlic, minced
⅓ cup chopped fresh parsley
3 (8-ounce) packages shredded Cheddar Cheese

¾ cup slivered almonds, toasted, chopped
1 (4-ounce) jar diced pimentos with juice
2 teaspoons Worcestershire
Hot pepper to taste

In mixer, cream mayonnaise and cream cheese, or use bowl with whisk. Add remaining ingredients; mix well. Serve as a spread with crackers or on bread for sandwiches. Add more mayonnaise to use as a vegetable dip.

ALTERNATE:
mixing bowl

Use your mixer (or mixing bowl) for both of these recipes.

mixer

mixing bowl;
spatula

A Very Cheesy Cheese Ball

The method makes it easy; the variety of cheeses makes it tasty.

1 (8-ounce) package shredded extra sharp Cheddar cheese

1 (8-ounce) package cream cheese, softened

4 ounces blue cheese, crumbled

½ stick unsalted butter, softened

2 tablespoons minced onion

1 tablespoon Worcestershire

1½ teaspoons Tabasco

1 garlic clove, minced

Dash of pepper

Minced fresh parsley (optional)

Minced fresh chives (optional)

Finely chopped nuts (optional)

Mix all ingredients, except parsley, chives, and nuts until smooth, about 1 minute. Line a bowl with plastic wrap so that it overhangs the rim by at least 4 inches. Transfer cheese mixture to bowl with spatula, press overhanging plastic flush to the cheese, and refrigerate until firm, about 3 hours.

Remove cheese from bowl by gripping edges of plastic wrap. Gather edges of plastic wrap together and twist, shaping the cheese into a ball. Remove plastic wrap. Roll cheese in parsley and chives, or nuts; transfer to serving plate. Serve with crackers. Serves 15–20.

Lisa Brady, Bob Warden, and Meredith Laurence are the on-air cook's essentials guests who are always cookin' something good in the QVC kitchen.

Cheese and Pepperoni Pinwheels

This light, flaky hors d'oeuvre is simple to make—impressive and addictive.

½ cup grated Asiago cheese
¾ teaspoon dried thyme
¾ teaspoon dried oregano
¼ teaspoon ground black pepper
1 sheet frozen puff pastry, thawed

2 tablespoons honey-Dijon mustard, divided
24 pepperoni slices, divided
1 large egg, beaten

mixing bowl

cookie sheets

Mix cheese and spices in medium mixing bowl. Cut puff pastry crosswise in half to form 2 rectangles. Spread 1 tablespoon mustard over 1 rectangle, leaving 1-inch plain border at 1 long edge. Place 12 pepperoni slices in single layer on mustard. Top pepperoni with half the cheese mixture. Brush plain border with egg. Starting at side opposite plain border, roll up pastry, sealing at egg-coated edge. Transfer pastry roll, seam side down, to a baking sheet. Repeat with remaining pastry rectangle, mustard, pepperoni, cheese mixture, and egg. Chill rolls until firm, about 30 minutes, or wrap and chill up to 1 day.

Preheat oven to 400°. Cut each pastry roll into about 30 (¼-inch-thick) rounds, and place on cookie sheets. Bake until golden, about 15 minutes.

cookie sheet

mixing bowl

Cheesy Pepperoni Puffs

Nice for a luncheon with a green salad, or as a buffet hors d'oeuvre.

2 packages (6 each) puff
  pastry shells
1 (8-ounce) package cream
  cheese, softened
1 (8-ounce) container sour
  cream
1 envelope spring vegetable
  dip seasoning
1 teaspoon Italian seasoning
½ cup minced onion

2 (3.5-ounce) packages
  pepperoni, chopped
1 cup shredded mozzarella
½ cup minced red and/or
  yellow bell pepper
2 tablespoons honey mustard
⅔ cup shredded Cheddar
  cheese
3 provolone slices, halved

Remove pastry shells from package; bake on cookie sheet according to package instructions. Remove from oven, cool a bit, then remove puffed-up top of each shell; set aside.

In mixing bowl, mix cream cheese and sour cream with vegetable dip mix and Italian seasoning; stir in minced onion, pepperoni, mozzarella, and bell pepper. Brush inside of each shell with honey mustard. Fill each shell with pepperoni mixture, and replace pastry tops. Return to oven at 350° and bake 15 minutes. Remove from oven; top some puffs with shredded Cheddar and some with halved provolone slices. Return to oven for a few minutes, until cheese melts over tops of puffs. Makes 12.

Asparagus Cheese Puffs

½ cup milk
¼ cup water
3 tablespoons unsalted butter
¾ teaspoon salt
¼ teaspoon cayenne pepper
¼ teaspoon ground
   coriander

¾ cup all-purpose flour
3 large eggs
4 ounces asparagus, trimmed
½ cup coarsely grated
   Gruyère cheese (2 ounces)
¼ cup freshly grated
   Parmesan cheese

saucepan

Bring milk, water, butter, salt, cayenne, and coriander to a boil in medium saucepan. Reduce heat to low, and add flour all at once. Using a wooden spoon, beat mixture until it pulls away from the bottom and sides of pan, about 1 minute. Let cool 4 minutes.

Put dough in a food processor and pulse 5–6 times to break it up. Add eggs, 1 at a time, and process, scraping down the sides, until combined and dough is smooth and shiny. Let cool slightly.

food processor

Preheat oven to 400°. Lightly butter 2 baking sheets. In a medium saucepan of boiling salted water, blanch asparagus until just tender, 2 minutes. Drain and rinse under cold running water; drain again thoroughly, and pat dry. Coarsely chop asparagus.

Mix asparagus, Gruyère, and Parmesan into dough. Spoon rounded teaspoons of dough onto prepared baking sheets 1 inch apart. Smooth tops of each puff with a lightly moistened pastry brush.

baking sheets

Bake puffs, 1 sheet at a time, on middle oven rack about 25 minutes, or until deep golden brown. Serve immediately. Puffs can be made up to a month ahead and frozen. Re-warm in a 350° oven.

mixing bowl

baking sheets

You'll need a baking sheet for both recipes.

Crab Rounds

These were a real hit at the Quail Ridge Press Christmas party.

1 (6½-ounce) can lump
  crabmeat, drained
1 cup mayonnaise
6 drops Tabasco
½ cup diced onion

1 cup shredded Cheddar
  cheese
¼ teaspoon curry powder
Mini bagels

Stir together all ingredients except bagels in a bowl. Spoon onto bagel halves. Place bagels on nonstick baking sheet, and bake at 400° for 10–15 minutes.

Pita Treats

This is so simple and yummy, it's almost funny.

4 (8-inch) pita bread rounds
¼ cup olive oil

2 teaspoons kosher or sea salt

With your kitchen shears, split each pita round in half. Stack the halves and cut into 6 wedges. Spread wedges on 2 or more nonstick cookie sheets and brush tops with oil. Sprinkle with kosher or sea salt.

Place baking sheets in 350° oven, spacing sheets for even baking (a convection oven at 325° works great). Bake until wedges begin to crisp, about 6 minutes. Turn wedges over and continue to bake until fully toasted, about 6 more minutes. Cool before serving.

The chips keep well wrapped in plastic wrap or in a closed tin for up to 4 days. Serve with dip, soup, or just as they are.

Asian Dipping Sauce

¼ cup soy sauce
1 clove garlic, minced
1 tablespoon minced ginger
1 tablespoon peanut oil
2 tablespoons honey

1 tablespoon rice wine
vinegar, or champagne
vinegar
Pinch of chile flakes

Combine all ingredients in 1-quart saucepan. Heat to a simmer. Remove from heat; serve with pot stickers or other Asian appetizers.

saucepan

Sunny Honey Mustard

Great on sandwiches, on top of cheese and crackers, or as a dip.

1 cup mustard
½ cup honey

½ cup brown sugar
1 teaspoon Worcestershire

Mix all ingredients with a whisk in a small mixing bowl or blender. Jar and refrigerate. Makes 2 cups.

mixing bowl;
whisk

When you use the small bowl to mix, you can put the storage lid on and store in the fridge until you are ready to use.

ALTERNATE:
blender

If they're not surrounded by food, Barbara and Gwen love to be surrounded by cookbooks.

mixing bowl

electric skillet

casserole

ALTERNATE:
casserole
with trivet

Norwegian Meatballs

This is one of my favorite dishes from Aunt Norma's (the caterer) New Year's Eve smorgasbord, for which she was famous. The secret to the rich flavor and color of these meatballs is adequate browning. First you brown the meatballs well. Then you brown flour in butter to make the gravy. Take the time to make sure the flour changes color without burning. — Bob Warden

2 pounds ground beef
¼ pound ground pork
1 egg
Salt and pepper to taste
⅓ teaspoon mace
⅓ teaspoon ground ginger

2 slices bread
Butter or margarine
1 medium onion, sliced
  (optional)
⅓ cup flour
Salt and pepper to taste

Combine first 6 ingredients in mixing bowl. Remove and discard crusts from bread (makes lighter meatballs) and moisten lightly with water; tear in pieces. Add to meat mixture. Knead this mixture thoroughly with your hands 5–10 minutes. Wash hands and wet them with cold water; roll meat mixture into walnut-sized balls, or even smaller, if you like.

In electric skillet on medium heat, melt a small amount of butter or margarine. Add meatballs and onions, if desired, and brown them on all sides; cook in the drippings, adding more butter, if necessary, stirring frequently until meatballs are golden brown and onion is translucent. Remove with slotted spoon and distribute in 3-quart casserole dish.

Make a brown gravy by adding flour to butter remaining in pan. Cook, stirring, over low heat until flour has turned golden brown. Gradually pour in enough hot water to achieve desired consistency; stir until gravy is thick and smooth (scrape all browned particles from pan into gravy). Season with salt and pepper. Pour gravy over meatballs, cover, and bake in a 350° oven about 45 minutes.

Editor's Extra: This makes enough for a party. Easy to halve.

bread and breakfast

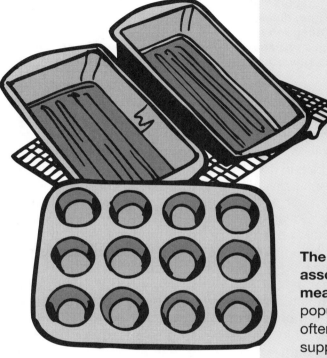

The dishes normally associated with morning meals have become so popular that they are often served for lunch and supper, too. When are omelets or pancakes or French toast not enjoyable? This chapter has recipes not just for rolls and cornbread, but sandwiches and frittatas and dressings, and even some compotes that go well with breakfast. Dive into morning food—it's good anytime!

saucepan

mixer

bundt pan

Orange Breakfast Bread

⅓ cup milk
½ cup butter or margarine
⅓ cup plus 1 tablespoon
  sugar, divided
½ teaspoon salt
1 package active dry yeast
¼ cup warm water

2 eggs
3½–4 cups all-purpose
  flour, divided
1½ cups ricotta cheese
½ cup orange marmalade
2 teaspoons orange peel

Combine milk, butter, ⅓ cup sugar, and salt in a small saucepan. Heat over low heat until butter melts and sugar dissolves. Cool to lukewarm. Dissolve yeast in warm water in mixer bowl. Add lukewarm milk mixture, eggs, and 2 cups flour. Mix with dough hook 2 minutes. Continue mixing while adding remaining flour, ½ cup at a time, until dough clings to hook and cleans sides of bowl. Knead 3–5 minutes longer, or until dough is smooth and elastic. Place in greased bowl, turning to grease top. Cover; let rise in warm place, free from draft, until doubled in bulk, about 1 hour.

Place ricotta cheese, orange marmalade, orange peel, and remaining 1 tablespoon sugar in clean mixer bowl. Mix 30 seconds.

Punch dough down. Roll into a 10x14-inch rectangle. Spread cheese mixture evenly over dough. Roll dough tightly from 10-inch side, pinching seams to seal. Pinch ends together to form a ring and place in a Bundt pan. Cover; let rise in a warm place, free from draft, until doubled in bulk, about 1 hour. Bake at 350° for 35–40 minutes. Remove from pan immediately and cool on wire rack.

Banana-Cranberry-Nut Bread

Cranberries add just the right amount of tartness, and nuts add just the right amount of crunch to this recipe.—Jeri Estok

6 whole ripe bananas
4 large eggs
1¼ cups oil
4 cups all-purpose flour
3 cups granulated sugar

1 teaspoon baking soda
1 teaspoon salt
1 cup chopped nuts (pecans or walnuts)
1 cup chopped cranberries

Grease 2 loaf pans and dust with sugar. Using a stand mixer, mix together bananas, eggs, and oil until bananas are completely liquefied. In separate bowl, combine flour, sugar, baking soda, and salt with a whisk. Add all dry ingredients to the mixer bowl, and mix just until completely blended. Fold in nuts and cranberries. Pour batter into prepared pans. Bake at 350° for 45–60 minutes or until toothpick comes out clean when inserted into the middle of bread. Turn out immediately onto cooling rack. Can be served immediately or frozen for later use.

loaf pans

mixer

Easy Pumpkin Bread

My mother's recipe . . . one that I make every fall. My son Jake loves this so much he bakes it at college and shares it with his roommates. Boy, has he gotten popular.—Jenny Repko

3⅓ cups flour, sifted
2 teaspoons baking soda
1½ teaspoons salt
1 teaspoon cinnamon
1 teaspoon nutmeg
3 cups sugar

1 cup oil
4 eggs
⅔ cup water
1 (16-ounce) can pumpkin
1 cup chopped nuts
1 cup raisins

Preheat oven to 350°. Sift dry ingredients into bowl. Make a well in center of dry ingredients. Add oil, eggs, water, and pumpkin. Mix just until smooth. Stir in nuts and raisins. Divide batter into 2 greased and floured 9x5-inch loaf pans. Bake 70 minutes, or until bread tests done. Cool.

Alternate Method: These make great muffins or mini muffins, too. Just bake 30 minutes or so for regular; 18 for mini muffins, or till done.

mixing bowl
You will love the nonskid feature of these mixing bowls.

loaf pans;
muffin pans

loaf pans

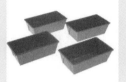

ALTERNATE:
mini loaf pans

Everyone will want to take a loaf home with them, so you might want to make these in the mini loaf pans.

mixing bowls

Cherry Eggnog Loaf

Who says you have to have traditional fruitcake for holidays? This pretty loaf takes the cake!

2½ cups all-purpose flour	**2 eggs, lightly beaten**
¾ cup sugar	**1 teaspoon vanilla**
1 tablespoon baking powder	**½ cup chopped walnuts**
½ teaspoon ground nutmeg	**½ cup coarsely chopped**
1¼ cups eggnog or	**candied red cherries**
half-and-half	**¼ cup chopped candied**
1 stick butter, melted and	**orange peel**
cooled	**½ cup chopped dates**

Preheat oven to 350°. Grease 2 (9x5-inch) loaf pans. Combine flour, sugar, baking powder, and nutmeg in large bowl. Stir eggnog, butter, eggs, and vanilla in medium bowl until well blended. Add eggnog mixture to flour mixture. Mix just until all ingredients are moistened. Stir in nuts, cherries, orange peel, and dates. Spoon into prepared pans.

Bake 40–45 minutes or until wooden toothpick inserted into center comes out clean. Cool in pans 15 minutes. Remove from pans and cool completely on wire rack. Store tightly wrapped in plastic wrap at room temperature.

Alternate Method: Shorten bake time to about 25 minutes (350° oven) if using mini loaf pans.

Barbara's grandsons, Bryce and Bailey, follow the recipe for making great muffins.

Always Ready Raisin Crunch Muffins

Healthy and tasty for breakfast or any time.

8 cups Raisin Bran Crunch cereal
¾ cup raisins
1¼ cups Splenda
5 cups flour
5 teaspoons baking soda
3 tablespoons wheat germ

1 packet Butter Buds
Egg substitute equivalent to 4 eggs
1 cup canola oil
1 quart skim milk, mixed with 3 tablespoons lemon juice

In a huge bowl, mix first 7 ingredients. In a separate bowl, mix remaining ingredients and pour over dry mixture. Store batter, covered, in refrigerator for up to 6 weeks.

For regular muffin pan, fill cups ⅔ full and bake at 375° for 16–18 minutes. For mini muffin pan, fill cups almost full, and bake at 350° for 14 minutes.

muffin pan
The muffin pan is used in both recipes.

Oatmeal Blueberry Muffins

Have these waiting for your overnight guests when they come in for breakfast. My daughter Heather did just that when she entertained our friends at her house. Marie and Judy are still "oohing" over those muffins.—Gwen McKee

½ cup butter, softened
1 cup sugar
2 eggs
1 cup mashed bananas
½ cup uncooked oats

1½ cups self-rising flour
1 teaspoon baking soda
½ cup chopped pecans
1 cup fresh blueberries

Cream butter; gradually add sugar, beating until light and fluffy. Add eggs, one at a time, beating well after each addition. Stir in mashed bananas. Combine oats, flour, and soda, stirring gently. Add to banana mixture. Fold in pecans and blueberries. Spoon batter into floured and greased regular muffin pans. Bake at 350° for 30 minutes. Makes 24 muffins.

mixer

toaster oven
broiler pan

toaster oven

Rolls in the Mornin'

Make-ahead easy . . . morning-coffee marvelous!

¼ cup chopped nuts
  (optional)
8 frozen dinner rolls
½ large package cook & serve
  (not instant) butterscotch
  pudding

¼ cup brown sugar
¼ teaspoon cinnamon
¼ cup butter, melted

Sprinkle nuts in bottom of toaster oven broiler pan. Place rolls on top of nuts. Sprinkle mixture of pudding, sugar, and cinnamon over rolls. Pour melted butter over all. Let sit on counter, uncovered, overnight.

The next morning, bake in toaster oven at 350° for 30 minutes. Invert onto platter. Enjoy!

Sticky Buns

These are so easy and so delicious. Better than store bought!

2 loaves bread dough, thawed
1 cup walnuts or pecans
  (optional)
1 cup dark or golden raisins
  (optional)
1 large package cook &
  serve vanilla pudding

¼ pound (1 stick) butter or
  margarine, melted
1 cup brown sugar
2 tablespoons milk
2 teaspoons cinnamon

baking pan

Grease a 9x13-inch baking pan. Sprinkle bottom of pan with nuts and raisins. Tear bread dough into walnut-size pieces. Place into pan in single layer. Beat remaining ingredients together and pour over dough. Cover with foil and refrigerate overnight.

Bake at 350° for 30–40 minutes, removing foil for the last 10 minutes to brown. Immediately flip onto plate and serve. Serves 8.

Editor's Extra: Got any leftovers? Take these with you for coffee break time at the office.

Almost Krispy Kremes

I remember my mom making these easy doughnuts for my sister and me when we came home from school. A treat worth passing on.—Melinda Burnham

2 (8-count) cans plain biscuits   Vegetable oil for fryer

Separate biscuit dough into individual biscuits. Poke a hole in center of each biscuit and stretch slightly. Drop into 375° oil and fry in electric deep fryer until golden brown. Drain on paper towels. Finish with either Glaze or Coating. Makes 16.

GLAZE:

⅓ cup powdered sugar   Water

Place sugar in mixing bowl; add enough water to make a slightly thick consistency. Dip doughnuts into Glaze and return to paper towels. Glaze will harden as doughnut cools.

COATING:

1 cup granulated sugar   1 tablespoon cinnamon

Mix sugar and cinnamon. Roll warm doughnuts in mixture and tap off excess.

electric deep fryer

ALTERNATE: snack fryer

A snack fryer is great for small batches.

mixing bowl

Gwen and Barbara get help from friend Judy Tyler in determining if the rolls are done. The aroma said—YES!

electric deep fryer

Deep fryers are one of the most popular items with the backstage crew at QVC. They jump on these French toast sticks faster than we can make them.—Meredith

mixing bowl

everyday pan

Deep-Fried French Toast Sticks

Another QVC deep fryer specialty. Here's a way to have French toast and cornflakes all at the same time!

Vegetable or peanut oil	1 tablespoon orange juice
3 eggs	concentrate
1 teaspoon cinnamon	2 cups cornflakes
1 teaspoon sugar	1 loaf Italian Bread
1/4 teaspoon salt	Maple syrup

Fill deep fryer with the appropriate amount of oil and preheat to 360°. Combine eggs, cinnamon, sugar, salt, and orange concentrate in a mixing bowl. In another bowl, crumble cornflakes. Cut bread into 1-inch slices, then into sticks about 1 inch wide. Dip bread sticks into egg mixture, then coat with cornflakes. Deep-fry coated bread sticks in hot oil 1–2 minutes, or until cornflakes are brown and crispy. Serve with maple syrup. Serves 8.

Apple Cinnamon French Toast

2 tablespoons butter, divided	French bread, sliced 1½
1/4 cup sugar, divided	inches thick
1 teaspoon cinnamon	5 eggs
1/4 teaspoon nutmeg	1 cup milk
2 apples, peeled, cored, and	1/2 teaspoon vanilla extract
sliced	

Melt 1 tablespoon butter over medium-high heat in 10-inch everyday pan. Add 2 tablespoons sugar, cinnamon, and nutmeg to the pan and mix well. Remove pan from heat and add apples, fanning them out in an attractive pattern. Place bread on top of apples, fitting the pieces together tightly.

Combine eggs, milk, remaining sugar, and vanilla; pour over bread. Let mixture rest 1–24 hours in the fridge.

Dot with remaining butter and bake in a 350° oven 1 hour. When ready to serve, invert French toast onto a plate so that apples are on top. Serves 8.

Baked Banana French Toast

This is so good, it will become a breakfast staple.

**French bread, cut into
  1½-inch cubes**
**2 bananas, sliced ½ inch
  thick**
½ cup currants
6 eggs

1½ cups milk
¼ cup maple syrup
2 teaspoons cinnamon
2 tablespoons sugar
6 tablespoons butter, cubed

sauté pan

Preheat oven to 375°. Arrange bread cubes tightly in a 500° oven-safe 10-inch sauté pan. Wedge banana pieces in among the bread cubes. Sprinkle currants on top. Combine eggs, milk, maple syrup, cinnamon, and sugar. Pour over bread and press slightly to help soak up egg mixture. Let pan sit 15 minutes.

Dot pan with butter, and bake in a 375° oven until everything is brown and slightly puffed, 35–45 minutes. Serves 4–6.

Editor's Extra: We love this so much that I have devised tasty alternatives: substitute raisins, cut dried fruit, or even chocolate-covered raisins for the currants. To halve the recipe, use 1 hoagie roll, cut into 1-inch pieces. Cook only 25–30 minutes. Serves 2–3.

electric deep
fryer

Apple Fritters

These are always a favorite at QVC. The only problem is that you have to wait for them to cool a little before digging in!

2 cups flour
1 tablespoon baking powder
½ cup sugar
1 tablespoon salt
2 eggs
1½ cups milk
2 tablespoons butter, melted

5 Granny Smith apples, peeled,
    cored, and cut into rings
    or wedges
1–3 quarts vegetable or
    peanut oil
Powdered sugar for dusting
Maple syrup (optional)

Combine flour, baking powder, sugar, salt, eggs, milk, and melted butter. Mix well. Let the batter rest at least 15 minutes.

Fill your deep fryer with the appropriate amount of oil and preheat to 375°. Dip apple rings or wedges into batter, and gently drop into hot oil. Deep-fry until fritters are golden brown and crispy. Drain on paper towels and dust with powdered sugar. Serve with maple syrup, if desired. Serves 6.

Editor's Extra: Don't soak the apple pieces in water, but be sure to cut them just before you need them. Otherwise the batter won't stick properly.

sauté pan

Breakfast Apple Pancake for Two

This is a fun breakfast for Barney and me, and sometimes the perfect thing for a light supper. Sometimes we like fresh lemon juice and powdered sugar on top. Yum!—Gwen McKee

2 tablespoons butter
2 eggs, or ⅔ cup egg
    substitute
⅓ cup milk
2 teaspoons sugar
¼ cup flour

½ teaspoon vanilla
1 tablespoon plus ¼ teaspoon
    brown sugar, divided
1 Granny Smith apple, peeled
    and thinly sliced
¼ teaspoon cinnamon

blender

Melt butter in 10-inch sauté pan (500° oven-safe) in 425° oven. Put eggs, milk, sugar, flour, and vanilla in blender, and mix for a minute. Take pan out of oven as soon as butter is melted and stir 1 tablespoon brown sugar into it. Place apple slices in butter. Sprinkle with cinnamon and remaining brown sugar. Pour blended mixture slowly over apples. Bake 18–20 minutes until puffed and browned. Good served with melon slices or grapes. Serves 2.

Banana, Raisin, and Oatmeal Pancakes

A nice healthy way to start the day. My kids love this one. I make a double batch and freeze some.—Jenny Repko

1 cup old-fashioned oats
1 cup all-purpose flour
¼ cup golden brown sugar, packed
1½ teaspoons baking powder
½ teaspoon baking soda
¼ teaspoon ground cinnamon
¾ cup plain yogurt

¾ cup whole milk
3 large eggs
½ teaspoon vanilla extract
2 ripe bananas, mashed, divided
1 cup raisins
½ stick unsalted butter, melted
Additional melted butter

skillet

ALTERNATE:
electric griddle

Whisk first 6 ingredients in medium bowl. Whisk yogurt, milk, eggs, and vanilla in another medium bowl to blend. Whisk dry ingredients into yogurt mixture just until blended. Fold in mashed bananas, raisins, and melted butter.

Brush nonstick skillet or electric griddle with additional melted butter; heat over medium heat. Working in batches, pour batter by ⅓ cupfuls onto skillet or griddle. Cook pancakes until bubbles form on top and bottoms are golden brown, about 2 minutes. Turn pancakes over and cook until golden brown, about 2 minutes. Serves 6.

breakfast griddle

What goes better with pancakes than bacon and eggs? This griddle is perfect for all three.

ALTERNATE: electric skillet

My mother always used an electric skillet for making pancakes. The temperature remains constant and you can make the perfect pancake over and over again.—Meredith

Light and Lovely Cornmeal Pancakes

You'll make these again and again.

1 cup all-purpose flour	**¼ teaspoon salt**
¾ cup cornmeal	**3 egg yolks**
2 tablespoons sugar	**1½ cups milk**
1½ teaspoons baking powder	**3 tablespoons vegetable oil**
	3 egg whites

Combine all dry ingredients. Combine egg yolks, milk, and vegetable oil. Whisk (or whip) egg whites until soft peaks form. Add milk mixture to dry ingredients, mixing well. Carefully fold egg whites into batter.

Heat lightly greased griddle over medium heat (electric skillet at 350°). Pour batter into pan, making pancakes of desired size. Cook 1–2 minutes or until little bubbles appear on one side of pancake. Turn over and cook other side. Serve immediately or keep warm.

Editor's Extra: These are so good, you may forget the butter and syrup! A nice variation is to add ¼ cup more milk and/or a mashed banana.

Puffy Pancake

This is a Warden family version of traditional German puffy pancakes. It is still the must-have breakfast whenever my children come to visit. While very easy to make, it looks remarkably impressive, and so my children used to make it whenever they had friends stay overnight as a simple but striking morning meal. It can be served with hot pie fillings, powdered sugar, syrup, fresh fruit, or just with butter. Our favorite is a fruit and berry compote. —Bob Warden

½ cup butter
2 cups milk

2 cups all-purpose flour
8 large eggs

baking pan

blender

Heat oven to 450°. Place butter in center of 9x13-inch baking pan. Place pan in oven for about 10 minutes, until butter is melted and dark brown, but not burned. While butter is melting, mix milk, flour, and eggs in a blender until smooth. Once butter is melted, open oven door and pull out rack, leaving pan in oven. Pour batter into center of pan. Close door and bake 30–40 minutes, until pancake has risen high not only on the edges, but in the center, and the edges are dark golden brown. Serve immediately. Serves 4–6.

Editor's Extra: Make sure you get everyone to the table before removing the pancake from the oven. You want to eat it piping hot.

The kitchen has always been a place for the Warden family to bond. David, Becca, Susan, Rachel, and Abby share a laugh.

saucepan

Cinnamon Oatmeal

2 cups milk
2 cups water
2 cups rolled oats
½ teaspoon salt

⅔ cup currants
1 tablespoon cinnamon
¼ cup brown sugar

Bring milk and water to a boil in 3-quart saucepan. Add oats and stir well. Add remaining ingredients and stir. Reduce heat and simmer until oats are tender. Adjust seasonings to taste. Serves 6–8.

Editor's Extra: Chopped dates or raisins can sub for currants.

baking pan

I like the covered choice when I am making enough to store for several days. —Bob

Baked Oatmeal

This is great because you can make it the night before, refrigerate it, and simply bake it in the morning.

½ cup cooking oil
½ cup sugar
1 egg
3 cups quick oats
2 teaspoons baking powder

½ teaspoon salt
1 cup milk
1 teaspoon cinnamon
½ cup raisins (optional)
½ cup nuts (optional)

Preheat oven to 350°. Cream oil, sugar, and egg in mixer. Add all other ingredients and mix. Pour into 9x13-inch baking pan. Bake 30 minutes. Serve warm with milk. Serves 6.

ALTERNATE:
casserole

I like the choice of the beautiful oval casserole with trivet when I take it right to the table. —Bob

Irish Omelet

We made this omelet on air for a St. Patrick's Day show. That show was filled with potatoes, potatoes, and more potatoes!—Bob Warden

4 eggs, separated
1 large potato, cooked and mashed
Juice of ½ lemon
1 tablespoon chopped chives
Salt and pepper to taste
1 tablespoon butter

Beat egg yolks, and combine with mashed potato. Mix well. Add lemon juice, chives, salt and pepper. Beat egg whites to stiff-peak stage, and fold into potato mixture. Heat 8-inch skillet over medium-high heat and add butter. Add potato mixture and cook, turning once, until both sides are golden. You may finish dish in oven, if desired.

skillet

Use skillet for both recipes on this page.

Omelet with Sausage, Spinach, and Pine Nuts

1 tablespoon pine nuts
2 teaspoons butter
3 eggs, well beaten
Salt and pepper to taste
2 ounces sausage, cooked
12 spinach leaves

Toast pine nuts in an 8-inch skillet over medium-high heat, until lightly browned; remove from pan and set aside. Heat same skillet over medium-high heat; add butter. Whisk eggs in small bowl; season with salt and pepper. When butter is melted and foamy, add eggs. Pull eggs back from the sides of the pan, allowing un-set eggs to cook. When eggs are almost set, add sausage, toasted pine nuts, and spinach. Fold omelet in half, wilting the spinach. Yields 1 serving.

mixing bowl; whisk

sauté pan

Oval pans always make beautiful presentation pieces!

mixing bowl

Sausage and Roasted Red Pepper Frittata

I like to bake this in the oval Technique sauté pan and take it right to the table.—Meredith Laurence

1 Italian sausage, casing removed and meat crumbled
¼ cup roasted red pepper strips
Salt and pepper to taste
2 fresh basil leaves, sliced
4 eggs, lightly beaten
¼ cup shredded Monterey Jack cheese
Fresh basil for garnish

Preheat oven to 500°. Heat 500° oven-safe 10-inch sauté pan over medium-high heat. Add sausage to pan and cook through. Drain all but 1 teaspoon grease. Add roasted red pepper strips and heat through. Season to taste with salt and pepper. Add fresh basil, and toss together well.

Lightly beat eggs in a mixing bowl and season with salt and pepper. Add eggs to skillet and stir around for 1 minute or so, until they just start to set on the bottom. Sprinkle cheese on top and transfer pan to a 500° oven. Bake 5–7 minutes or until frittata has puffed up and egg is set. The top should be lightly brown. If more color is desired on the frittata, hold the skillet under the broiler for 30 seconds or so. Garnish with fresh basil. Serves 2–4.

Chilaquiles

This breakfast takes me back to the meals that some of the prep cooks would make for all the cooks on the line when I was working in restaurants in California.—Meredith Laurence

3 tablespoons olive oil
2 corn tortillas, cut into strips
½ onion, chopped
1 teaspoon chili powder
½ teaspoon ground cumin
½ red chile pepper, chopped
½ green chile pepper, chopped

½ cup chorizo sausage, cooked and crumbled
6 eggs, beaten
Salt and pepper to taste
1 avocado, sliced
1 tomato, sliced
1 tablespoon chopped cilantro leaves

Heat olive oil in 12-inch sauté pan over medium-high heat. Add corn tortilla strips and fry until crispy. Remove from pan and set aside. Discard all but 1 teaspoon oil.

Add onion and sauté 2–3 minutes. Add chili powder, ground cumin, and peppers. Cook until all vegetables are tender. Stir in cooked sausage and heat through. Add eggs to pan, and stir to cook until set. Return crispy corn tortilla strips to the mixture, and season to taste with salt and pepper. Garnish plates with avocado and tomato slices, and sprinkle cilantro leaves over all. Serves 4–6.

sauté pan

OPTION:
santoku knife

Chopping ingredients with the santoku knife makes this a snap.

Joe's Favorite
Chile Relleno Casserole

This is a favorite of my son, Joseph, who loves spicy food—though he turns bright red and breaks out in a cold sweat with even mild salsa. It can be made milder or hotter by using different types of peppers.—Bob Warden

8–10 large jalapeño peppers
½ pound mozzarella cheese
4 eggs

1 (12-ounce) can evaporated milk

Wash jalapeños. Slice each pepper down one side; remove seeds. Put one slice cheese (about 1x3x½-inch) into each pepper. Whisk eggs and milk together in a bowl. Lay peppers in a greased casserole dish. Pour egg mixture over peppers. Bake at 350° until firm, 45–50 minutes. Serves 4–6.

mixing bowl; whisk

casserole

sauté pan;
saucepan

Sausage and Grits
Breakfast Casserole

1 pound bulk sausage
½ cup uncooked grits
2 tablespoons butter
1 cup shredded Cheddar
cheese

¾ cup milk
2 large eggs
Salt and pepper to taste
Chopped fresh parsley for
garnish

Brown sausage in 10-inch sauté pan until crumbly; drain and set aside. Cook grits per package directions in 2-quart saucepan. Stir in butter and cheese, and cook just enough to melt.

Measure milk in mixing bowl, then beat in eggs, salt and pepper. Stir into grits mixture. Pour over sausage in pan. Bake in 350° oven 40–50 minutes until set. Garnish with chopped fresh parsley. Serve with buttered biscuits or toast, and fresh fruit. Serves 4–5.

mixing bowls

Make-Ahead
Breakfast Bake

1 pound sausage, cooked,
drained, and crumbled
3 slices bread, cubed
4 eggs, slightly beaten

1 cup shredded Cheddar
cheese
1 cup milk
½ teaspoon salt

Mix all together in large bowl; place in greased large baking dish or 9x13-inch baking pan. Refrigerate overnight.

Bake at 350° for 35 minutes. Cut into squares and serve hot. This may be frozen before cooking. If frozen, thaw in refrigerator overnight before baking. Serves 6.

stoneware
baking dish

Aunt Norma's Butterflake Rolls

This family favorite came to us from Aunt Norma, a Norwegian immigrant who worked part time as a caterer. My adult children demand it for all Christmas, Thanksgiving, birthday, holiday, Sunday . . . well, come to think of it, just about all dinners. —Bob Warden

mixer

1 (14-ounce) can sweetened condensed milk
1 can hot tap water
½ cup sugar
1 tablespoon yeast
1 tablespoon salt
2 eggs, beaten
5–6 cups bread flour
1½ sticks butter, softened, divided

cookie sheet

Combine milk, hot water, sugar, yeast, and salt. Add eggs. Add flour. Mix ingredients in a mixer with the dough hook, and knead for several minutes. When dough is very smooth and elastic, turn onto an oiled surface and roll out with rolling pin into a rectangle. Spread with ½ stick butter, fold in half, turn 90 degrees, and roll out again. Repeat 2 more times. Continue until you have used up all the butter. You will have several thin layers of dough piled up on one another.

Cut dough into 1- to 2-inch squares. Space on a nonstick cookie sheet about ½–1 inch apart and allow to rise until doubled in bulk. Bake at 350° until golden brown. Be careful not to burn the bottom; use a top oven shelf. Best served fresh and warm.

The chef and the cook. It's a feast when cook's essentials meets BEST OF THE BEST.

roaster pan

square skillet

Turkey Dressing at Its Best

Gwen's family always made bread dressing, and husband Barney's family made cornbread dressing. This is a perfect blend of the two, and makes enough for the whole family.

4 tablespoons unsalted butter	1 tablespoon Cajun seasoning
2 tablespoons olive oil	½ teaspoon red pepper
1 large onion, chopped	½ teaspoon sugar
½ bell pepper, chopped	Salt and black pepper to taste
1 large stalk celery, chopped	4 cups crumbled Cornbread
8 large mushrooms, chopped	2 cups cubed wheat bread
2 cloves garlic, minced	(or white)
6–7 cups chicken or turkey	1 cup seasoned bread
broth	stuffing (or crushed croutons)

Heat butter and olive oil in roaster pan. Add chopped vegetables in order listed, and sauté until soft. Add broth; stir; add seasonings; stir again. Add breads and stir. Mixture should be loose, almost liquid-like. Bake at 375° for 30–50 minutes till softly firm. Bring on the cranberry sauce. Serves 8–10.

CORNBREAD:

Crusty on the outside, moist on the inside.

¼ cup plus 1 tablespoon	⅔ cup milk
vegetable oil, divided	1 cup self-rising cornmeal mix
1 small egg, or 2 tablespoons	
liquid egg substitute	

Heat oven to 450°. Pour 1 tablespoon oil into 8-inch square skillet and put in oven while it is preheating. Mix remaining ingredients and pour into warmed oil. Bake 10–13 minutes or till golden brown on top. When used for dressing, crumble by hand or in food processor. Makes about 4 cups crumbs.

Dried Cherry Cornbread Stuffing

½ cup butter
1 onion, finely chopped
2 ribs celery, finely chopped
2 cloves garlic, minced
1 tablespoon finely chopped
  thyme

2 cups dried cherries, soaked
  in ½ cup sweet Marsala
½ cup chicken stock
3 quarts crumbled cornbread
½ cup walnuts, toasted
Salt and pepper to taste

Heat an electric roaster or stovetop casserole pan over medium-high heat. Add butter, and sauté onion and celery until translucent. Add garlic and thyme, and continue to cook 1 minute. Add cherries and Marsala to the pan. Add chicken stock, and bring to a boil. Toss in crumbled cornbread and toasted walnuts. Season with salt and pepper. Cook in roaster at 375°, or transfer casserole pan to a 375° oven for 35–45 minutes, or until cornbread is lightly browned on top. Serves 8.

electric roaster

This can be made in any casserole dish, but when burner and oven space are at a premium during the holidays, use an electric roaster for your dressing.

Cornbread Hotcakes

2 cups self-rising cornbread
  mix
1 large egg, beaten

1½ cups buttermilk
3–4 tablespoons oil

Thoroughly combine cornbread mix, egg, and buttermilk in bowl. Add oil; mix well. Oil an 11-inch square skillet; heat, then pour batter, about the size of pancakes, onto surface. Reduce heat and cook until bubbles form on top side, and underside is brown. Turn over and increase heat to brown other side. Continue making hotcakes until all batter is used. Serves 6–8.

Editor's Extra: If you like "corny bread," add a small can of drained corn to batter. A little Tabasco gives it a kick.

square skillet
with press

ALTERNATE:
electric griddle

casserole

ALTERNATE:
stoneware
baking dish

Crawfish & Sausage Cornbread

1 bunch green onions, chopped
1 stick butter
3 eggs, slightly beaten
2 cups cornmeal, yellow or white
¼ cup flour
2 teaspoons baking powder
1 tablespoon sugar
1 teaspoon salt
1½ cups milk
1 (17-ounce) can whole-kernel corn, drained
1 pound frozen peeled crawfish tails, thawed and drained
8 fully cooked sausage links, chopped
1 tablespoon jalapeño slices
2 cups shredded sharp Cheddar cheese

Brown onions in butter. In a large mixing bowl, combine eggs, cornmeal, flour, baking powder, sugar, salt, and milk. Add onions and butter to mixture. Stir in corn, crawfish tails, sausage, jalapeño slices, and cheese. Pour into a greased 3-quart baking dish. Bake at 375° for 35 minutes, or until firm in the middle and well browned on top.

baking pan

Puffy Cheese Sandwiches

4 slices bread, divided
2 slices Cheddar cheese
1 egg
½ cup milk
Pinch of salt
Pinch of pepper
Pinch of dry mustard

Place 2 bread slices in greased 7x11-inch baking pan. Cover each with a cheese slice and remaining slices of bread. Whisk egg in bowl; then add milk and seasonings. Pour over sandwiches. Cover and refrigerate until milk is absorbed (overnight is fine). Bake in 350° oven 23–26 minutes until browned. Makes 2 sandwiches.

mixing bowl

Holly's Monte Cristo Sandwiches

This recipe is flexible. It can easily be made for one or for an entire group. These sandwiches are delicious and fun!—Holly Hardy

Bread slices (white or wheat bread), 3 slices per serving
1 (1-pound) block Velveeta cheese
Thinly sliced ham
Thinly sliced turkey
Onion ring batter mix
Vegetable oil for frying
Powdered sugar, honey, or jelly for topping (optional)

santoku knife

electric deep fryer

To assemble sandwiches, using a chef's knife, remove bread crusts on all sides. To stack sandwiches (kids can help with this part), place first layer of bread on a clean, flat surface, and place a slice of ham on bread, then a ⅛-inch-thick slice of cheese on ham. (The cheese acts as the "glue" to keep the layers together.) Next, put another slice of bread, another slice of cheese, and a slice of turkey, folded to fit inside edges. Top with remaining slice of bread; press together firmly. Cut in half diagonally; set sandwiches aside.

Mix onion-ring batter mix with water in shallow bowl according to package directions. The batter should have a pasty thickness to it, so it's not too watery, but not so thick that it pulls the bread apart. Heat oil in deep fryer. When oil is hot, immerse a sandwich in the batter to cover all sides. Carefully drop sandwiches one at a time in oil, and let cook about 5 minutes. They are cooked completely when the batter gets crispy and doesn't stick to your cooking utensil. Use tongs to remove from oil, and set on plate to drain.

If desired, top sandwich with your choice of toppings: powdered sugar, honey, or jelly.

Holly fixes her sandwiches in the Quail Ridge Press kitchen. Yum!

mini muffin pan

ALTERNATE:
muffin pan
I like to use the covered bakeware to take these as hostess gifts. —Bob

Surprise Broccoli Cheese Muffins

When Melinda Burnham brought these muffins to the Quail Ridge Press office for us to try, we declared that on a scale of one to ten, ten being the best . . . these muffins are a twenty!

CHICKEN CHUTNEY FILLING:

1 (8-ounce) package cream cheese, softened
1 (9-ounce) jar mango chutney
1 (6-ounce) package cooked chicken strips, chopped into small pieces

Mix cream cheese, mango chutney, and chicken. Set aside.

MUFFINS:

2 cups Bisquick baking mix
1 (10-ounce) package frozen chopped broccoli, thawed and drained
1 cup shredded mild Cheddar cheese
⅔ cup milk

Mix all ingredients. Fill greased mini muffin pans and bake at 400° for about 10 minutes, or until slightly browned on top. Remove from oven and let cool completely. Remove Muffins and slice in half horizontally.

Put spoonfuls of Chicken Chutney Filling on bottom half of each Muffin and top with remaining Muffin piece. Garnish with a dab of cream cheese and a carrot curl, if desired. Makes 24.

Alternate Method: Bake 15 minutes in a regular-size muffin pan.

*Melinda is ready to pop these beauties in the oven.
So good, they disappeared fast.*

Cinnamon-y Apple Compote

6 Granny Smith apples, peeled and quartered
1 cinnamon stick
½ cup sugar
1 teaspoon salt

Pinch of nutmeg
2 cloves
¼ teaspoon ground ginger
¼ cup water

Combine all ingredients in a 3-quart saucepan. Bring to a simmer and allow to cook 30 minutes or until desired consistency is reached. Allow mixture to cool. Remove cloves and cinnamon stick, and serve lukewarm. Turn out into serving dish, or serve over pancakes or French toast.

saucepan

Ginger Pear Compote

Compotes make such a nice, refreshing change from maple syrup on pancakes and French toast, and they also go nicely with meats to brighten up a dish.

4–6 Bartlett pears
⅓ cup sugar
¼ cup water

2 tablespoons lemon juice
2 tablespoons grated gingerroot

Peel, core, and cut pears into ½-inch pieces. Combine all ingredients in a 2-quart saucepan. Bring to a simmer and cook over medium-low heat until pears are soft and sauce is a slightly thickened consistency. Cool slightly before serving.

Editor's Extra: This is also great over ice cream or in mini shells or over biscuits.

ALTERNATE:
electric saucepan

Use a saucepan for both of these recipes.

saucepan

Blueberry Star Anise Compote

This was one of the first things I made on QVC when I was doing The Tuesday Night Cooking Class. *You'll keep your guests guessing at what that flavor is.*
—*Meredith Laurence*

**3 cups blueberries, frozen
  or fresh**
⅔ cup sugar
¾ cup water
2 teaspoons lemon juice

1 cinnamon stick
1 star anise
¼ teaspoon salt
Pinch of pepper

Combine all ingredients in 2-quart saucepan. Stir well. Bring mixture to a boil. Reduce heat, and simmer 30 minutes or until desired consistency is reached. Remove cinnamon stick and star anise. Turn out into a serving vessel (preferably glass), or ladle over pancakes or French toast.

Editor's Extra: Star anise is a star-shaped, licorice-flavored spice, a part of the five-spice powder used in Chinese cooking.

soups, chilies, and stews

Ahhh, soup! It warms the body and the spirit. The secret to great-tasting soup is good seasoned stock that wraps itself around all the ingredients. Longer cooking makes for more flavor absorption, so enjoy the wonderful aroma while your pot of soup is simmering.

easy pour stockpot

Using this pot enables you to easily drain fat.

Spanish Cheese Soup

1 pound ground chuck
2 cups water (or more)
1 cup whole-kernel corn
1 cup chopped, peeled potatoes
1 cup chopped celery
½ cup sliced carrots

½ cup chopped onion
4 beef bouillon cubes
1 (16-ounce) jar Cheez Whiz with jalapeño, or 1 pound Velveeta Mexican Mild, cubed

Brown meat in stockpot, then drain fat. Add all other ingredients, except cheese. Cook slowly 1–1½ hours. Just before serving, add cheese and allow to melt. Serve with cornbread or hush puppies to make a good meal. It freezes well. Serves 6.

electric stockpot

ALTERNATE:
stockpot

It's-A-Snap Cheese Soup

This is so easy. Make it when you're caught with hungry people and have nothing prepared. It's delicious, warming, and a snap! A nice salad makes this a quick and satisfying meal.

¼ onion, chopped
1 stalk celery, chopped
1 carrot, chopped
1 (14-ounce) can chicken broth

2 cups milk
¼ cup flour
¼ teaspoon paprika
1 cup shredded Cheddar cheese

Place vegetables in 6-quart electric stockpot with chicken broth; heat to boiling. Turn to SIMMER, cover, and let simmer about 15 minutes. Measure milk in measuring bowl; whisk in flour and paprika; whisk this into soup. Heat only until slightly bubbly. Cut cheese into chunks, and stir into soup. Serve with crackers or crusty bread. Serves 4.

Zesty Broccoli Cheese Soup

So quick and easy, you'll want to fix it all the time.

1 (14-ounce) can chicken broth
1 (10¾-ounce) can cream of chicken soup, undiluted
1 crown broccoli, chopped
½ (1-pound) block Velveeta Mexican Mild, cubed

Combine broth, soup, and broccoli in 2-quart saucepan. Bring to a boil; reduce heat and simmer until broccoli is tender, 3–5 minutes. Add cubed cheese; stir frequently as cheese melts. Serves 4–6.

saucepan

ALTERNATE:
electric
saucepan

Joe's Favorite Potato Cheese Soup

My son, Joseph, would have eaten this every day for every meal if we had let him. This delicious, hearty soup is fantastic on cold and rainy days.
—Bob Warden

4 large potatoes
1 small onion, finely chopped
2 slices bacon, browned well and crumbled
2 tablespoons bacon grease
1 (12-ounce) can evaporated milk, or 1½ cups milk or cream
¾ cup grated cheese (Cheddar or mixed cheeses)
¼ cup grated Parmesan cheese
1 tablespoon dill weed (not dill seed)

Peel and chop potatoes and onion; cover with water, and simmer in 4-quart electric stockpot about 30 minutes or until tender. Mash with a potato masher while still in water. Simmer another 45 minutes. Add bacon, bacon grease, milk or cream, cheeses, and dill. Mix well and heat, but don't boil. Serves 4.

electric
stockpot

ALTERNATE:
stockpot

chef's pan

blender

Homemade Cream of Mushroom Soup

2 ounces dried wild
  mushrooms
2½ cups chicken stock,
  divided
2 tablespoons butter
1 onion, chopped
1 clove garlic, minced

½ teaspoon chopped fresh
  thyme leaves
6 cups sliced mushrooms
3 tablespoons flour
1 cup cream
1 tablespoon sherry
Salt and pepper to taste

Reconstitute dried mushrooms in a little warm chicken stock and let sit 30 minutes. Drain mushrooms, reserving soaking liquid. Pass soaking liquid through a very fine strainer; reserve liquid.

Melt butter in 4-quart chef's pan; sauté onion until tender and translucent. Add garlic and fresh thyme; cook for an additional minute. Add fresh mushrooms and stir well. Add reconstituted dried mushrooms. When fresh mushrooms are cooked and tender, sprinkle in flour. Stir to coat all mushrooms; cook 2–3 minutes. Add remaining chicken stock and reserved liquid; bring mixture to a boil. This will thicken soup somewhat. Simmer 10–15 minutes to blend all flavors. Purée soup in a blender or food processor until smooth. Return puréed soup to pan. Add cream and sherry; season to taste with salt and pepper. Serves 4–6.

Cabbage Patch Soup

A great make-ahead dish, this soup is even better the next day.

1 medium head cabbage, shredded
1 medium onion, chopped
2 carrots, sliced very thin
2 ribs celery, sliced thin
3 (14-ounce) cans chicken broth
½ stick butter
3 tablespoons flour
1 teaspoon salt
½ teaspoon black pepper
½ teaspoon red pepper
2 cups milk
1 cup heavy cream
2 cups cubed ham
1 teaspoon dried basil
2 teaspoons dried parsley

electric
stockpot

In 8-quart electric stockpot, combine cabbage, onion, carrots, celery, and chicken broth; bring to a boil. Cover and simmer about 15 minutes until vegetables are soft. Melt butter in saucepan. Stir in flour, salt, and peppers until thickened. Gradually stir in milk and cream with a whisk. When it has thickened somewhat, stir into the cabbage pot. Add ham, basil, and parsley; heat thoroughly without boiling. Serves 6–8.

Editor's Extra: Some people say this is just as good without the ham—I know better!

ALTERNATE:
stockpot

Creamy Carrot Soup

Pretty and sooo good!

1 green pepper, chopped
1 large onion, chopped
3 tablespoons olive oil
1 tablespoon butter
6–8 carrots, sliced thinly
2 potatoes, peeled, diced
1 tablespoon minced garlic
1 tablespoon minced fresh basil
3 (14-ounce) cans chicken broth
1 tablespoon Greek seasoning
1 (12-ounce) can evaporated milk
Parmesan cheese for garnish (optional)

stockpot

In large stockpot, sauté green pepper and onion in oil and butter until soft. Stir in carrots, potatoes, garlic, basil, and chicken broth; bring to a boil, then simmer about an hour.

Season, add milk, and return to a simmer. Serve with Parmesan cheese sprinkled on top, if desired. Serves 8–10.

stockpot

OPTION:
mini food chopper

This is perfect for chopping small amounts of veggies.

ALTERNATE:
kohaishu knife

When I'm in a hurry, I use the electric food chopper, but sometimes I just like the pleasure of using a good knife. — Bob

Talk-About-Good Split Pea Soup

On a cold winter day, this can't be beat!

1 pound dried split peas	**1 smoked ham hock, or 1 cup**
½ cup chopped celery	**chopped ham**
1 cup chopped onion	**1 teaspoon Cajun seasoning**
½ cup chopped carrot	**1 teaspoon salt, or to taste**
1 clove garlic, minced	**Dash of red pepper**
2 tablespoons butter or	
vegetable oil	

In a stockpot, cover peas with water to about an inch above; soak overnight.

Next day, sauté celery, onion, carrot, and garlic in butter or oil (or use a combo) in your 10-inch sauté pan. Drain and reserve liquid from peas. Add enough water to make a total of 10 cups liquid; set aside. Put sautéed vegetables, ham hock or ham, and seasoning into pot with peas. Add the reserved 10 cups liquid. Bring to a boil; cover and simmer, stirring occasionally, 3 hours. Serves 6–8.

Bob got a taste of true southern hospitality when he visited with Barbara's mom in Brandon, Mississippi.

Black Bean Soup

1 pound black beans	1 bay leaf
4 (¼-inch) slices bacon	3 quarts water
1 onion, chopped	1½ tablespoons salt
2 ribs celery, chopped	Pepper to taste
½ teaspoon cumin seed, ground	Sour cream for garnish
	Cilantro for garnish

electric
stockpot

Soak black beans in water at least 8 hours or overnight. Drain soaking liquid and discard. Heat a large stockpot over medium heat. Add bacon and render fat. When bacon is crispy, remove from stockpot and set aside. Drain all but 1 tablespoon of fat. Sweat onion and celery in bacon fat until soft. Add ground cumin and bay leaf, and stir well. Add drained black beans and water. Cook 45 minutes or until beans are very soft. Add salt and pepper to taste. (Be sure to wait until the end of the cooking to add salt. Adding salt at the beginning of the cooking will prolong the time and make the beans tough.)

When beans are very soft, purée soup with a blender, food processor, or immersion blender. (For smoothest texture possible, pass soup through a food mill. This is recommended for this soup due to the skins on the black beans.) Return soup to stockpot over low heat. Garnish soup with reserved bacon, sour cream, and fresh cilantro. Makes 10–12 servings.

Editor's Extra: Soups should simmer—never boil—while cooking. A tall pot works best for stocks that simmer for hours since it keeps evaporation to a minimum. You can freeze all soups. Best if used within a month of freezing, a bit longer if it has been puréed.

ALTERNATE:
stockpot

Make the recipe in the stockpot, then store and reheat the leftovers in the smaller pot.

blender

electric
stockpot

ALTERNATE:
dutch oven

*A good pot is
almost as important
as the ingredients
that go in it.
Especially for cream
or cheese soups,
you must have a
good pot with
a heavy bottom that
conducts heat
evenly and avoids
hot spots.*

Seven-Bean Soup

This is one of my daughter Rachel's favorites, and one of the first things she made once she got an electric stockpot of her own. As with most soups, this has many potential variations.—Bob Warden

1½–2 cups pinto, garbanzo, kidney, lima (or butter), pink, navy, white, cranberry, black, or other dried beans
1 large onion, chopped
1 (16-ounce) can tomato sauce, or puréed whole tomatoes
1 (14-ounce) can beef broth
1 can corned beef, or cooked shredded beef, or 1 pound hamburger meat (optional)
Salt and pepper to taste
Cumin to taste
Garlic to taste
Grated cheese or apple cider vinegar

Soak bean mixture in water overnight, if possible. Drain soaking water and rinse beans. In electric pot, cover with fresh water, and add onion. Simmer for several hours, adding water as needed to keep beans covered.

Add tomato sauce or tomatoes, broth, corned beef or hamburger, and salt, pepper, cumin, and garlic to taste. Continue to simmer until flavors are blended. Serve with grated cheese or apple cider vinegar. Serves 6–8.

Editor's Extra: You can buy a whole variety of beans in one package. You might might want to buy single bean packages to make up your own variety, then wrap in fun packages or jars for gifting.

Cream of Pumpkin Soup

It is quite well-known amongst my acquaintances, that the only thing in the world I don't seem to like eating is pumpkin! That I developed and tested this recipe is a miracle.—Meredith Laurence

2 tablespoons butter
1 onion, finely chopped
1 carrot, finely chopped
2 cloves garlic, minced
3 thyme sprigs
½ cup white wine
2 quarts canned pumpkin

2 cups water
6 cups chicken stock
2 cups heavy cream
4 tablespoons salt
1 teaspoon pepper
3 tablespoons sugar
1 teaspoon nutmeg

Heat stockpot over medium-high heat. Add butter; melt. Add onion and carrot; cook until vegetables are soft and onion is translucent. Add garlic and thyme; cook an additional 30 seconds. Add wine and simmer until almost all wine has disappeared. Add pumpkin, water, and chicken stock; bring to a simmer. Simmer an additional 15–20 minutes. Remove from heat, stir in the heavy cream, and season to taste with salt, pepper, sugar, and nutmeg. Serves 16.

Editor's Extra: Easy to halve or quarter recipe for fewer servings.

stockpot

ALTERNATE:
electric
stockpot

OPTION:
santoku knife

Chopping ingredients with the santoku knife makes this a snap.

All kinds of ideas are cooked up in the Best Room at Quail Ridge Press. Taking this idea from conception to completion was an arduous task . . . but has endeared our friendships.

saucepan

ALTERNATE:
electric
saucepan

blender

stockpot

Quick Cream of Tomato Soup

This is the best quick tomato soup I have ever had.—Bob Warden

1 (28-ounce) can whole tomatoes, chopped or blended briefly
1 (12-ounce) can evaporated milk

½ teaspoon baking soda
1 milk can full of water

Combine tomatoes with milk; bring to a boil. Remove from heat; add soda and water. Serves 3–4.

Editor's Extra: If you want to give this simple recipe some pizzazz, add a dash or two of Italian or other seasoning. Good served with a few oyster crackers and/or parsley flakes on top.

Roasted Tomato and Lentil Soup

10 tomatoes, halved horizontally
10 garlic cloves, unpeeled
6 cups water
½ cup chopped fresh basil
1 bay leaf
1 carrot, cut into 3-inch pieces
1 onion, quartered

2 ribs celery, cut into 3-inch pieces
1 pound lentils
Salt and pepper to taste
1 tablespoon olive oil
1 onion, chopped
2 ribs celery, chopped
2–4 cups chicken stock

Place tomato halves and garlic cloves on a cookie sheet, and roast in a 400° oven 1 hour, or until garlic cloves are soft and tomatoes have split and are tender. Purée tomatoes in a blender. Press garlic out of its skin and add to tomato purée. Bring water, basil, bay leaf, carrot, quartered onion, and celery pieces to a boil in a 6-quart stockpot. Once at a boil, add lentils and stir. Simmer lentils until tender, 20–30 minutes. Season with salt and pepper.

In a separate pot, heat olive oil, and lightly sauté chopped onion and celery until tender. Add tomato purée and simmer. Strain lentils and remove large pieces of carrots, celery, and onion. Add lentils to the tomato base, and thin with chicken stock to desired consistency. Serves 12.

Grocery Store Roasted Chicken Soup

When the flu bug was making its rounds while I was babysitting grandchildren away from home, necessity was the mother of invention for this chicken soup! With a little meat left on the bones of the roasted chicken bought out of desperation at the grocery store for the previous night's meal, I made some delicious chicken soup. —Gwen McKee

1 chicken carcass with some meat
1 quart water
1 large onion, chopped
1 stalk celery, chopped
1 tablespoon minced garlic
3 large mushrooms, chopped (optional)
1 tablespoon olive oil
1 tablespoon butter
1 tablespoon minced parsley
½ teaspoon sugar

Boil carcass in water in 8-quart electric pot, then simmer at least 30 minutes, covered. Remove carcass to plate with slotted spoon, making sure all bones are removed from stock. When cool enough to handle, pick any remaining meat off bones and add back to stock. Sauté vegetables in oil and butter. When limp, add to stock with parsley, sugar, and any additional seasoning you may like (grocery store chickens are usually well seasoned). Simmer, covered, another half hour or so. Makes 4–6 warming cups of good-for-what-ails-you soup. The kids like buttered toast dipped in their broth . . . and so do we! Serves 4–6.

Editor's Extra: Good soup is made from good stock. You can call yourself a good cook if you have stock in your freezer, because it enhances the flavor of anything you add it to so nicely. It's easy; purée cooked vegetables or boil turkey bones or seafood peels, etc. Cook them in water with seasoning, then freeze in ice cube trays; when frozen, transfer to an airtight freezer bag.

electric stockpot

ALTERNATE: stockpot

OPTION: mini food chopper

stockpot

ALTERNATE:
electric
stockpot

When using any electric stockpot, make sure it is set on high SIMMER. *Anything higher will boil away your soup.*

Turkey Rice Soup

This is another use-up-the-leftovers-from-the-holidays dish. I get a great sense of satisfaction out of turning one meal into a completely different meal. —Meredith Laurence

1 tablespoon olive oil
3 carrots, peeled and diced
3 ribs celery, diced
1 onion, peeled and diced
2 leeks, sliced
3 cloves garlic, minced

2 teaspoons dried sage
2 teaspoons dried thyme
1 turkey carcass with some
    meat
2 cups white rice, cooked
Salt and pepper to taste

Heat stockpot over medium-high heat. Add oil. Add carrots, celery, onion, and leeks to the pot and cook until translucent. Add garlic, sage, and thyme, and cook an additional minute. Add turkey carcass to the pot (break bones if necessary to fit), and cover with cold water. Bring to a simmer and skim off any foam that rises to the surface. Simmer 2–3 hours, replenishing water if surface drops too low. Remove carcass and pick off all meat. Return meat to the pot. Discard bones.

Add rice to soup, and heat through. Season with salt and pepper. Soup will continue to thicken over time. If necessary, thin with stock. Serves 10.

Headed home after a busy time in the South.
"Y'all come back soon."

Quick-As-A-Flash Chicken Corn Chowder

1 pound (about 6 strips) chicken fajita strips
1 small onion, chopped
2 teaspoons minced fresh garlic
2 tablespoons butter
2 cups milk
1 (10¾-ounce) can cream of chicken soup
1 (10¾-ounce) can cream of potato soup

1 (15-ounce) can sweet corn, drained
1 (15-ounce) can stewed tomatoes, drained
1 (4-ounce) can chopped green chiles
2 tablespoons minced fresh cilantro
2 teaspoons ground red pepper
1 cup shredded Monterey Jack cheese

stockpot

ALTERNATE:
electric saucepan

Cut chicken strips into bite-size pieces. In large stockpot, sauté onion and garlic in butter until soft, not brown. Stir in milk, soups, corn, tomatoes, chiles, cilantro, and pepper. Bring to a boil. Add chicken pieces, reduce heat, and simmer, uncovered, 8–10 minutes, stirring often. Add cheese; cook and stir until cheese melts. Serve at once. Makes 4–5 servings.

Editor's Extra: Salt soups and stews toward the end of cooking—it gives the other flavors time to develop. Taste from time to time, adding salt gradually. You can always salt at the table. But if soup gets too salty, add a raw peeled potato (remove before serving).

dutch oven

ALTERNATE:
cast-iron
casserole

OPTION:
santoku knife

You can't make this recipe without a good knife, and the santoku is the only one you need.

Spicy Corn and Black Bean Chili

2 teaspoons olive oil
1 small onion, finely diced
1 carrot, finely diced
1 rib celery, finely diced
½ red pepper, finely diced
½ orange or yellow pepper, finely diced
1 jalapeño pepper, finely diced
1 clove garlic, minced
1½–2 tablespoons chili powder, or to taste
1 teaspoon ground cumin
1 (28-ounce) can diced tomatoes
1½ cups corn kernels, fresh off cob, or frozen
1 (16-ounce) can black beans, drained
1 teaspoon salt
Pepper to taste
1 cup grated Cheddar cheese
½ cup sour cream
¼ cup freshly chopped cilantro

Heat a Dutch oven over medium-high heat 2–3 minutes. Add olive oil. Sauté onion, carrot, celery, and peppers 5–6 minutes, or until onion is soft and translucent. Add garlic, chili powder, and cumin; continue to cook another 2 minutes. Add tomatoes and bring to a simmer. Simmer 20 minutes. Add corn and beans; simmer another 20 minutes. Season to taste with salt and pepper. Serve with grated cheese, sour cream, and cilantro. Serves 6.

Chicken Chili

This is a nice version of chili, without the beef. My friend at university started making this, having learned it from his mother. The rest of us loved it!
—Meredith Laurence

6 slices bacon, chopped
2 onions, finely chopped
2 ribs celery, finely chopped
2 red bell peppers, finely chopped
2 green bell peppers, finely chopped
1½ cups corn kernels, drained
¾ cup canned green chiles, drained
4 cloves garlic, minced
1–2 tablespoons chili powder
2 teaspoons ground cumin
3 cups canned tomatoes, drained

3 cups cannellini beans, cooked or canned, drained
3 cups kidney beans, cooked or canned, drained
3 cups shredded, cooked chicken (1½-inch pieces)
3 cups chicken stock
Salt and pepper to taste
Sour cream (optional)
Cheddar cheese, grated (optional)
Scallions, finely chopped (optional)

stockpot

ALTERNATE:
electric
stockpot

OPTION:
knife set

Heat a stockpot over medium heat. Add bacon and render out all fat until bacon is almost crispy. Remove bacon with a slotted spoon and set aside. Drain all but 2 tablespoons bacon fat. Add onions, celery, and red and green peppers to pan; sauté 5 minutes over medium-high heat, until onion is tender. Add corn, green chiles, and garlic; continue to cook an additional 2 minutes.

Add chili powder and cumin; combine well. Add tomatoes, both beans, bacon, and chicken; combine with vegetables. Add chicken stock and bring to a boil. Reduce heat to a simmer and cook 30–40 minutes, until all ingredients are tender, and flavors have blended well. Season to taste with salt and pepper. Serve with sour cream, grated cheese, and chopped scallions as optional garnishes. Serves 8–10.

skillet

I use a large skillet to brown the pork. This way I can do it all at once instead of in batches. —Bob

ALTERNATE:
electric stockpot

Chunky Spicy Chili

Makes a lot, so invite a crowd.

1 pound boneless beef chuck steak, cut into 1-inch pieces
1 pound pork tenderloin, cut into 1-inch pieces
¼ cup all-purpose flour
1 tablespoon oil
1 (10-ounce) can hot Ro-Tel tomatoes, undrained
1 (10-ounce) can mild Ro-Tel tomatoes, undrained

3 (15-ounce) cans pinto beans, undrained
1 (12-ounce) can beer
½ cup chopped red onion
2 tablespoons chili powder
1 teaspoon cumin
1 teaspoon cilantro
½ teaspoon garlic powder
½ teaspoon salt
1 (12-ounce) can tomato paste

In large bowl, combine beef, pork, and flour; toss to coat evenly. Heat oil in large skillet over medium-high until hot. Add meat; cook and stir until no longer pink.

Put all ingredients into stockpot; mix well. Cover; cook on SIMMER 4–5 hours or until beef and pork are fork-tender. Serves 12.

In the annex, live audiences get this view of the meticulous preparation that goes into the setup before each product is ready to go on air.

Skillet Turkey Bean Chili

1 pound ground turkey breast
1 (14-ounce) can beef broth
1 large onion, finely chopped
1 green bell pepper, seeded
  and diced
1 package chili seasoning
2 teaspoons chili powder
½ teaspoon garlic powder
1 teaspoon salt
1 teaspoon red pepper flakes
½ teaspoon ground allspice
  (optional)
¼ teaspoon ground cinnamon
  (optional)
¼ teaspoon paprika
2 (15-ounce) cans black beans,
  rinsed and drained
2 (14-ounce) cans crushed
  tomatoes in tomato purée,
  undrained
2 teaspoons apple cider
  vinegar

saute pan

Heat 12-inch nonstick sauté pan over high heat. Add turkey, beef broth, onion, and bell pepper. Cook and stir, breaking up turkey, until turkey is no longer pink.

Add chili seasoning, chili powder, garlic powder, salt, red pepper, allspice, cinnamon, and paprika. Reduce heat to medium-low; simmer 10 minutes. Add beans, tomatoes, and vinegar; bring to a boil. Reduce heat to low; simmer 20–25 minutes or until thickened to desired consistency. Garnish as desired. Serves 4–6.

ALTERNATE:
lipped skillet

I think the lipped skillet is the perfect alternative for this recipe, as it is a combination fry pan and saucepan.
—Bob

square pan with
bacon press

stockpot

Gwen's Hankerin' Gumbo

In the South, it is some sort of violation to ignore a good hankerin' for a favorite dish. My Louisiana roots dictate times when I just have to have a bowl of good gumbo! Here's a recipe to make and freeze, so you have a stash in case you get one of those hankerin's! Just boil some rice and serve with hot buttered French bread. Oh, man, that's good!—Gwen McKee

8 slices bacon
6 tablespoons flour
9–10 cups chicken stock
2 pounds frozen cut okra
4 packages frozen chopped
  seasoning vegetables
1 tablespoon chopped garlic
1 (28-ounce) can chopped
  tomatoes

1 (10-ounce) can Ro-Tel
  tomatoes
5 bay leaves
½ teaspoon thyme
½ teaspoon red pepper
1 tablespoon Cajun seasoning
2–3 pounds raw shrimp,
  peeled
1 pound crabmeat

Fry bacon in square pan using bacon press; drain bacon on paper towels. Set aside. Sprinkle and stir flour into grease, and brown on medium heat.

Transfer roux (flour and grease mixture) to stockpot, then stir in chicken stock, and bring to a boil. Add all other ingredients, except bacon, shrimp, and crabmeat. Bring back to a boil, and simmer slowly about 3 hours.

Add shrimp and crabmeat, cooking only about 5 minutes. Crumble in crisp bacon. Remove from heat. When cooled some (this takes an hour or so), transfer to freezer containers, or save for the next day. If you think it tastes good now, wait till those flavors have time to marry.

Lamb and Spring Vegetable Stew

1 pound lamb stew meat, trimmed of fat
¼ cup flour
1 teaspoon salt
¼ teaspoon freshly ground black pepper
2 teaspoons olive oil
1 onion, rough chopped
1 rib celery, rough chopped
1 carrot, rough chopped
1 clove garlic, crushed
1 bay leaf
4 sprigs thyme
4 cups chicken stock, divided

6 baby potatoes, quartered
2 small carrots, sliced on the bias
6 pearl onions
1 cup green beans, sliced into 1-inch long pieces
1 cup frozen sweet peas
12 cherry tomatoes, halved
1 teaspoon salt
¼ teaspoon freshly ground black pepper
4 tablespoons chopped fresh parsley

casserole

ALTERNATE: electric stockpot

Heat a casserole pan or electric stockpot over medium heat 2–3 minutes. Dredge lamb pieces in mixture of flour, salt, and pepper, shaking off any excess. Add oil to pot and brown meat in batches until browned all over. Set meat aside.

Add onion, celery, carrot, garlic, bay leaf, and thyme to the pot and cook 4–5 minutes. Return meat to pot and add 2 cups chicken stock. Bring mixture to a boil, then simmer one hour at 325°.

While lamb simmers, prepare remaining vegetables. When lamb has simmered an hour, remove meat from casserole and set aside in a bowl. Strain liquid in casserole, discarding solid matter and saving sauce. Return sauce and meat to casserole and bring to a boil. Add potatoes, carrots, and onions. Add remaining stock to cover vegetables and meat. Simmer 20 minutes.

Add green beans and simmer another 15–20 minutes. Add peas and cherry tomatoes and simmer another 5 minutes. Season to taste with salt and pepper, and garnish with freshly chopped parsley.

Best Ever Oven Beef Stew

dutch oven

ALTERNATE:
pressure cooker

2 pounds stew beef, cubed
1 (1-pound) bag mini carrots
2 onions, cut in eighths
3 stalks celery, cut
⅓ cup tapioca
¾ teaspoon Mrs. Dash Table Blend seasoning
2 teaspoons sugar
¼ teaspoon cayenne pepper
½ teaspoon basil
1½ cups low-sodium V-8 Juice
2 Yukon gold potatoes, peeled, cubed

Place all but potatoes in Dutch oven or big casserole; cover. Bake at 325° for 2 hours. Stir and add potatoes. Cook 1 more hour. Serve with a green salad and crusty French bread or cornbread. Serves 6–8.

Alternate Method: To make this in a pressure cooker, cook on HIGH pressure 30 minutes.

"Hungary" for Beef Stew?

electric stockpot

ALTERNATE:
pressure cooker

2 pounds beef stew meat
6 unpeeled new potatoes, cut into ¾-inch pieces to equal 3 cups
1 medium onion, chopped
½ cup all-purpose flour
Salt to taste
1 tablespoon paprika (Hungarian)
½ teaspoon peppered seasoned salt
1 teaspoon cayenne
¼ teaspoon caraway seed
1 tablespoon minced garlic
1 (14-ounce) can beef broth
1½ cups frozen sweet peas, thawed
½ cup sour cream
1 (8-ounce) package sliced fresh mushrooms

Preheat 5- to 8-quart electric stockpot to 400°. Toss beef, potatoes, onion, flour, salt, paprika, seasoned salt, cayenne, caraway seed, and garlic in stockpot until well mixed. Stir in broth. Reduce heat to SIMMER. Cover and cook 7–8 hours. Stir in peas, sour cream, and mushrooms. Cover and cook about 15 more minutes or until peas are tender. Serves 6.

Alternate Method: Cook on HIGH in pressure cooker 40 minutes, then release pressure and proceed with stirring in peas, sour cream, and mushrooms; cook uncovered another 5 minutes.

Tuscan Ham, Bean, and Cabbage Stew

The convenience of packaged coleslaw mix in your supermarket makes this stew a snap to prepare.

1 tablespoon margarine or butter
1 tablespoon olive or vegetable oil
1 pound fully cooked ham, chopped
1 large onion, coarsely chopped
1 tablespoon celery flakes
1 clove garlic, finely chopped
4 cups chicken broth
2 chicken bouillon cubes
1 (28-ounce) can stewed Italian-style tomatoes, undrained

6 ounces uncooked bowtie pasta (farfalle)
1 cup coleslaw mix
1 (6-ounce) package baby spinach
1 tablespoon chopped fresh basil, or 1 teaspoon dried basil leaves
2 (15-ounce) cans Great Northern beans, rinsed and drained
1 teaspoon coarsely ground black pepper
1 bay leaf

Heat margarine and oil in Dutch oven or electric stockpot over medium heat. Cook ham, onion, celery flakes, and garlic in margarine mixture, stirring occasionally, until onion is tender. Stir in broth, bouillon, and tomatoes, breaking up tomatoes. Heat to boiling.

Stir in pasta. Heat to boiling; reduce heat. Cover and simmer about 10 minutes or until pasta is tender. Stir in remaining ingredients. Heat to boiling; reduce heat. Simmer uncovered about 3 minutes or until cabbage is tender. Makes 8 servings.

dutch oven

ALTERNATE:
electric stockpot

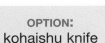

OPTION:
kohaishu knife

Chopping ingredients with the kohaishu knife makes this a snap.

electric roaster

ALTERNATE:
electric
stockpot

Movie Night Pork Stew

This is so good, so easy . . . and leftovers are equally heavenly!

4 lean pork chops
1 teaspoon Mrs. Dash Table
    Blend seasoning
4 Yukon gold potatoes,
    peeled, chunked
6 medium carrots, peeled,
    chunked

1 onion, peeled, chunked
1 clove garlic, minced
⅓ envelope ham seasoning
1 cup hot water
½ teaspoon coarsely ground
    pepper

Turn roaster oven or electric stockpot to 375° for 5 minutes. Add pork chops and season with Mrs. Dash; turn after 3 minutes; season other sides. Add vegetables and garlic. Dissolve ham seasoning in hot water, and add to pot. Sprinkle pepper on top. Stir slightly, cover, and lower temperature to 200°. Cook 2–3 hours. Makes 4–6 servings.

You can go to a movie, and come home to a great smelling house. Toast some whole-wheat bread and pour a little of the stew juice over diagonal slices on the plate, cut up a fresh pear, and pour the Cabernet! You might want to light the candles for this one.

Editor's Extra: Look for Goya Ham-Flavored Concentrate in the Mexican section of your supermarket. It comes in a box with several envelopes.

salads

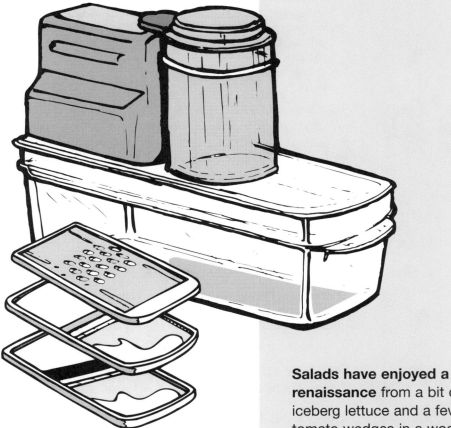

Salads have enjoyed a renaissance from a bit of iceberg lettuce and a few tomato wedges in a wooden bowl to a multi-ingredient, beautifully dressed masterpiece. Now served in fancy plates and bowls, salads are indeed the choice main meal for many, with merely the addition of some good bread and a nice glass of wine.

mixing bowl

utensils

Nice to have the right tools when you need them.

OPTION:
mini food chopper

So handy for all fine chopping.

mixing bowl; whisk

Black Bean-Salsa Salad

1 (15-ounce) can black beans, rinsed and drained
1 cup canned corn, drained, or thawed, frozen corn
1 (7-ounce) jar roasted red bell peppers, packed in garlic and olive oil
⅓ cup pineapple-chipotle salsa
2 tablespoons balsamic vinegar
2 ounces mozzarella cheese, cut in small cubes
½ cup chopped red or yellow onion, divided

Place all ingredients except cheese and 1 tablespoon onion in medium mixing bowl. Toss gently to blend well. Let stand 15 minutes to absorb flavors. Just before serving, gently fold in all but 2 tablespoons of cheese. Sprinkle remaining cheese and remaining onion on top. Serves 6–8.

Beans and Rice Salad

2 cups cooked long-grain rice
1 (16-ounce) can black beans, drained and rinsed
1 cup diced plum tomatoes
1 green bell pepper, diced
½ cup chopped red onion

Combine all salad ingredients in large bowl.

VINAIGRETTE:
3 tablespoons white wine vinegar
2 teaspoons Dijon or Creole mustard
1 teaspoon ground cumin
½ teaspoon salt
¼ teaspoon black pepper
½ teaspoon hot pepper sauce
½ cup olive oil

Mix all ingredients except olive oil. Whisk in olive oil slowly. Toss with salad. Let stand 30 minutes at room temperature or 3 hours in refrigerator before serving.

Rice Mandarin Salad

½ pound 4-rice blend (wild, brown, white, red)
3 cups chicken stock or water
½ cup cashew pieces
1 cup golden raisins
¼ cup chopped mint (optional)
Grated rind of 1 orange
4 green onions, sliced
¼ cup olive oil
⅓ cup orange juice
Ground black pepper
1 (11-ounce) can Mandarin oranges, drained
Lettuce leaves

chef's pan

Rinse rice in cold water; drain. Bring liquid to a boil in 2-quart chef's pan. Add rice and simmer, covered, according to package instructions, about 30 minutes; should not need draining. Mix remaining ingredients with rice (except lettuce) and let it stand for a minimum of 2 hours. Serve at room temperature over lettuce leaves. Serves 8.

Mediterranean-Style Salad

1 bag chopped salad mix
1 bag chopped romaine lettuce
Sweet grape tomatoes
1 cucumber, chopped
1 (16-ounce) can garbanzo beans, rinsed and drained
1 (5¾-ounce) can jumbo pitted black olives, drained
1 (14-ounce can) quartered artichoke hearts, drained
1 (16-ounce) jar marinated vegetables (mushrooms, carrots, onions, jalapeño peppers)
1 (7-ounce) jar roasted red peppers packed in garlic and olive oil, drained
2 (6-ounce) packages grilled chicken strips
Grated Romano and Asiago cheeses (optional)

measuring bowl

Assemble all ingredients in large salad bowl. Top with grated Romano and Asiago cheeses, if desired.

mini food
processor

saucepan

Tabbouleh Salad

This is a fantastic summer salad, and is a favorite among my children. Yum! Yum! Yum!—Bob Warden

¾ cup whole wheat berries
3–4 large cucumbers, peeled and chopped
5–8 ripe tomatoes, chopped
1 (14-ounce) can water-packed artichoke hearts, drained
1 (8-ounce) package feta cheese, crumbled
1 (4-ounce) can pitted olives, cut in half
½ cup chopped green onions, including tops
2–3 tablespoons chopped fresh parsley

1–2 tablespoons chopped mint (optional)
1–2 tablespoons chopped fresh basil
1 tablespoon chopped fresh oregano
2–3 garlic cloves, minced
⅓–½ cup good quality olive oil
¼ cup lemon juice
Salt and freshly ground black pepper to taste

Grind wheat berries in food processor as for cracked wheat cereal. Use a strainer to eliminate as much chaff as possible. Put into a 2-quart saucepan and add a generous amount of salted water. Boil until tender, about 1–1½ hours. Drain, rinse well, and chill.

Add all ingredients and adjust seasoning to taste. Chill well. This salad improves with age. Serves 10–12.

Much of the work involved in putting a cookbook together happens outside of the kitchen. Gwen and Bob work tirelessly on the computer compiling recipes and writing copy.

Salad for Two with Style

This salad has class written all over it.   Delicious and impressive.—Gwen McKee

¼ cup coarsely cut pecans
8 cups cut mixed lettuces
1 medium tomato, cut small
1 tablespoon creamy poppy
** seed dressing**
1½ tablespoons red wine
** vinegar**
6 canned asparagus spears
1 teaspoon McCormick Salad
** Supreme**

Toast pecans in toaster oven tray for one MEDIUM toast cycle. Allow to cool. In a large bowl, mix greens, tomato, and cooled pecans. Mix dressing and vinegar; toss with salad and serve on 2 plates. Cross asparagus over top and sprinkle with salad seasoning. Serves 2.

Editor's Extra: Buy small bottles of salad dressings along with a variety of flavored vinegars. They are wonderful mixed, and nobody misses the fat.

toaster oven tray

mixing bowl

Glazed Walnut Apple Salad

Don't taste the walnuts after cooking . . . because you will have none left for the salad.

1 tablespoon butter
½ cup sugar, divided
Dash of cayenne
1 cup walnuts, large cut
⅔ cup apple cider vinegar
⅓ cup light olive oil
1 bunch romaine lettuce,
** torn into pieces**
4 Pink Lady apples, cored,
** cut bite-size**
⅓ cup feta cheese

Melt butter with ¼ cup sugar and cayenne in skillet; add walnuts and stir, cooking only until glazed. Cool. Mix vinegar with oil and remaining ¼ cup sugar. Arrange torn lettuce on 8 salad plates, then apples, then walnuts on top. Sprinkle with feta cheese. Add dressing right before serving. Serves 8.

skillet

mixing bowl

skillet

OPTION:
mixing bowl

Spring Mix Pear Surprise Salad

Freshly squeezed orange juice gives this just the right touch.

ORANGE-SESAME VINAIGRETTE:

4 teaspoons sesame seeds
½ cup vegetable oil
6 tablespoons fresh orange juice
1 tablespoon red wine vinegar

4 scallions, sliced thin
2 teaspoons honey
1 teaspoon grated ginger (optional)
½ teaspoon salt

Toast sesame seeds in dry skillet over medium heat, stirring until golden, 3–5 minutes. Shake toasted seeds together with remaining ingredients in a jar or mixing bowl with a tight-fitting lid. The dressing can be refrigerated for up to 3 days. Bring to room temperature and shake vigorously before using. Great on a hearty green salad. Makes about 1 cup.

SALAD:

1 (4-ounce) package spring mix
1 bunch watercress
2 pears, cored and sliced thin
½ cup walnuts, toasted

½ cup Orange-Sesame Vinaigrette
3 ounces blue cheese, crumbled

Combine spring mix, watercress, pear slices, and toasted walnuts in salad bowl. Toss with vinaigrette and crumbled blue cheese just before serving. Serves 6.

Editor's Extra: When toasting sesame seeds, you have to toss or stir every few seconds. You want golden brown, not burned.

Layered Salad with Creamy Chili Tomato Dressing

Pretty enough for special occasions . . . easy enough for every day! Not only is this a complete meal, it makes a beautiful presentation if layered in a large glass bowl.

LAYER AS FOLLOWS:

Romaine lettuce
Spinach leaves
Mushrooms, raw, sliced
Pepperoni, sliced
1 bunch green onions, chopped
Frozen asparagus spears, thawed and chopped
1 (14-ounce) can artichoke hearts, quartered and drained

1 (8-ounce) package shredded mozzarella cheese with sundried tomato and basil
1 (6-ounce) package cooked chicken strips, chopped
Romaine lettuce
Spinach leaves
½ (6-ounce) jar pickled mild banana peppers, sliced
1 (4-ounce) package real bacon bits

CREAMY CHILI TOMATO DRESSING:

1 cup ranch dressing
¼ cup honey mustard
2 teaspoons horseradish

1 (14¼-ounce) can diced tomatoes, chili seasoned, drained (reserve juice)

In a mixing bowl, mix dressing ingredients with a whisk, leaving large pieces of tomato in the dressing. Add just enough tomato juice to flavor and tint to a dark peach color.

mixing bowl; whisk

Barbara and Gwen test recipes all the time— it's all about "taste, taste, taste."

easy pour
stockpot

saucepan

*Once you use a
pot with a storage
lid, you will think of
other ways to save
on the dishwashing.*

Frog Eye Salad

*This is the salad that our five-year-old neighbor Stacy would never eat, once
we told her its name. We got the recipe from family friends, and it became a
staple at picnics, church functions, and holiday parties.—Bob Warden*

1 (8-ounce) package acini di
  pepe pasta
1 cup sugar
2 tablespoons flour
1½ teaspoons salt
3 tablespoons lemon juice
2 eggs, beaten
1⅔ cups reserved pineapple
  juice
1 (20-ounce) can crushed
  pineapple, drained (reserve
  juice)

2 (20-ounce) cans pineapple
  chunks, drained (reserve
  juice)
3 (11-ounce) cans Mandarin
  oranges, drained
2 cups miniature
  marshmallows
2 (16-ounce) containers
  Cool Whip, or 2 pints heavy
  whipping cream, whipped

In large stockpot, prepare pasta per package directions. Drain,
rinse, and cool.

In saucepan, mix sugar, flour, salt, and lemon juice.
Gradually whisk in eggs and pineapple juice. Cook over moderate heat until thickened. Cool. Combine this mixture with
cooled pasta. Cover and refrigerate overnight.

Add both pineapples, oranges, marshmallows, and Cool
Whip or whipped cream. For holidays, add green food coloring
and chopped maraschino cherries. Combine well and refrigerate. Serves 12.

Editor's Extra: Instead of the sugar-flour-egg-pineapple juice mixture, you may substitute 1 (3-ounce) package vanilla pudding mix prepared with pineapple juice rather than milk.

A Different Aspic

3 (3-ounce) packages
  raspberry gelatin
1¼ cups boiling water
3 (16-ounce) cans stewed
  tomatoes

6 drops Tabasco
1 (6-ounce) package pine nuts

Dissolve gelatin in boiling water in medium saucepan. Stir in stewed tomatoes, breaking them up with a spoon. Add Tabasco and pine nuts. Mix well and pour into lightly oiled 3-quart tube pan; chill until firm. Unmold onto salad greens and fill center with Sour Cream Dressing.

SOUR CREAM DRESSING:
1 pint sour cream
1 tablespoon creamy
  horseradish

¼ teaspoon salt
½ teaspoon sugar

Combine ingredients, and serve over salad. Serves 12.

saucepan

tube pan

Cranberry Jell-O Salad

Grandma Emily used to make this every Thanksgiving at her house on Josephine Street in Berkeley. It became an essential part of not only Thanksgiving, but also Christmas dinner. In my children's opinions, it is still the perfect centerpiece for a holiday table. —Bob Warden

1 (3-ounce) package
  cranberry-flavored gelatin
2 tablespoons sugar
1 (12-ounce) package fresh
  cranberries

1 orange, peeled, deseeded
½ cup chopped celery
½ cup chopped walnuts
½ teaspoon orange zest

Prepare Jell-O in medium saucepan according to package directions, adding 2 tablespoons sugar with the hot water. Grind cranberries and orange in food processor in batches. Add to Jell-O. Add remaining ingredients. Pour into mold and chill well. Serves 6.

saucepan

mini food
processor

blender

Using a blender will keep ingredients from separating.

ALTERNATE:
food processor

Refreshing Dressing for Your Salad

This is good on any green salad. Add some fruit, nuts, croutons . . . yum!

Juice of 2 lemons (¼ cup)
⅓ cup olive oil
¼ cup vegetable oil
1 teaspoon minced garlic
1 teaspoon sugar

½ teaspoon black pepper
½ teaspoon salt
¼ teaspoon thyme
½ teaspoon dried oregano

Mix all in blender. Blend again before pouring on salad greens.

Fabulous French Salad Dressing Treat

My good friend Harriette Treat sent me this old recipe that her mother used to make in the 50s. It's even easier to make these days with a blender. And it is definitely a treat.—Gwen McKee

1 onion
1 (10¾-ounce) can tomato soup, undiluted
½ cup white vinegar
1 teaspoon dry mustard

⅔ cup granulated sugar
½ cup oil
1 tablespoon Worcestershire
1 teaspoon salt

Quarter onion and place in blender container with all ingredients. Blend on high speed or liquefy about 30 seconds or until thoroughly blended. Can be kept in the refrigerator 2–3 months—if it lasts that long!

Editor's Extra: You can also grate the onion in the food processor, then add all ingredients.

Vegetables and fruits are the body's best friends. They are loaded with vitamins, minerals, antioxidants, fiber . . . and are recommended for virtually all diets. Whether you grow your own, buy them fresh, or grab the little box from the freezer, vegetables can be cooked quickly and easily in a variety of ways—and in a variety of vessels—to capture their natural goodness.

square pan with bacon press

Anytime you have to brown and drain away the fat, pour spouts save you time. When you need crisp bacon, the press is a must.

Sautéed Brussels Sprouts with Bacon in Mustard Sauce

If someone you know says they don't like Brussels sprouts, ask again after they taste these.

6 strips bacon	2 tablespoons Dijon mustard
2 pounds Brussels sprouts	1 teaspoon salt
2 tablespoons butter, unsalted	1 teaspoon pepper

Using square pan with bacon press, cook bacon crisp, then drain, cool, and break into pieces. Trim brussels sprouts; cut an "X" in base, then boil in salted water approximately 10 minutes. Drain water. Add butter and Dijon mustard to hot brussels sprouts. Season with salt and pepper. Yields 10 servings.

saucepan

Our Favorite Asparagus Casserole

This family-favorite recipe has been in my family for years. —Dana Walker

1 (6-ounce) jar Old English cheese	Salt and pepper to taste
1 cup grated mild Cheddar cheese	2 (15-ounce) cans asparagus spears, drained well
1 (10¾-ounce) can cream of mushroom soup	1 (8-ounce) can English peas, drained well
1 (2-ounce) jar pimentos, drained (optional)	4–6 hard-boiled eggs, sliced
	Cracker crumbs for topping

casserole

In a 2-quart saucepan over low heat, melt cheeses in soup with pimento, salt, and pepper. In 3-quart casserole, layer asparagus, peas, and boiled eggs; cover with cheese sauce. Top with cracker crumbs. Bake in 350° oven for 30–45 minutes. Let stand 15–20 minutes before serving. Serves 6–8.

Festive Broccoli Bake

I love the variety of flavors in this tasty side dish. It's easy and really delicious. Nice for the big holiday dinners or a potluck dinner.—Jenny Repko

1 (16-ounce) package broccoli florets, thawed and drained
2 (14½-ounce) cans stewed tomatoes
2 tablespoons cornstarch
1 teaspoon sugar
1 teaspoon Italian seasoning, divided
¼ teaspoon black pepper

1½ cups shredded mozzarella cheese
4 tablespoons butter or margarine, melted
2 tablespoons grated Parmesan cheese
2 cups unseasoned dry bread cubes, crushed

Preheat oven to 350°. Place broccoli in single layer in 10-inch everyday pan, cutting any large florets in half. Combine tomatoes, cornstarch, sugar, ¾ teaspoon Italian seasoning, and pepper. Pour over broccoli. Sprinkle mozzarella cheese over tomatoes. Combine melted butter with remaining ¼ teaspoon Italian seasoning and Parmesan cheese. Toss with dry bread cubes. Sprinkle over broccoli mixture. Bake 30 minutes. Makes 8 servings.

everyday pan

ALTERNATE:
casserole

Broccoli and Cauliflower Sauté

This was a recipe I learned when working at a restaurant in San Francisco. It's also great mixed in with pasta.—Meredith Laurence

2 tablespoons olive oil
2 cups broccoli florets, sliced from stem through floret
2 cups cauliflower, sliced from stem through floret
¼ cup pine nuts, toasted

¼ cup golden raisins, plumped in hot water
3 cloves garlic, minced
Salt and pepper to taste
2 tablespoons finely chopped parsley

Heat sauté pan over medium-high heat. Add olive oil. Sauté broccoli and cauliflower in oil, browning well, and cooking until tender. Add pine nuts, raisins, and garlic; toss. Heat through. Season to taste with salt and pepper, then add in parsley. Serves 6–8.

sauté pan

ALTERNATE:
electric skillet

skillet

ALTERNATE:
electric skillet

Grammy's Creamed Spinach

My mother loves spinach, and has been making variations of this recipe for a long time. It must be good for you . . . she's 92. —Gwen McKee

4 (10-ounce) packages frozen chopped spinach	**2 tablespoons chopped garlic**
¼ cup water	**2 tablespoons Worcestershire**
½ stick butter	**4 ounces cream cheese, cut into chunks**
1 medium onion, chopped	**½ pint heavy cream**
Seasoned salt to taste	**1 cup grated cheese**

Steam spinach in water in very large skillet, covered, just until totally melted. Drain in a colander.

In same skillet, melt butter and sauté onion until soft. Add drained spinach and seasoned salt; sauté about 4 minutes. Add garlic, Worcestershire, cream cheese, and cream; stir until mixed. Bring to a boil, then simmer about 10 minutes. Pour into greased casserole. Sprinkle with cheese. Bake in pre-heated 350° oven about 5 minutes, or until cheese is slightly browned. Serves 8–10.

Editor's Extra: If making ahead, refrigerate before adding cheese. Bake about 20 minutes to heat thoroughly, then add cheese and bake until browned. May use half Worcestershire and half soy sauce, or all soy sauce.

Gwen's family (Janet, Hal, and Ann) toast Grammy's birthday. We make her spinach now, but she evaluates and tells us how good it is.

Braised Greens with Bacon

Ahh . . . the divine swine! Bacon makes everything taste great.

½ pound bacon, chopped
   into ½-inch pieces
1 onion, sliced
2 cloves garlic, minced
2 pounds bitter greens*
   washed, stemmed, and
   chopped

1 cup chicken stock
Salt and pepper to taste

chef's pan

ALTERNATE:
cast-iron
casserole

Heat a 4-quart chef's pan over medium heat. Add bacon and cook until almost crisp. Add onion and cook until tender. Add garlic and cook an additional minute. Toss in greens and stir well. Add chicken stock and a little salt and pepper. Be careful not to overseason the food at this point. Reduce heat to a simmer.

Cover pan; braise greens until they are wilted and tender. Season again with salt and pepper to taste. Serve as a side dish, or mix into pasta with Parmesan cheese. Serves 4.

Editor's Extra: Any bitter greens such as collard, kale, Swiss chard, etc. can be used.

Perfectly Perfect Greens

1 tablespoon canola oil
⅓ cup diced lean ham
1 clove garlic, minced
1 small onion, diced
3 cups water

3 tablespoons pepper vinegar
1 teaspoon sugar or Splenda
2 pounds washed greens
   (mustard, turnip, or collard)

easy pour
stockpot

ALTERNATE:
pressure cooker

In stockpot, heat oil; sauté ham, garlic, and onion about 5 minutes on medium-high heat. Add water, vinegar, sugar, and greens. Bring to a boil, then cover and simmer about ½ hour or until tender. Serves 6.

Alternate Method: Cooking in a pressure cooker takes only 10 minutes on HIGH setting.

square pan with
bacon press

Chard Stems with Bacon and Cream

4 slices bacon, chopped
2 cups chard stems, sliced
¼ inch

1 clove garlic, minced
½ cup heavy cream
Salt and pepper to taste

Cook bacon in skillet over medium-high heat. When bacon is crispy, add chard stems and sauté until al dente. Add garlic; cook an additional 30 seconds. Add cream and bring to a simmer. Simmer for a few minutes to slightly thicken the liquid. Season to taste with salt and pepper. Serves 2–3.

Braised Leeks au Gratin

If you've never experienced leeks, this is a great way to get to know them. It's an easy preparation that you'll find yourself making over and over again.

1 tablespoon butter
2 leeks, cleaned and cut into
2½-inch pieces
Salt and pepper to taste
½–1 cup chicken stock

½ cup coarse bread crumbs
½ cup shredded mozzarella
cheese
¼ cup grated Parmesan
cheese

everyday pan

Preheat oven to 425°. Heat a 500° oven-safe everyday pan over medium-high heat. Add butter and melt. Sauté leeks in butter until lightly browned. Season to taste with salt and pepper, and add enough chicken stock to barely cover leeks. Cover pan, lower heat to simmer, and braise leeks until almost tender to a knife point. Remove lid, increase heat, and continue to cook until almost all the liquid has disappeared. Remove pan from heat. Combine bread crumbs and cheeses; sprinkle mixture on top of leeks. Transfer pan to a 425° oven and bake until cheese melts and bread crumb topping is a light brown color. Serves 4.

Editor's Extra: This recipe can be used for any variety of vegetables as long as the vegetable is cooked before applying the bread crumb topping. Try using steamed broccoli, cauliflower, or carrots sautéed with fresh thyme. Roasted tomato halves with herbs also make an excellent gratin.

French-Fried Turnip Fingers

Southerners will fry anything!

½ cup all-purpose flour
1 tablespoon cornstarch
1 teaspoon seasoned salt or
  Cajun seasoning

1 teaspoon Greek seasoning
4 or 5 turnips, peeled, sliced
  into fingers
Oil for frying

Combine flour, cornstarch, and seasonings in large bowl or plastic bag. Add turnips and shake to coat thoroughly. Set aside while oil is heating in electric deep-fryer (this gives the coating time to set). Add coated turnips to hot oil, not over-crowding in basket. Cook 3–5 minutes, then drain on paper towels; cover with another paper towel while frying another batch. Serves 6–8.

electric deep
fryer

ALTERNATE:
chicken fryer

Mamean's Turnip Soufflé

My mother developed this recipe when we had an abundance of turnips in our garden . . . delicious!—Barbara Moseley

½ stick butter
¼ cup minced onion
2 tablespoons all-purpose
  flour
3 cups mashed, cooked
  turnips

1 teaspoon salt
½ teaspoon white pepper
2 teaspoons sugar
2 eggs, separated

Melt butter in 10-inch skillet; add onion and sauté until tender. Add flour and stir to blend. Add turnips, salt, pepper, sugar, and beaten egg yolks. Mix well. In a small bowl, whisk egg whites until stiff and fold into turnip mixture. Bake at 350° for 35–40 minutes. Serves 4.

skillet

OPTION:
stoneware
baking dish

Though cook's essentials skillets can go right in the oven, Barbara likes to transfer the mix-ture into a buttered casserole dish.

double boiler

stoneware
baking dish

Grandma Barlow's Creamed Onions

This recipe was adapted from a dish Grandma Barlow always served at Thanksgiving. —Bob Warden

4 white onions, peeled and
   cut into quarters
4 tablespoons butter, melted
4 tablespoons flour
1 cup heavy cream
¼ teaspoon freshly ground
   nutmeg

½ teaspoon freshly ground
   pepper
Salt to taste
Buttered bread crumbs
Grated provolone cheese

Steam onions in double boiler until tender, retaining 1 cup of onion steaming water. In a small saucepan, mix butter and flour; add cream and onion water. Cook sauce until thick; add steamed onions. Add nutmeg, pepper, and salt to taste. Turn into greased baking dish and top with bread crumbs and cheese. Bake at 350° until hot and bubbly. Serves 4–6.

steamer

This is so nice to steam both green beans and onions at the same time.

skillet

Green Beans with Caramelized Onions

2 pounds fresh green beans
1 pound pearl onions, peeled
¼ cup butter or margarine

¼ cup firmly packed brown
   sugar

Arrange green beans in lower steamer basket of electric steamer and onions in top basket. Cover and steam 5 minutes; check onions, they may need to come off at this time. Return green beans to steam for another 5–7 minutes.

Melt butter in large heavy skillet over medium heat; add brown sugar, and cook, stirring constantly, until bubbly. Add onions, and cook, stirring constantly, 3 minutes. Add green beans; cook, stirring constantly, until thoroughly heated. Yields 8 servings.

Green Beans with Shallots, Hazelnuts, and Rosemary

½ cup skinned hazelnuts
5 pounds green beans
5 shallots, sliced in rings
2 tablespoons rosemary

8 tablespoons olive oil
1 teaspoon salt
1 teaspoon pepper

lipped skillet

Toast hazelnuts; chop lightly. Trim one end of green beans. In saucepan, blanch beans in salted water. In lipped skillet, sauté shallots and rosemary in olive oil. Toss together beans, shallot mixture, hazelnuts, salt, and pepper. Yields 20 servings.

Editor's Extra: To get the skins off hazelnuts, put hot toasted nuts in a clean tea towel. Collect all the ends of the towel around the nuts and rub the nuts together. Most of the skins will fall off.

OPTION:
steamer

Easy to steam beans rather than blanching.

Pressure-Steamed Veggies

1 pound green beans
1 pound carrots, sliced
½ inch on bias

1 cup chicken stock
Butter
Italian seasoning

Place green beans and carrots on separate sides of pressure cooker. Add stock and cook under HIGH pressure 2 minutes. Drain stock and add butter and Italian seasoning to the warm vegetables. Serves 6–8.

Alternate Method: This will take about 20 minutes in a large covered stockpot.

pressure cooker

ALTERNATE:
stockpot

dutch oven

ALTERNATE:
cast-iron
casserole

Beans and More

All of my favorites in one pot . . . I like to use fresh vegetables when possible.
—Barbara Moseley

2 cups frozen lima beans, or
   1 (15-ounce) can lima beans
½ cup water
1 (14½-ounce) can tomatoes,
   okra, and corn
½ cup frozen chopped onion,
   bell pepper, and celery mix

1 teaspoon bacon drippings
   or cooking oil
½ teaspoon salt
¼ teaspoon black pepper
½ teaspoon sugar
2 strips bacon, crisply fried,
   crumbled

In 4-quart Dutch oven or bean pot, place lima beans in ½ cup water. Add undrained tomatoes, okra, and corn. Add chopped vegetables, bacon drippings, and seasonings. Cook on medium-low heat 25–30 minutes; or until beans are tender. Add crumbled bacon and stir in. Delicious served with hot cornbread.

square pan with
bacon press

ALTERNATE:
electric skillet

Rainbow Succotash

4 slices bacon, chopped
1 onion, chopped
1 clove garlic, minced
1 (16-ounce) package frozen
   lima beans
1 (10-ounce) package frozen
   corn kernels

½ cup chopped roasted red
   pepper
Salt, pepper, and sugar to taste
2 tablespoons chopped parsley
1 cup cherry tomatoes, halved
½ cup half-and-half

Preheat skillet over medium heat. Cook bacon until almost crispy. Drain all but 1 tablespoon of fat. Add onion and cook until tender. Add garlic, lima beans, and water per package directions on the lima beans. When lima beans are tender, add corn and red pepper. Heat through for 5 minutes. Season to taste with salt, pepper, and sugar. Toss in parsley and cherry tomatoes. Add half-and-half; heat through briefly. Serves 6.

Pressure Cooker Baked Beans

I never made baked beans at home until I got a pressure cooker. It's so easy, so fast, and so tasty. — Meredith Laurence

1 pound dried navy beans
**1/2 pound bacon, chopped
   into 1/2-inch pieces**
1 onion, diced small
2 cloves garlic, minced
1/4 cup molasses

1/4 cup ketchup
1/4 cup brown sugar
1 teaspoon dry mustard
1 bay leaf
Water
1–2 teaspoons salt, or to taste

pressure cooker

Soak navy beans in water overnight, or quick-soak by bringing water to a boil, turning off heat, and letting beans sit for 1 hour. Drain. Heat pressure cooker and cook bacon pieces until almost crispy. Remove bacon pieces and set aside. Drain bacon fat.

ALTERNATE:
electric
stockpot

Return bacon to pressure cooker; add onion and garlic, and continue to cook 2–3 minutes. Add beans and remaining ingredients to pressure cooker, with enough water to just cover the beans (about 2 cups). Bring mixture to a boil. Cover securely with pressure cooker lid and cook under HIGH pressure 30 minutes. Let pressure release naturally. Season to taste again. If beans have too much liquid, turn pressure cooker on without the lid and allow the sauce to reduce until desired consistency is reached, about 5 minutes. Serves 6–8.

Alternate Method: To make in a regular or electric stockpot, simply cook baked beans for 1 1/2–2 hours on high SIMMER.

dutch oven

ALTERNATE:
cast-iron
casserole

Gwen's Favorite Way to Cook Beans

It's not necessary to soak them all night. How long beans cook isn't what makes the beans soft and delicious—how they cook is.—Gwen McKee

1 pound dry beans
1 tablespoon olive oil
1 big onion, chopped
½ green pepper, chopped
1 clove garlic, minced
1 meaty ham bone, or a cube
  of salt pork, or ham chunks,
  or 3 strips bacon, minced

2 tablespoons brown sugar
1 tablespoon minced jalapeño,
  or 1 tablespoon chili powder
1 tablespoon Cajun seasoning
Fritos (optional)

Pour beans in a Dutch oven with 8 cups water. Bring to a boil, covered with a lid you can vent open. Remove from heat, close vent on lid, and do not take lid off at all!

After an hour or so of no peeking, put back on medium-low, and heat till the lid is showing steam.

Now stir in a tablespoon of olive oil. Simmer, covered with vent open, 1–2 hours. Stir from time to time to see if you need to add more water, but be sure it is hot water.

Now stir in onion, green pepper, garlic, and meat of choice. Add brown sugar, jalapeño or chili powder, and seasoning. Simmer at least another 45 minutes or for several hours. If too dry, add more hot water; if too thin, cook longer to reduce liquid, and/or crush a few Fritos and add to pot. Serves 8.

Editor's Extra: Sometimes I add browned ground meat or sausage, tomatoes, sometimes a little barbecue sauce, molasses, maybe a touch of smoke flavoring, or different seasonings. Beans are good for you. This is a good recipe to have fun being creative with them.

Peas Please

I grew up thinking peas and cornbread were a staple in everybody's dining. Even though I now know others don't have the same feeling for these delicious southern dishes, I still enjoy my peas with cornbread fritters on the side.

—*Barbara Moseley*

electric saucepan

1 (16-ounce) package frozen purple hull peas
½ teaspoon salt
½ teaspoon black pepper
½ teaspoon sugar
½ cup chopped, cooked ham
1 onion, quartered
Water to cover

Place all ingredients in electric or 3-quart saucepan. Cook on high until boiling; turn heat down to medium and continue cooking 30–35 minutes or until peas are done. Watch the water level; do not let the peas dry out. Serves 6.

Can-tastic Black-Eyed Peas

Don't wait for New Year's to indulge in this wonderful vegetable. Serve it with stuffed bell peppers and cornbread for a truly southern meal.

ALTERNATE:
saucepan
Use a saucepan for both recipes.

2 strips bacon, chopped
¼ cup chopped onion
1 teaspoon minced garlic
2 (16-ounce) cans black-eyed peas, undrained
½ teaspoon sugar
Dashes of black and red pepper

Fry bacon in a saucepan for a minute; add onion and garlic; sauté another 2 minutes. Add peas with sugar and peppers. Heat to boiling, then simmer 8–10 minutes. Add a little hot water if it gets dry. Some like to dip cornbread in the juice, so be sure it's juicy! Serves 4–5.

skillet

roasting pan

Zucchini Gondolas

Lively, delicious, beautiful, and fun! And did I mention easy? You'll be the talk of the town with this presentation. —Gwen McKee

3 medium-size zucchini
⅓ pound seasoned ground
**   sausage**
½ cup chopped onion
1 clove garlic, minced
½ cup chopped green pepper
1 small tomato, seeded,
**   chopped**

1 tablespoon chopped
**   pimentos**
¼ cup bread crumbs
**   (plain or seasoned)**
½ cup grated Parmesan
**   cheese**
¾ cup shredded mozzarella
**   cheese**

Cut zucchini in half lengthwise. Scoop out pulp, leaving ½-inch shell; reserve ½ cup seedless pulp; set shells aside. Cook sausage, onion, garlic, and green pepper in medium skillet over high heat until browned; drain. Stir in tomato, pimentos, bread crumbs, Parmesan, and reserved pulp. Spoon into zucchini shells, shaping a little higher at each end, then place in large roasting pan or casserole. Divide mozzarella into each gondola. Bake in 350° oven till cheese melts, about 25 minutes. Serves 8.

Editor's Extra: To make this a highlight of your Italian dinner, be creative with cuts of red bell pepper stuck into each end to emphasize the gondola shape. Before serving, lean Italian breadsticks against gondola for steering poles.

Bob and Carole Haffey have fun before a Today's Special Value presentation.

Yellow Bird Bell Peppers

My mother-in-law made the best stuffed peppers. It took me years to come close. Once you master the method, the deviations are fun to try. With a substitution of colorful saffron rice, these please . . . it's as simple as that. Some people eat only the stuffing, but I eat the peppers, too.—Gwen McKee

stoneware baking dish

3 large or 4 medium bell peppers
⅔ cup minced onion
1 clove garlic, minced
1 tablespoon butter
½ pound ground beef
½ cup chopped ham
½ cup yellow saffron rice, cooked

Dash of red pepper
Dash of salt
2 (8-ounce) cans tomato sauce, divided
½ cup apple juice
½ cup water
½ cup sour cream
⅓ cup shredded Cheddar cheese

everyday pan

Cut peppers in half lengthwise; seed, stem and wash. Drop into 6-quart pot of boiling, lightly salted water; turn off heat and let peppers sit in water 5 minutes. Drain on paper towels; put in baking dish.

Preheat oven to 350°. Sauté onion and garlic in everyday pan in butter. Mix with ground beef, ham, cooked rice, seasonings, and 1 can tomato sauce. Stuff this mixture into peppers. In separate bowl, mix remaining can tomato sauce, apple juice, water, and sour cream. Pour over peppers in baking dish. Bake 40 minutes. Top peppers with cheese, and bake an additional 20 minutes. Superb! Serves 6–8.

OPTION:
steamer

I like using this steamer instead of parboiling the peppers; just steam enough to take the "hard edge" off. —Bob

Roasted Corn and Red Pepper Polenta

saucepan

OPTION:
jellyroll pan

4 cups milk
6 cups water
2 cups cornmeal
½ pound butter
4 ears corn, roasted, kernels
   removed

3 red bell peppers, roasted,
   peeled, and diced small
Salt and pepper to taste

Combine milk and water in saucepan and bring to a boil. As soon as it boils, whisk in cornmeal, stirring constantly. (Avoid letting the milk and water boil for too long, or milk will curdle.) Bring polenta back to a boil, then immediately reduce heat to a simmer. Cook, stirring frequently, until polenta is tender, about 20–30 minutes. Add butter, corn kernels, and red peppers. Season to taste with salt and pepper. Serves 6.

Editor's Extra: For hard polenta, pour polenta into a greased jellyroll pan and let cool. When polenta has set, cut it into desired shape and grill, sauté, or fry.

Corn Bake Ranchero

baking pan

ALTERNATE:
casserole

1 (7-ounce) package southern
   cornbread mix
1 (1.2-ounce) package ranch
   fiesta salad dressing mix
2 eggs, beaten
⅓ cup butter or margarine,
   melted
1 cup sour cream
1 (16½-ounce) can cream-
   style corn

1 (12-ounce) can corn with red
   and green bell peppers,
   drained
1 (4-ounce) can mushroom
   stems and pieces, drained
1 cup shredded sharp Cheddar
   cheese

Preheat oven to 350°. In large bowl, combine cornbread mix and salad dressing mix. Stir in eggs, butter, and sour cream just until moistened. Add remaining ingredients, except cheese. Pour into greased 9-inch-square baking pan or 10-inch casserole. Sprinkle cheese evenly over top. Bake until toothpick inserted in center comes out clean, 50–60 minutes. Serves 8–10.

Colorful Corn Pudding

2 (11-ounce) cans whole-kernel corn, drained
⅓ cup chopped bell peppers (red and green)
¼ cup flour
2 tablespoons self-rising cornmeal
1 tablespoon sugar
3 tablespoons butter, melted
¾ cup milk
2 eggs
Few dashes cinnamon
Few dashes nutmeg
Salt and pepper to taste
Paprika

Put corn and peppers into a blender and blend for a minute. Add remaining ingredients except paprika, and process until smooth. Pour into greased 2-quart baking dish, scantily sprinkle paprika over top, and bake in 350° oven for 35 minutes. Serves 6.

blender

stoneware baking dish

Rave Corn Pudding

My lifelong friend and neighbor, Gayle, makes this every Christmas and brings me the leftovers because I love it so much. I've made it for special occasions and everyone raves about it. So easy to put together.—Jenny Repko

⅓ cup sugar
3 tablespoons cornstarch
3 eggs
½ stick butter, sliced
1 (16-ounce) can cream-style corn
1 (12-ounce) can evaporated milk

Preheat oven to 350°. Blend all ingredients in food processor. Place in shallow pan. Bake 1 hour. Serves 4–6.

food processor

sauté pan

ALTERNATE:
casserole

Mimi's Creamed Corn Casserole

1 onion, chopped
⅓ cup chopped bell pepper
½ stick butter
1 (15-ounce) can creamed corn
1 (15-ounce) can shoepeg corn
1 (11-ounce) can whole-kernel corn
½ teaspoon sugar
½ teaspoon white pepper
½ teaspoon salt, or to taste
3 ounces cream cheese, chunked
2 eggs, beaten
½ cup sour cream
30 Ritz Crackers, crushed, divided
Spray butter

In sauté pan, sauté onion and pepper in butter. Add corn, seasonings, and cream cheese; heat until cream cheese is melted. Take off fire and add beaten eggs, sour cream, and half the cracker crumbs. Refrigerate now, if making ahead.

Allow casserole to come to room temperature before baking. Sprinkle remaining crumbs over top and spray generously with spray butter. Bake at 350° about 20–30 minutes until browned on top. Serves 6–8.

saucepan

Sweet Carrots with a Touch of Cinnamon

People who think they don't like carrots almost always love these.

1 (16-ounce) bag baby carrots
½ teaspoon salt
2–3 tablespoons butter
¼ cup brown sugar
¾ cup miniature marshmallows
⅛ teaspoon cinnamon

In 2-quart saucepan, put carrots and salt in water to cover; bring to a boil, then simmer 15–20 minutes. Drain all but about ¼ cup water. Add remaining ingredients and stir until marshmallows are melted. Serves 5–6.

Tomatoes Meritage

FOUR TOWERS:

4 large ripe tomatoes
1 eggplant, cut into 8 pieces no wider than tomatoes
2 large roasted red peppers, cut into 8 pieces no wider than tomatoes
8 marinated or grilled portobello mushrooms, same diameter as tomatoes

8 slices fresh mozzarella cheese, no bigger than tomatoes
Olive oil for drizzling
Salt and pepper to taste
12 fresh basil leaves for garnish

baking sheet

Slice tomatoes into 8 round slices approximately ½ inch thick. Place 4 tomatoes on a baking sheet approximately 2 inches apart. Build up with a round of eggplant, then a piece of pepper, then a portobello, then a slice of mozzarella; repeat so there are 2 of everything (you may need a toothpick to help keep the tower upright.) Drizzle with olive oil, salt, and pepper, and bake at 350° about 30 minutes or until eggplant is very tender.

saucepan

BALSAMIC REDUCTION:

2 cups balsamic vinegar

Put balsamic vinegar in a 1-quart saucepan and simmer until the consistency will coat a spoon.

RED PEPPER SAUCE:

2 cups chopped roasted red and/or yellow bell peppers

1 teaspoon minced garlic
Salt and pepper to taste

food processor

Put ingredients in a food processor or blender and purée, then push through a fine sieve. Transfer into a squeeze bottle.

Transfer each tower to a white plate and drizzle with both sauces. Place the basil either on top or scatter around plates. If you would like to add more color to the plate, top with a teaspoon of thick pesto.

skillet

OPTION:
kohaishu knife

A kohaishu knife is so nice for slicing tomatoes.

pizza pan

mini food processor

Fried Red Tomatoes

¾ cup bread crumbs
¼ cup grated Parmesan cheese
½ teaspoon dried oregano

1 teaspoon salt
¼ teaspoon pepper
2 firm tomatoes
2 tablespoons butter

Combine bread crumbs, Parmesan, oregano, salt, and pepper. Slice tomatoes ½ inch thick. Coat with bread crumb mixture. Heat 12-inch skillet over medium heat and melt butter. Brown tomatoes in butter, turning once. Serves 3–4.

Easy Tomato Basil Pizza

Barney and I love basil on tomatoes. This is a quick lunch or supper you'll fix again and again!—Gwen McKee

3 (7-inch) refrigerated pizza crusts
1½ cups shredded mozzarella or Swiss cheese, divided
2 large or 3 small tomatoes, sliced

2 tablespoons grated Parmesan cheese
1 tablespoon refrigerated basil herb blend (or snipped basil)
¾ cup mayonnaise
1 teaspoon minced garlic

Preheat oven to 375°. Place pizza crusts on pizza pans or large cookie sheets. Divide and sprinkle half the Swiss or mozzarella cheese on the crusts. Place sliced tomatoes on top. In food processor, mix remaining ingredients, including remaining cheese, and dollop onto tomatoes. Bake for 20 minutes. Serves 2–3.

Editor's Extra: Refrigerated basil herb blend is in a green tube found near the fresh basil in produce. It keeps a lot longer, and is so simple to use.

Potato Potsy

Cooking for two? This easy, tasty dish also assures leftovers are mighty tasty the next day.

1 tablespoon butter
1 tablespoon vegetable oil
1 large onion, sliced in half
   rings
4 medium potatoes

2 stalks celery
1 teaspoon minced garlic
1 tablespoon minced parsley
Salt, black pepper, and red
   pepper to taste

Place butter and oil in electric saucepan on 270°. Add onion. Stir occasionally while peeling and slicing potatoes and celery. Add sliced potatoes, celery, garlic, parsley, and seasonings to pot. Cook about 25 minutes, stirring every 5 minutes or so till done. Serves 4.

electric
saucepan

ALTERNATE:
saucepan

Potatoes au Fromage

My daddy loved good, tasty food. Being Irish, potatoes were a favorite of his, but they had to be tasty, too. He always liked them when Mother put cheese on top.—Gwen McKee

8 cups sliced peeled red
   potatoes
1 large onion, sliced
1 teaspoon minced garlic
1 tablespoon chopped parsley
1 teaspoon salt

½ teaspoon black pepper
1 (10¾-ounce) can cream
   of mushroom soup
1 cup sour cream
2 cups shredded Cheddar
   cheese

Heat everyday pan (500° oven-safe) on medium-high heat. Throw in potatoes, onion, garlic, parsley, and seasonings. Stir while partially browning. Add soup, cover, and lower heat; simmer about 30 minutes. Stir in sour cream. Sprinkle cheese over top, and bake in 400° oven 15 minutes till cheese is slightly browned. Serves 8.

everyday pan

*Technique or 500
series cookware is
safe to 500°.*

ALTERNATE:
mandoline

VEGETABLES • 103

casserole

saucepan

everyday pan

ALTERNATE:
stoneware
baking dish

Scalloped Potatoes with Bacon

Good with anything—steak, hamburgers, pork chops, fried chicken . . . it's just plain good.

8 cups sliced, peeled red potatoes
½ cup minced onion
¾ cup chopped green pepper
1 (10¾-ounce) can cream of celery soup

1 (8-ounce) package cream cheese, cubed
1½ cups heavy cream or milk
1 teaspoon seasoned salt
5 slices bacon, cooked, crumbled

Place potatoes, onion, and bell pepper in casserole, stirring to mix. In 2-quart saucepan, heat remaining ingredients except bacon. Pour over potato mixture; bake in 350° oven 1 hour. Sprinkle bacon pieces over top and bake another 15 minutes. Serves 8.

Crunchy Potato Cakes

A great way to use leftover mashed potatoes.

2 cups leftover mashed potatoes
1 large egg, beaten
½ onion, chopped
1 cup shredded Cheddar cheese or cheese blend

½ teaspoon Greek seasoning
½ cup crushed cornflakes
1 teaspoon toasted sesame seeds

Mix potatoes with egg, onion, cheese, and seasoning. Form into balls or cakes. Roll in mixture of cornflakes and toasted sesame seeds. Bake in lightly greased everyday pan or baking dish at 350° for 20–25 minutes. If top is not browned to your liking, turn cakes over and bake another 5 minutes. Serves 3–4.

Joe-tatoes

saucepan

Using a saucepan with a drain lid makes draining potatoes a snap.

My son, Joseph, developed this recipe as a teenager, and he used to eat it by the gallon. It is the one thing he is required to make at any holiday gathering— they are so good they don't even need gravy. My daughter, Rachel, brought these to a work Christmas party one year. Every one of the twenty people there demanded the recipe.—Bob Warden

6–10 large potatoes, washed and diced (with or without peels)
½–1 pound butter

1–2 cups sour cream
½–1 pint whipping cream
Salt and pepper to taste

Wash and dice potatoes. Boil in saucepan until very tender. Drain potatoes and mash them in the pan to keep them warm. Add butter and sour cream, then add whipping cream to desired consistency. Use a mixer to whip the ingredients together. Serves 6–8.

mixer

Potato and Ham Casserole

2 tablespoons unsalted butter
1 tablespoon flour
2 cups heavy cream
1 clove garlic, slivered
½ teaspoon dried thyme
½ teaspoon salt
¼ teaspoon black pepper
1–2 pounds pound deli-sliced ham

2–3 baking potatoes, peeled and sliced thin
½ yellow onion, sliced thin
½ cup grated Parmesan cheese
2 tablespoons finely chopped parsley

skillet

In a skillet, melt butter, then stir in flour. Add cream. Stir, then bring to a boil to thicken. Add garlic, thyme, salt, and pepper; let simmer until reduced slightly, about 10 minutes. In a greased baking dish, layer ham, potatoes, onion, and sauce until pan is full (2–3 layers). Top with Parmesan cheese. Bake in 350° oven 45–60 minutes. Cool completely. Sprinkle with parsley. Serves 6.

ALTERNATE:
stoneware
baking dish

mixer

baking pan

Mais Oui Potato Casserole

Pronounced "may-wee," it's French for, "but yes." One bite and you'll agree.

5 pounds potatoes, peeled, cubed
½ teaspoon salt
1 stick butter, softened
1 (8-ounce) package cream cheese, softened

1 (16-ounce) container French onion dip
1 teaspoon garlic salt
1–2 cups grated Cheddar cheese (optional)

Boil potatoes in lightly salted water till tender; drain. Beat potatoes well with mixer. Add butter, cream cheese, onion dip, and garlic salt; beat well again. Transfer to buttered 9x13-inch baking pan. Bake at 350° for 35 minutes, or until browned around edges. If cheese is desired, sprinkle on top during last 15 minutes of baking. Serves 6–8.

baking sheet

OPTION:
santoku knife

You need a good knife for this recipe.

Twice-As-Nice Potato Spears

2 sweet potatoes, peeled and cut into wedges or fries
2 white potatoes, cut into wedges or fries
⅓ cup Italian dressing

⅓ cup grated Parmesan cheese
1 tablespoon chopped fresh parsley

Preheat oven to 375°. Toss potatoes with dressing. Place on lightly greased baking sheet. Cook 30 minutes. Turn potatoes; cook an additional 30 minutes, sprinkling with cheese during the last 5 minutes. Sprinkle with parsley. Serves 8.

Sweet Potato Gratin

1 cup heavy cream
1 cup whole milk
4 cloves garlic, smashed
Salt and freshly ground black
  pepper
1–2 pinches nutmeg

2 pounds sweet potatoes,
  peeled, sliced ⅛–¼ inch
  thick
2 cups grated Parmesan
  cheese
Chopped parsley for garnish

cast-iron
saucepan

OPTION:
mandoline

*If you have ever
tried to cut sweet
potatoes evenly
with a knife, you
are really going to
love using this
mandoline slicer.*

Preheat oven to 425°. Combine heavy cream, milk, and garlic in a large, straight-sided (500° oven-safe) saucepan. Bring mixture to a boil on stovetop and simmer 10 minutes. Discard smashed garlic cloves and season to taste with salt, pepper, and a pinch or 2 of nutmeg (the nutmeg should have a faint taste—not too strong). Remember the potatoes will absorb a lot of the salt as they cook, so season well at this stage.

Add potatoes to simmering cream mixture. Stir them around to make sure everything is well-blended. If you like, you can carefully shingle the top layer of potatoes so that the presentation is beautiful at the end. Sprinkle Parmesan on top and transfer pan to oven; bake 30–45 minutes. The top of the gratin should be nicely brown and the potatoes should be tender to a knife point. Remove from oven and allow to cool and set slightly before serving. Garnish with chopped parsley. Serves 8.

*Young Bob tends his garden. Growing your own vegetables
always leads to healthier, tastier foods.*

saucepan

OPTION:
knife set

OPTION:
food processor

A food processor makes perfect chutney if you are careful to pulse fruits just a few times, then again after adding remaining ingredients.

Mango-Apricot Chutney

Spruce up a bland plate with this pretty and tasty chutney.

1 mango, diced
½ cup chopped dried apricots
⅓ cup brown sugar
½ jalapeño pepper, diced small
¼ cup cider vinegar

2 tablespoons currants
3 tablespoons water
1½ teaspoons lime juice
Salt to taste
¼–½ teaspoon minced garlic

Combine all ingredients in a 2½-quart saucepan; bring to a boil. Reduce heat and simmer for 30 minutes, stirring occasionally. Serve warm, or place in a jar in refrigerator and serve later cold.

pasta, rice, etc.

Pasta and rice dishes are so perfect for one-dish creations for buffets, potlucks, tailgates, and just good hearty family meals. Most can be made ahead and frozen. They lend themselves to creativity, as it is so easy to substitute or add favorite ingredients and seasonings.

stockpot;
skillet

mixing bowl

baking pan

Garden Vegetable Lasagna

Some nights we just want a break from meat, so I came up with the lasagna option. Try it, you won't miss the beef!—Jenny Repko

8 uncooked lasagna noodles
1 tablespoon olive or
  vegetable oil
1 garlic clove, minced
3 cups frozen broccoli cuts
1½ cups (about 4 ounces)
  sliced fresh mushrooms
1 medium red, yellow, or
  orange bell pepper, coarsely
  chopped (about 1 cup)

1 egg
1 (16-ounce) container ricotta
  cheese
1 teaspoon dried Italian
  seasoning
1 (26- to 28-ounce) jar chunky
  vegetable tomato pasta sauce
2 cups shredded 6-cheese
  Italian cheese blend

Cook lasagna noodles as directed on package in large stock-pot. Drain; place in cold water to cool. Meanwhile, heat oven to 350°. Heat oil in large skillet over medium-high heat until hot. Add garlic, broccoli, mushrooms, and bell pepper; cook 3–4 minutes or until vegetables are crisp-tender, stirring frequently. Remove from heat. If necessary, cut broccoli into smaller pieces. Beat egg in small bowl with wire whisk. Add ricotta cheese and Italian seasoning; mix well. Drain cooled lasagna noodles. Spread ½ cup pasta sauce in ungreased baking pan. Top with 4 noodles, overlapping as necessary, half of ricotta mixture, half of cooked vegetables, half of remaining pasta sauce (about 2¼ cups), and 1 cup shredded cheese. Repeat layers, starting with noodles. Bake for 45–50 minutes or until hot and bubbly. If cheese is getting too brown, cover baking dish loosely with foil. Let stand 15 minutes before serving. Makes 8 servings.

Thoughtful Vegetable Lasagna

I have had many vegetarian friends, and sometimes cooking a meal for them takes just a little more thought. Here's a dish they love.—Meredith Laurence

2 pounds ricotta cheese
1 cup grated Parmesan cheese
1 cup shredded Swiss cheese
2 eggs
2 teaspoons salt
½ teaspoon pepper
3 cups marinara sauce
1 pound lasagna noodles, cooked

½ pound spinach, cooked
½ pound sliced fresh mushrooms
2 yellow squash, sliced thin, lengthwise
25 leaves fresh basil, sliced thin

Preheat oven to 375°. Mix cheeses, eggs, salt, and pepper in mixing bowl. In casserole dish, layer ⅓ marinara sauce, ⅓ noodles, ⅓ cheese mixture, ½ the vegetables, and ½ the basil; repeat. Finish with remaining marinara, noodles, and cheese mixture. Bake in 375° oven for 1 hour. Cool. Serves 8–10.

mixing bowl

casserole

Cooking and serving in one pan helps save on dishwashing. This casserole comes with a trivet to keep your counter and table safe.

Cooking on the island is a given when Mimi cooks with grand-kids. Eva is a natural at separating sticky lasagna noodles.

Home-Style Macaroni and Cheese

saucepan

No need for a colander with this drain and pour saucepan.

casserole

If you have kids, you most likely make macaroni and cheese. I used the boxed variety for years, but once I came up with this homemade version, I never went back. It's healthier for the kids, too!—Jenny Repko

½ stick butter
1 medium yellow onion, diced
¼ cup all-purpose flour
4 cups milk
2 cups cubed sharp white
   Cheddar cheese
1 cup sour cream
Salt and freshly ground pepper
1 pound pasta such as
   macaroni or rigatoni
⅓ cup seasoned bread
   crumbs

In a 2-quart saucepan, melt butter over medium-high heat. Add diced onion and cook until just beginning to brown. Add flour and stir to make a paste. Add milk and stir until the sauce is thick, about 15–20 minutes. Stir in cheese. Add sour cream and stir. Season with salt and freshly ground pepper. Cook pasta according to directions on package in pasta pot with drain lid. Drain and place into a buttered casserole dish. Stir sauce into pasta. Sprinkle with bread crumbs. Bake in pre-heated 350° oven 20–25 minutes until the top begins to brown and casserole bubbles. Serves 6.

Chicken Mac

1½ cups heavy cream
1 pound Cheddar cheese,
  cut into cubes
½ cup Dijon mustard
1 (12- to 16-ounce) package
  chicken tenders, cooked
  and cubed
1 (12- to 16-ounce) package
  skinless, boneless chicken
  thighs, cooked and cubed

1 (10-ounce) can Ro-Tel
  tomatoes
1 cup sliced shiitake
  mushrooms
1 white onion, chopped
1 teaspoon cayenne pepper
12 ounces uncooked elbow
  macaroni
2 tablespoons grated
  Parmesan cheese

Combine cream, cheese, and mustard in medium saucepan; cook and stir over low heat until cheese melts and mixture is smooth. Stir in chicken, tomatoes, mushrooms, onion, and cayenne pepper. Remove from heat.

Cook macaroni according to package directions in pasta pot with drain lid; drain. Add cheese mixture; toss until well coated. Preheat oven to 350°. Spoon macaroni mixture into greased shallow 2-quart baking dish. Cover and bake 15–20 minutes. Stir; sprinkle with Parmesan cheese. Bake, uncovered 5 more minutes. Let stand 10 minutes before serving. Refrigerate leftovers. Makes 6–8 servings.

saucepan

pasta pot

stoneware
baking dish

stockpot;
sauté pan

Pasta Putanesca

When I was first learning to cook, my mother had a book of pasta recipes and this one stood out. I remember cooking it over and over again in her kitchen, adding my own touches over the years. This is a favorite of mine.

—*Meredith Laurence*

1 pound spaghetti
1 tablespoon olive oil
6–8 anchovy fillets, drained
  and chopped
1 clove garlic, minced
2–3 large tomatoes, chopped

12 black olives, pitted and
  chopped
2 tablespoons capers, rinsed
  and chopped
Fresh basil, chopped
Salt and pepper to taste

Bring a large stockpot of salted water to a boil. Boil spaghetti until al dente, or just tender to the tooth. Drain pasta well, and return to stockpot.

Meanwhile, heat a nonstick sauté pan over medium heat. Add olive oil and anchovies, and cook until anchovies start to melt. Add garlic and sauté about 30 seconds. Add tomatoes, olives, and capers and toss together well. Bring mixture to a simmer and let it cook gently while the pasta is boiling.

Add basil to sauce, then add mixture to drained pasta. Season to taste with salt and pepper. (Be careful when adding salt because anchovies are already very salty.) Serve in pasta bowls or on plates, and garnish with more fresh basil. Serves 8.

Food stylists Holli and Bobbi Cappelli work with Gwen at QVC to make every dish look irresistible for the camera.

Island Pasta

I first had this pasta on the island of St. John, and have been making it for friends and family ever since. This pasta keeps very well, and can be served hot or cold. — Holli Cappelli

1 tablespoon peanut oil
2 shallots, minced
6 green onions, minced
1 tablespoon minced fresh garlic
1 (4-ounce) jar chopped pimientos, drained
3 tablespoons light brown sugar
1 tablespoon clover honey
5 tablespoons white balsamic vinegar

2½ teaspoons roasted sesame oil
4 tablespoons soy sauce
1½ teaspoons grated fresh ginger
1 teaspoon finely chopped candied ginger
1 cup peanut butter
1½ cups chicken or vegetable broth
1 pound cooked pasta (your choice)

GARNISHES:

3 green onions, finely chopped
¾ cup chopped peanuts
1 (8-ounce) can pineapple tidbits, drained

1 medium red bell pepper, finely chopped
1 (3-ounce) can coconut flakes
1 cup shredded cooked chicken

Heat peanut oil in large skillet, and sauté the shallots and onions until tender. Add minced garlic and chopped pimientos. Mix well and sauté 3–4 minutes. Mix brown sugar, honey, vinegar, sesame oil, soy sauce, and gingers in a small bowl; whisk well. Lower heat and whisk in brown sugar mixture; mix well. Add peanut butter and whisk again. Over low heat, add broth until mixture has the consistency of a pasta sauce. Taste the sauce and season to your liking. Heat over medium heat until hot. Serve immediately over cooked pasta of your choice (I have used cooked oriental noodles or cooked spaghetti). Garnish with your choice of toppings and serve. Serves 8 as a main or 12 as a side dish.

skillet

OPTION:
mini food chopper

So handy for all fine chopping.

skillet

pasta pot

OPTION:
mandoline

Great for slicing onions this thin.

Pasta with Butternut, Sage, and Cream

2 tablespoons butter
1½ cups butternut squash, diced ¼ inch
1 onion, thinly sliced
1 clove garlic, minced
4 leaves sage, chopped

½ cup heavy cream
Salt and pepper to taste
½ pound pasta, cooked
1 whole sage leaf, fried, for garnish
Parmesan cheese, grated

Heat large skillet over medium-high heat. Add butter. Sauté squash and onion until soft and slightly brown. Add garlic and sage and continue to cook for another minute. Reduce heat and add cream. Season with salt and pepper. Toss with pasta and adjust seasonings, if necessary. Garnish with fried sage leaf and grated Parmesan cheese. Serves 6–8.

Ever ridden a Segway? When Meredith gets a lesson from Gwen's husband Barney in Quail Ridge Press' warehouse, Bob makes sure to capture it with his camera.

Pasta Carbonara

I like to keep things simple and am drawn to the classics of cooking. This is a classic. — Meredith Laurence

1 pound pasta, any shape
1 pound sliced bacon, chopped
½ cup grated Parmesan cheese
4 eggs, lightly beaten
1 cup heavy cream
Salt and freshly ground black pepper
Fresh parsley, chopped

pasta pot

Cook pasta in boiling salted water. Drain and reserve, keeping pasta as warm as possible. Cook chopped bacon in a large everyday pan over medium-high heat until almost crispy. Combine Parmesan, eggs, and heavy cream in a separate bowl. As soon as the bacon is cooked sufficiently, add pasta to pan and toss well to coat; reheat slightly. Stir in eggs, cheese, and cream mixture over low heat for a minute or two, until the sauce thickens slightly. Season to taste with salt and pepper; sprinkle with freshly chopped parsley for garnish. Serves 6–8.

everyday pan

Rachel's Alfredo Sauce

My daughter, Rachel, first made this for her boyfriend on Valentine's Day. Everybody loves it. — Bob Warden

2 sticks butter, divided
¾–1 quart whipping cream, divided
2 (8-ounce) packages cream cheese
2 ounces grated Parmesan cheese
2 ounces grated Asiago cheese
2 ounces grated mozzarella cheese
2 ounces grated provolone cheese
2 ounces grated Romano cheese
Salt, pepper, and garlic powder to taste

saucepan

Melt 1 stick butter in 3-quart saucepan. Slowly add 2 cups whipping cream, whipping as you add. Cut cream cheese into small squares, adding pieces one at a time, whipping the mixture until each piece is melted. Begin to add additional whipping cream as needed to keep mixture creamy and liquid. Add cheeses one ounce at a time, whipping and stirring until completely melted, adding more whipping cream as needed to keep mixture creamy and liquid. Add salt, pepper, and garlic powder to taste. Serve over fettuccini, or your favorite pasta.

OPTION:
mandoline
The mandoline is great for grating cheese.

crêpe pan

cookie sheet

If you have silicone bakeware, this recipe loves it. Cook's essentials insulated cookie sheets work great, too.

Homemade Manicotti

HOMEMADE CRÊPES:

6 eggs
6 cups water
3 cups flour

2 teaspoons vegetable oil
2 cups shredded mozzarella cheese

Place eggs in a large bowl; lightly whip eggs. Add water; whip water and eggs while adding flour one cup at a time until smooth. DO NOT overwhip!

Use paper towels to coat bottom and sides of crêpe pan or 9-inch skillet with oil. Once oil is hot, ladle in just enough batter to lightly coat bottom of pan. Gently but quickly roll pan to ensure crêpe is evenly distributed. When crêpe is dry on top, slide out of pan onto wax paper. Fill crêpe with approximately ¼ cup Filling, and roll gently. Place filled crêpes on a cookie sheet or in a roasting pan. Top crêpes with mozzarella cheese. Bake at 300° until cheese is melted and Filling is heated, approximately 20 minutes. Serves 8.

FILLING:

32 ounces fresh whole-milk ricotta cheese
3 cups chopped fresh Italian parsley
1 tablespoon dried basil
2 egg yolks
¾ cup roasted pine nuts

1 cup chopped onion, caramelized
1 teaspoon chopped garlic (or to taste)
Salt and pepper to taste
¼ cup chopped figs or raisins (optional)

Combine all ingredients in a large bowl and fold together using silicone spatula until well incorporated.

Editor's Extra: Though this stands alone deliciously, it's also good to pour spaghetti sauce on crêpes before topping with mozzarella.

Brown Rice with Sunflower Seeds and Red Grapes

A staple for all the summer recipes. I bring it to family reunions and inevitably someone wants the recipe. This summer salad recipe is also served at my catering business.—Jenny Repko

1 medium onion, finely
  chopped
1 stalk celery, finely chopped
1 tablespoon oil
1–2 tablespoons finely
  chopped fresh thyme, or
  1 teaspoon crushed dried
  thyme leaves

1 cup uncooked brown rice
2½ cups chicken broth
2 tablespoons shelled
  sunflower seeds
¾ cup halved seedless red
  grapes

skillet

In 10-inch skillet, cook onion and celery in oil until onion is crisp-tender. Stir in thyme and rice. Add chicken broth. Bring to a boil. Reduce heat; cover and simmer 45–50 minutes or until liquid has been absorbed and rice is tender. Stir in sunflower seeds and grapes. Serves 8.

ALTERNATE:
electric skillet

Stir-Fried Rice with Color Cooked In

2 teaspoons vegetable oil,
  divided
2 eggs, lightly beaten
3 green onions, sliced
1 cup chopped ham, small
  dice
1 tablespoon freshly grated
  ginger
1 clove garlic, minced
1 cup sliced mushrooms

1 carrot, thinly sliced on
  the bias
½ cup sweet peas (frozen is
  fine)
1 green or red bell pepper,
  diced small
4 cups cooked rice
Salt and pepper to taste
1 tablespoon soy sauce

chef's pan

Heat 1 teaspoon oil in 4-quart chef's pan or wok over medium-high to high heat. Add eggs and cook until scrambled into curds. Remove eggs from pan and set aside. Add remaining vegetable oil, green onions, and ham, and sauté 2–3 minutes. Add ginger, garlic, mushrooms, carrot, peas, and pepper, and sauté 2–3 minutes. Add rice and stir around to heat through and break up. Season with salt and pepper. Return eggs to pan, toss with soy sauce, and season to taste. Serves 8.

Editor's Extra: Nice to serve sweet and sour sauce alongside.

steamer

skillet

Grill marks on the chicken will make this a more appetizing dish.

Confetti Rice

A great way to spruce up steamed rice.

½ cup white basmati rice
½ cup chopped red pepper
1 green onion, chopped
1 cup frozen corn
2 teaspoons minced garlic
⅔ cup water
1 (6-ounce) package frozen
   fajita chicken strips,
   chopped

¼ cup chopped, packed
   cilantro leaves
Freshly ground pepper to taste
Salsa (optional)
Sour cream (optional)

Place rice, pepper, green onion, corn, and garlic in rice bowl of electric steamer. Add water. Place in steamer tray, filling water level to medium, and steam uncovered for 40 minutes. Let mixture rest for 5 minutes after time is up. Brown chicken strips in skillet. Add rice mixture, cilantro, and black pepper. Serve with salsa and sour cream, if desired. May be served hot or cold. Serves 4–5.

Editor's Extra: You may prepare your own chicken strips with chicken tenders and a package of taco seasoning; grill in skillet until done. Then prepare recipe as above.

When Bob Bowersox and Meredith Laurence get together on the set, you know there's going to be some good cookin' goin' on!

Simply Spanish Rice

1 tablespoon vegetable oil
¾ cup finely chopped onion
½ green pepper, finely chopped
2 cloves garlic, minced

2¼ cups long-grain rice
3 (29-ounce) cans stewed tomatoes
½ tablespoon chili powder
1½ teaspoons salt

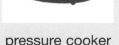

pressure cooker

Heat vegetable oil in at least a 6-quart pressure cooker. Sauté onion, pepper, and garlic until soft. Add rice and stir to coat. Add tomatoes, chili powder, and salt. Lock lid in place, and cook under HIGH pressure 10 minutes. Release pressure manually, and fluff rice with a fork. Serves 8–10.

Alternate Method: To cook in regular or electric stockpot, bring to a boil, then lower heat to a simmer and cook for 30 minutes.

ALTERNATE:
electric
stockpot

Mexican Rice with Chicken

2 teaspoons olive oil
1 small onion, finely diced (about ½ cup)
½ green pepper, finely diced (about ½ cup)
1 clove garlic, minced
½ teaspoon dried cumin
1 cup long-grain rice
2 cups cooked and shredded chicken

1 (28-ounce) can diced tomatoes
1 cup chicken stock
1 teaspoon salt
½ teaspoon freshly ground black pepper
½ jalapeño pepper, seeds removed, chopped
3 tablespoons chopped fresh cilantro (optional)

Heat a cast-iron casserole over medium-high heat 2–3 minutes. When casserole is hot, add olive oil and sauté onion and green pepper until onion is translucent (about 4 minutes). Add garlic and cumin, and continue to sauté another minute. Add rice and stir to coat well with the oil. Continue to cook, stirring constantly, for another minute.

Add shredded chicken along with tomatoes, chicken stock, salt, pepper, and jalapeño. Stir well. Bring mixture to a boil. Cover and lower heat. Let chicken and rice simmer 20 minutes. Check rice for doneness and fluff gently with a fork. Garnish with the fresh cilantro, if desired. Serves 8.

cast-iron
casserole

This colorful cast-iron casserole makes a beautiful presentation when you take it directly to the table.

skillet

I like using the skillet with the drain spout when I'm in a hurry, and I use the electric skillet set on WARM when I want everyone to help themselves at their leisure. —Bob

ALTERNATE:
electric skillet

Shrimp and Sausage Jambalaya

¾ pound chorizo, sliced in
   1-inch pieces
1 pound chicken thighs
1 onion, chopped
1 green bell pepper, chopped
1 stalk celery, chopped
2 cloves garlic, minced
1¾ cups uncooked rice
1 (28-ounce) can chopped
   tomatoes
1 (6-ounce) can tomato paste
1½ teaspoons salt
½ teaspoon dried thyme
1 bay leaf
¼ teaspoon cayenne pepper
1¾ cups water
1–1½ pounds medium
   shrimp, peeled and deveined
Salt and pepper to taste
Freshly chopped parsley

Preheat large skillet over medium-high heat. Add chorizo to skillet, and brown. Remove and set aside. Brown chicken thighs in skillet, and set aside with sausage. Drain all but 1–2 tablespoons grease. Add onion, green pepper, and celery; sauté until tender. Add garlic and cook an additional minute or two. Add rice and toss to coat well. Add tomatoes, tomato paste, salt, thyme, bay leaf, cayenne, and water. Return chicken and sausage to pan. Bring mixture to a simmer, cover pan, reduce heat, and simmer 30–40 minutes.

Add shrimp to skillet and toss gently to incorporate into rice mixture. Cover skillet and continue to cook another 10–15 minutes or until shrimp is cooked, rice is tender, and almost all the liquid has disappeared. Season to taste with more salt and pepper, if necessary. Garnish with freshly chopped parsley. Serves 6–8.

Editor's Extra: Chorizo is highly seasoned pork sausage.

Pork and Sausage Jambalaya

Jambalaya has become the best known rice dish in America.

dutch oven

electric stockpot

¼ cup Crisco or bacon drippings
2 pounds cubed pork
1 pound andouille, sliced
2 cups chopped onions
2 cups chopped celery
1 cup chopped bell pepper
¼ cup diced garlic
7 cups beef or chicken stock
2 cups sliced mushrooms
1 cup sliced green onions
½ cup chopped parsley
Salt and cayenne pepper to taste
Dash of hot pepper sauce
4 cups uncooked rice

In a large Dutch oven, heat Crisco or bacon drippings over medium-high heat. Sauté cubed pork until dark brown on all sides, and some pieces are sticking to the bottom of the pot, approximately 30 minutes. (This is very important as the brown color of jambalaya is derived from the color of the meat.) Add andouille and stir-fry an additional 10–15 minutes.

Drain oil except for 1 large spoonful. Add onions, celery, bell pepper, and garlic. Continue cooking until all vegetables are well caramelized. (Be very careful as vegetables will tend to scorch since the pot is so hot.) Add beef stock, bring to a rolling boil, and reduce heat to a simmer. Cook all ingredients in stock approximately 15 minutes for flavors to develop.

Add mushrooms, green onions, and parsley. Season to taste using salt, cayenne pepper, and hot sauce (season a little heavily because rice will require some seasoning). Add rice, reduce heat to very low, cover, and allow to cook 30–45 minutes, stirring at 15-minute intervals. Serves 8–12.

Editor's Extra: When making a roux, serious Cajun cooks prefer cast iron.

buffet pan

ALTERNATE:
cast-iron
saucepan

These pans are great for both of these recipes, and so nice to take to the table.

Jambalaya Tah-Die-Fah

This classic jambalaya can be prepared ahead of time. A meal in a dish, it needs only a salad and some good crusty bread to feed lots of happy folks . . . including the chef.—Gwen McKee

1 pound smoked sausage, sliced	**1–2 teaspoons Cajun seasoning**
2 medium onions, chopped	**3 dashes red pepper**
1 small bell pepper, chopped	**1 tablespoon Worcestershire**
3 cloves garlic, minced	**1 cup uncooked rice**
⅓ cup chopped mushrooms (optional)	**2½ cups water**
½ pound ham chunks	**1 tablespoon chicken bouillon granules**

Brown sausage in 10-inch buffet pan. Add vegetables, mushrooms, if desired, and ham chunks, then seasonings. Stir and cook 8–10 minutes until softened. Add rice, water, and bouillon; stir and bring to a boil. Reduce to simmer. Cover and cook about 30 minutes. Stir, then leave covered until ready to serve. Refrigerates well. Serves 6–8.

Editor's Extra: Cajuns make jambalaya for parties because it serves a lot of people. At tailgates, they use huge iron pots and stir with boat paddles.

Salsa Red Bean Jambalaya

½–1 pound smoked sausage, sliced	**1 cup diced tomatoes**
1 (15½-ounce) can red beans, drained	**1 cup salsa**
	2–3 cups cooked rice

Fry sausage briefly in buffet pan, and drain on paper towels. Heat beans, tomatoes, and salsa in same pan; add rice and sausage; stir and simmer covered about 15 minutes. Serves 4–5.

Green Onion and Cheese Soufflé

2 tablespoons unsalted butter
3 tablespoons all-purpose flour
1 cup milk, room temperature
½ cup grated Gruyère cheese
½ cup grated Parmigiano-Reggiano cheese
6 ounces pancetta, finely chopped (optional)

2 bunches green onions, cleaned and sliced on the bias into ½-inch slices
2 teaspoons Dijon mustard
8 eggs, separated
Salt and pepper to taste
1 teaspoon cream of tartar (omit if using a copper bowl)

saucepan; skillet

stoneware casserole

ALTERNATE:
mini cassoulets

Preheat a medium saucepan over medium-high heat. Add butter and melt until frothy. Add flour, reduce heat to medium, and cook, stirring constantly 2–3 minutes, creating a roux. Remove pan from heat, and add milk, whisking vigorously. Return pot to heat and bring mixture to a boil so sauce will thicken. (This is a basic white sauce.)

Again, remove pan from heat and add grated cheeses, stirring well to melt. In a large skillet, cook chopped pancetta over medium heat. When pancetta is fully cooked and a little crispy, add green onions and sauté briefly. (If you are not including the pancetta, simply sauté the green onions in a tablespoon of butter.) Add pancetta, green onions, mustard, and egg yolks to cheese sauce. Season to taste with salt and pepper. (Be sure to season well or overseason slightly, since this mixture will be diluted by the egg whites later.) Let this mixture cool completely.

Preheat oven to 375° and butter casserole or cassoulets. Whisk egg whites to soft-peak stage. In 3 stages, carefully fold egg whites into soufflé base. Transfer mixture to buttered casserole or mini cassoulets. Bake at 375° for 30 minutes (less for cassoulets) or until risen and lightly browned on top. The soufflé should jiggle only slightly when finished. Serves 6–8.

pie pan

mixer

Mushroom Swiss Onion Quiche

A superb quiche even real men will give thumbs up.

1 (8-ounce) package shredded
 Swiss cheese, divided
1 (9-inch) pastry shell, baked
¼ pound fresh mushrooms,
 sliced
1 small onion, finely chopped
4 eggs

1 cup heavy cream
1 teaspoon salt
2 tablespoons chopped parsley
Dash of hot pepper sauce
3 slices bacon, crisply cooked
 and crumbled

Place half the shredded cheese in pastry shell. Arrange sliced mushrooms on top of cheese. Arrange onion on top of mushrooms. Break eggs into a mixer bowl. Beat 3 minutes; add cream, salt, parsley, and hot pepper sauce; beat 1 minute; pour into shell. Top with remaining cheese and sprinkle with bacon. Bake at 350° for 30 minutes. Knife inserted in center will come out clean when done. Serve immediately. Yields 1 (9-inch) pie.

Many consider meat the anchor of the meal, planning it first, then side dishes and dessert around it. Whether you cook it on the stovetop, in the oven, or on the backyard grill, the trick is to achieve tenderness and flavor— the challenge of many a host and hostess. Tastily combined with pastas and vegetables and breads, meat enhances and complements, but it is usually the star of the show.

square skillet
with press

baking pan

skillet

ALTERNATE:
electric skillet

Italian Veal with Mushrooms and Cheese

8 veal cutlets, or enough scallops for 4 people
1 egg, beaten
Italian bread crumbs
Olive oil
2 tablespoons red wine vinegar
2 white onions, sliced

1 pound mushrooms, sliced
Jar of pasta or spaghetti sauce, or your own homemade red gravy
8 slices provolone cheese
¾ cup grated Parmesan cheese

Dip veal cutlets in egg, then bread crumbs. In 11-inch skillet with press, sauté cutlets in olive oil until well browned, and drain on paper towels. In a separate saucepan, drizzle olive oil and vinegar over onions and mushrooms. Cover and simmer over low heat until onions are opaque. In a 9-inch-square baking pan, layer ⅓ sauce, ½ the cutlets, ½ the onion-mushroom mixture, ½ the provolone cheese, and ⅓ the Parmesan cheese. Repeat layers. Top with remaining ⅓ sauce and ⅓ Parmesan cheese. Bake at 350° until bubbly. Serves 8.

Breaded Veal Cutlets in a Bed of Glazed Onions

A superb way to serve an outstanding-tasting meat.

¼ cup olive or vegetable oil
1 pound veal cutlets or cube steak
2 eggs, beaten
Salt and pepper to taste

12 crackers, crushed
¾ cup Italian bread crumbs
3 tablespoons butter
1 sweet onion, cut in half rings

Heat oil in large skillet. Dip cutlets into eggs, then into a mixture of seasoned cracker and bread crumbs. Fry on each side in oil until crusty and brown. Remove to plate. Melt butter in skillet; add onion slices, and sauté until golden.

When ready to serve, divide onions onto each plate. Return cutlets to skillet, and turn to high to briefly crisp on each side. Lay cutlets on top of onions. Serve with anything—this is a great go-with entrée. Serves 4.

Mac and Chili Meal

An easy, one-dish meal.

2 pounds ground venison
  or ground beef
1 (16-ounce) can chili beans,
  undrained
1 (15-ounce) can red kidney
  beans, undrained
1 (10-ounce) can Ro-Tel
  tomatoes, undrained
1 (8-ounce) can tomato sauce
½ cup frozen seasoning blend
  vegetables, or equivalent of
  chopped onion, pepper,
  and celery

½ teaspoon salt
½ teaspoon black pepper
½ teaspoon cumin
1 teaspoon garlic salt
1 (8-ounce) package elbow
  macaroni, cooked
1 cup grated Cheddar cheese

electric skillet

OPTION:
pasta pot

Brown meat in 12-inch electric skillet with lid. Drain. Add beans, Ro-Tel, and tomato sauce. Add vegetables and seasonings. Reduce heat and simmer 45–60 minutes. May add macaroni and toss, or serve over macaroni. Top with grated cheese. Serves 10.

*Bob's children, Rachel and Jonathan, bond with their
great grandparents at a family dinner.*

casserole

saucepan

mixing bowl

meatloaf pan

Barbecue Venison Meatballs

1 pound ground venison
  or ground beef
2 tablespoons milk
¼ cup soft bread crumbs

½ teaspoon ground sage
½ teaspoon salt
½ teaspoon garlic powder
1 egg, beaten

Combine all ingredients, mixing well. Shape with hands into 1-inch balls. Put in 3-quart casserole dish, and bake at 350° for 45 minutes, turning frequently. Drain and cover with Touch of Orange Barbecue Sauce. Cook another 15 minutes so that sauce coats meatballs well.

TOUCH OF ORANGE BARBECUE SAUCE:

1 cup (your choice) barbecue
  sauce

½ cup orange marmalade
¼ cup water

Combine ingredients in saucepan; bring to a boil and pour over meatballs.

Tasty Venison Meatloaf

This meatloaf is also good sliced thin and made into sandwiches.

1 pound ground venison
  or ground beef
1 cup cracker crumbs
1 egg, beaten
⅓ cup ketchup

2 tablespoons lemon juice
2 tablespoons Worcestershire
1 small onion, chopped
¼ cup chopped bell pepper
Salt and pepper to taste

Combine ingredients in large bowl; mixing by hand is best. Form into loaf and place in meatloaf pan with drain holes. Cook 45 minutes at 350°. Serves 4–6.

Monterey Meat Rolls

1 (8-ounce) can tomato sauce
1 (6-ounce) can tomato paste
1 teaspoon oregano, divided
1 pound ground chuck
½ pound ground veal
½ pound ground pork
1 small onion, finely chopped

¾ cup fresh bread crumbs
1 egg, beaten
½ teaspoon salt
¼ teaspoon pepper
2 cups shredded Monterey
   Jack cheese

Combine tomato sauce, tomato paste, and ½ teaspoon oregano in a small bowl. Set aside. Combine meats and onion in bowl. Add bread crumbs, egg, remaining oregano, salt, pepper, and ½ the tomato mixture to meat mixture. Mix thoroughly. Turn out onto wax paper and shape into 2 (9x5-inch) rectangles. Sprinkle cheese evenly over meat. Roll up, beginning at longest side. Press edges and ends of rolls together to seal. Place in 2 ungreased 9x5-inch meatloaf pans, seam side down. Bake at 350° for 1 hour. Drain excess fat (if not using drain pans). Pour remaining tomato mixture on top. Return to oven and bake 15 minutes more. Yields 10 servings.

Alternate Method: If using mini loaf pans, adjust the size of the rectangles to fit, and cook only 40 minutes.

meatloaf pans

ALTERNATE:
mini loaf pans

I like the mini loaf pans because they are quick cooking and you can make individual servings or freeze for future use. —Bob

food processor

muffin pan

meatloaf pan

Meatloaf Muffins

The kids will love this quick-and-easy burger dish, for sure. I have been known to use three frozen hamburger patties (thawed) when I'm out of ground beef . . . superb!—Gwen McKee

2 slices bread
7 crackers
¼ onion
¼ green pepper
Salt and pepper to taste

Basil to taste
1 pound ground beef
1 (8-ounce) can seasoned
 tomato sauce, divided

Crumb bread then crackers in food processor. Add onion and green pepper and pulse until chopped. Add seasonings, ground beef, and ½ can tomato sauce. Pulse only until mixed. Scoop into 6 greased muffin cups and top with remaining tomato sauce. Bake in preheated 350° oven 25–30 minutes. Easy to do in a toaster oven, too. Serves 3–4.

Italian-Style Meatloaf

Quail Ridge Press team member Lisa Flynt says she and her son Jack love to make and eat this tasty meatloaf. Leftovers are great reheated.

1½ pounds ground chuck
¾ cup old-fashioned oats
¼ cup chopped onion
1 egg
½ teaspoon salt
¼ teaspoon freshly ground
 pepper

¾ teaspoon garlic and herb
 seasoning
1 (8-ounce) can tomato sauce
4 ounces (1 cup) shredded
 mozzarella

Preheat oven to 350°. Mix beef, oats, onion, egg, salt, pepper, and seasoning. Knead 8–10 turns to blend well. Form into 4x8-inch loaf in meatloaf pan. Spread tomato sauce over top. Bake 50 minutes. Top meatloaf with cheese, and bake an additional 10 minutes.

Meatloaf of Champions

You can sneak lots of good-for-you ingredients into meatloaf as long as you have good seasonings to perk up the flavor.

½ cup crushed Wheaties
¼ cup bread crumbs
3 tablespoons Egg Beaters,
　or 1 small egg
¼ cup milk
¼ teaspoon garlic and herb
　seasoning

¼ teaspoon onion powder
1 teaspoon chopped parsley
Salt and white pepper to taste
⅔ cup ketchup, divided
1 pound lean ground beef

meatloaf pan

Preheat oven to 400°. Mix all ingredients except ground beef, using only ⅓ cup ketchup. Add ground beef, and mix all together with your hands. Shape into a loaf and place in loaf pan; cover with remaining ketchup, and bake 45–50 minutes. Serves 4–6.

Alternate Method: When using mini loaf pans, cook only 35–40 minutes.

ALTERNATE:
mini loaf pans

Cowboy Beef and Beans, Texas Style

A simple recipe that's bound to please.

1 pound lean ground beef
　or ground turkey
1 large onion, chopped
½ pound bacon, cut into
　pieces

1 (14½-ounce) can stewed
　tomatoes with jalapeños,
　garlic, and cumin, undrained
1 (28-ounce) can sweet and
　spicy baked beans

electric
stockpot

In large electric stockpot, cook ground beef and onion over medium heat 8–10 minutes, stirring frequently, until beef is thoroughly cooked; drain and set aside. In same stockpot, cook bacon over medium heat, stirring frequently, until bacon is brown and crisp; do not drain drippings. Add tomatoes; heat to boiling. With spoon, break up large pieces of tomato. Return beef mixture to stockpot. Stir in baked beans. Cover; cook on SIMMER 2–3 hours. Serves 8.

sauté pan

baking pan

Enchiladas Olé

1½ pounds ground beef
1 (1-ounce) package taco
  seasoning mix
1½ cups chicken broth,
  divided
1 (8-ounce) can tomato sauce
¼ teaspoon cayenne pepper
½ teaspoon salt
½ teaspoon black pepper

1–2 cloves garlic, crushed
Dash of Tabasco
1–2 shakes Worcestershire
2 large onions, chopped
1½ tablespoons olive oil
1 pound or more extra sharp
  Cheddar cheese
1 (10-inch) package flour
  tortillas

Brown ground meat in sauté pan; drain, if necessary. Shake taco mix over meat; stir. Cover with 1 cup chicken broth. Add tomato sauce, seasonings, and garlic. Add Tabasco and Worcestershire to taste. Cook on low heat 10 minutes. Sauté chopped onions in a little oil in saucepan until limp; set aside. Grate cheese; set aside.

Lightly coat a 9x13-inch baking pan or large casserole dish with oil. Spread tortillas, one at a time, with about 1 heaping tablespoon meat mixture (use slotted spoon) and a generous sprinkle of onions and cheese, then roll up. Roll them in the pan and push them together to make room as you go along. Spread any remaining onions over top of enchiladas. Add remaining chicken broth to remaining meat sauce mixture and pour evenly over all, being sure that there are no "dry" edges left. Top with remaining cheese. Cover with foil and bake at 350° about 30 minutes. Serves 8–10.

Editor's Extra: I substituted tomato-basil wraps when I had to make a fast meal for company with no time to go to the grocery for tortillas. I cut the larger-sized wraps in half before filling, so it made ten. Everybody loved them. I didn't cover the casserole while baking. Superb!

Upper Crust Pizza in a Pan

skillet

A very popular dish! Who doesn't like pizza?

1 pound ground beef
1 medium onion, chopped
½ medium bell pepper, chopped

¼ pound pepperoni, chopped
1 (7-ounce) can mushroom pieces, drained
1 (14-ounce) jar pizza sauce

In a large 500° oven-safe skillet, brown beef, onion, and bell pepper; drain. Stir in pepperoni, mushrooms, and pizza sauce. Bring to a boil, then simmer about 10 minutes, stirring a few times. Preheat oven to 400°.

UPPER CRUST:

1 cup milk
2 eggs
1 tablespoon oil
1 cup flour
½ teaspoon salt

1½ cups shredded mozzarella cheese
¼ cup grated Parmesan cheese

mixing bowl

In a mixing bowl, combine milk, eggs, and oil. Add flour and salt; mix another minute. Sprinkle mozzarella over top of meat mixture in skillet. Pour crust mixture evenly over this. Sprinkle Parmesan over top. Put skillet into preheated oven and bake 20–25 minutes or until crust is golden brown. Serves 6–8 (or maybe only 4 because it's soooo good!).

Gwen's grandson, Patrick, loves to cook, and is such a big fan of cook's essentials cookware, he requested some for Christmas.

skillet

ALTERNATE:
dutch oven

Easy-To-Please Beef Stroganoff

Nothing is more satisfying than a wonderful dish of beef stroganoff. It's one of my rotation dinners. — Gwen McKee

1½ pounds top sirloin or
   round steak, cubed
1 tablespoon butter
1 tablespoon oil
2 onions, chopped
1 teaspoon minced garlic
8 ounces fresh mushrooms,
   sliced
1½ teaspoons beef bouillon
   granules, dissolved in
   1½ cups hot water

1 tablespoon Worcestershire
Salt, black pepper, and red
   pepper to taste
3 tablespoons flour
1¼ cups sour cream
1 (12-ounce) package egg
   noodles, cooked
Parsley flakes (optional)

Place meat in melted butter and oil in 12-inch skillet over medium-high heat. Stir in onions and garlic after meat is somewhat browned. When onions are limp, add mushrooms. After 5 minutes or so, pour in hot bouillon and Worcestershire; season. Bring to a boil, then simmer, covered, 35–45 minutes. Stir flour into sour cream, then add to skillet; stir and cook gently another 10 minutes. Serve over drained noodles. Sprinkle with a little parsley, if desired. Serves 8.

Smothered Hamburger Steak with Gravy

Southerners like their gravy. I like to make this and serve it over rice or biscuits. I put the gravy on both. I found the cook's essentials electric skillet worked especially well for this.—Barbara Moseley

electric skillet

½ pound ground beef
½ cup frozen seasoning blend
  vegetables, or equivalent of
  chopped celery, green
  pepper, and onion

Dash of salt
¼ teaspoon pepper
1 (1-ounce) package onion
  soup mix

ALTERNATE:
skillet

Combine ingredients well, and form into hamburger-size patties. Place in heated electric skillet. Cook on medium-high heat until brown on both sides. Remove patties to plate, and keep warm while making Gravy. Leave drippings in skillet.

GRAVY:
1 or 2 beef bouillon cubes
1 cup warm water
2–3 tablespoons all-purpose
  flour

½ cup chopped onion

Dissolve bouillon cubes in water. Brown flour in drippings from meat. (If meat was very lean, you might have to add a tablespoon of oil to skillet.) Add chopped onion, and cook briefly before adding bouillon. Stir until well incorporated. Add steak back to Gravy; cover and simmer 15–20 minutes. Serves 2–3.

Three generations of Moseleys—Barbara, Mama Jean, and Meg—appreciate easy cleanup after a family meal.

electric griddle

ALTERNATE:
square skillet
with press

sauté pan

ALTERNATE:
electric skillet

Stuffed Hamburger Steaks

This is such an nice change from regular hamburger steak. My husband Lonnie gave these an A+.—Barbara Moseley

1 pound ground beef
1 teaspoon seasoned salt
½ teaspoon black pepper

1 (6-ounce) roll garlic cheese
Flour seasoned with salt and
pepper

Combine ground beef, seasoned salt, and black pepper. Shape into 6 patties. Slice cheese roll into ¼-inch slices. Place 1–2 slices on half the beef patties, and place remaining patties on top. Seal edges and dredge in seasoned flour. Pat flour into meat. Cook on electric griddle or in square skillet with press on medium heat. Cook slowly until brown on one side, then turn over and cook until brown on other side. Lower heat and simmer 15–20 minutes until thoroughly cooked.

Ruth's Green Pepper Steak

Grandma Ruth knew this was a favorite, so it was always an occasion for celebration when I came home and discovered it was on the menu.—Bob Warden

1½ pounds round steak
2 tablespoons soy sauce
½ cup flour

3 tablespoons oil
1 cup sliced green bell peppers
1 cup water

Pound meat to tenderize. Slice the meat against the grain into the thinnest possible strips. Brush each strip with soy sauce, and sprinkle with flour. In a sauté pan, brown steak strips in oil. Add green peppers, and sauté slightly. Add water and simmer just until peppers are tender. Serve with rice. Serves 6.

Filet Mignon with Peppercorn Sauce

1 tablespoon olive oil
2–4 filet mignon steaks
½ cup finely chopped
   shallots
2 cloves garlic, minced
1 tablespoon chopped fresh
   thyme
3 tablespoons green
   peppercorns, drained,
   rinsed, and chopped

½ cup red wine
1 cup beef stock
¼ cup heavy cream
Salt and pepper to taste
Chopped parsley for garnish

sauté pan

ALTERNATE:
electric skillet

Preheat sauté pan on high heat. Add oil. Sauté steaks 3–4 minutes per side for medium, adjusting the time for different degrees of doneness. Remove steaks to a plate and loosely tent with foil. Add shallots to the pan and sauté 1–2 minutes. Add garlic and thyme and sauté an additional minute. Add green peppercorns and heat through. Add red wine and bring to a boil. Add stock and return to a boil. Let mixture simmer until slightly reduced. Add cream, and season to taste with salt and pepper. Pour over steaks and garnish with parsley.

roasting pan;
wire rack

saucepan

Jalapeño Oven Ribs

Sweet and spicy is sinfully nice-y!

½ teaspoon liquid smoke
 (optional)
3 pounds boneless ribs
Seasoning salt
1 cup barbecue sauce,
 any style

½ cup jalapeño jelly or
 hot pepper jelly
2 tablespoons soy sauce
1 teaspoon minced garlic

Using a roasting pan with rack, pour water to reach halfway to rim of pan; add a little liquid smoke to the water, if desired. Lay greased rack over pan and lay ribs on rack. Sprinkle with seasoning salt. Put pan in oven and bake ribs at 275° for 3 hours. During the last 30 minutes of cooking time, mix barbecue sauce, jalapeño jelly, soy sauce, and garlic in a small saucepan. Heat mixture on low heat, stirring occasionally. Open oven and baste ribs with sauce (add more hot water, if evaporated). Increase oven temperature to 325°. Continue basting sauce over ribs until surface of ribs begins to crisp. Serves 6.

Olivia shares a bite—she knows that Mimi likes to taste.

Chinese-Style Ribs

Three kinds of pepper give these ribs their kick.

3½ pounds pork country-style ribs
6 green onions, chopped
¼ cup soy sauce
¼ cup molasses
2 tablespoons hoisin sauce
4 tablespoons brown sugar
2 tablespoons white wine vinegar
2 teaspoons toasted sesame oil
2 teaspoons lemon juice
½ teaspoon bottled hot pepper sauce
½ teaspoon ground ginger
½ teaspoon garlic powder
½ teaspoon chili powder
¼ teaspoon ground red pepper
¼ teaspoon black pepper
2 cups cooked rice

electric
stockpot

ALTERNATE:
pressure cooker

Place ribs in electric stockpot. In a small bowl, combine green onions, soy sauce, molasses, hoisin sauce, sugar, vinegar, sesame oil, lemon juice, hot pepper sauce, ginger, garlic powder, chili powder, ground red pepper, and black pepper. Pour sauce over ribs in cooker, turning to coat.

Cover, and simmer 8–10 hours. Transfer ribs to serving platter. Strain sauce; skim off fat, serve over ribs with hot cooked rice. Serves 8–10.

Alternate Method: To cook in pressure cooker, add ½ cup water and cook on HIGH 60 minutes.

Slow-Braised Beef Short Ribs

Every year a national cooking magazine asks the top 100 chefs their five favorite dishes, and short ribs is number one on most lists. I have tested these chef's recipes to determine the very best. This recipe combines the best features of the Best of the Best recipes from the Best chefs in the country. Judge for yourself . . . it is unquestionably THE BEST!—Bob Warden

sauté pan

ALTERNATE:
pressure cooker

Try these in the oven then in a pressure cooker. You might be surprised which way tastes the best.

¼ pound bacon, chopped
2 tablespoons olive oil
4 pounds short ribs, cut
    4 inches in length
Salt and freshly ground
    black pepper
6 large leeks, sliced ¼ inch
    thick
2 large carrots, finely chopped
1 onion, finely chopped
1 rib celery, finely chopped
4 cloves garlic, minced
3 sprigs fresh thyme
1 bay leaf
½ cup good red wine
1½ cups orange juice
4 cups chicken stock

Preheat a large sauté pan over medium-high heat. Add bacon and sauté until crispy. Add olive oil. Season short ribs well with salt and pepper; sear, in batches, if necessary, getting a good brown color on all sides of the ribs. When they are nicely browned, remove ribs from pan and set aside.

Pour off and discard fat that has accumulated in pan. Add leeks, carrots, onion, and celery to the pan and sauté a couple of minutes. Add garlic, thyme, and bay leaf and continue to cook another minute or so. Add wine and let simmer and reduce until it has almost entirely disappeared. Add orange juice and chicken stock and bring to a simmer. Return browned short ribs to pan. Reduce heat to very, very low and cover pan with tight-fitting lid. Let ribs simmer about 5 hours on the stovetop or in 300° oven. To get the perfect ribs, use an oven-proof meat thermometer and cook for 1 hour after internal temperature of ribs has reached 200°. The meat should be so tender that it "falls off the bone."

Remove ribs from pan and set aside, covered with foil. Increase the heat below the sauce and reduce the braising liquid until it has thickened slightly and is almost glaze-like. Return ribs to pan and coat in the sauce. Serve ribs over egg noodles and spoon sauce on top. The sauce can be strained for a smooth finish, if desired. Serves 4–6.

Alternate Method: To cook in pressure cooker, cook on HIGH pressure 60 minutes. Reduce liquid, after removing ribs, until it has thickened slightly.

BBQ Pulled Pork

2 tablespoons vegetable oil
4 pounds pork stew meat
  (such as shoulder of pork),
  cut into 1-inch cubes
2 onions, finely chopped
4 cloves garlic, minced
1 quart puréed tomatoes
3 cups water
½ cup Worcestershire
½ cup cider vinegar
¼ cup brown sugar
1 tablespoon dry mustard
2 teaspoons chili powder
2 teaspoons salt
1 teaspoon freshly ground
  black pepper

dutch oven

Heat Dutch oven over high heat or set pressure cooker on BROWN. Add some of the oil and sear pork in batches. Try not to overcrowd the pot, as this will prevent browning. When all pork has been browned and set aside, add onions and sauté 2 minutes. Add garlic for an additional minute; add remaining ingredients to pan, including browned pork. Simmer over low heat 2 hours in Dutch oven or 60 minutes in pressure cooker. (You can cook this in a 325° oven 3 hours or until the meat is so tender that it falls apart.)

ALTERNATE:
pressure cooker

Cool meat in sauce. Once cool, shred the pork. (One way to do this is to transfer the meat with a slotted spoon into a heavy-duty zipper bag and massage the pork until it breaks down. Another method is to use a table fork to shred the meat.) When all meat has been shredded, add enough remaining sauce back to just moisten the meat, making it the right consistency for your purpose. Season to taste with salt and pepper. Reheat to serve on sandwiches, incorporate into pasta, or serve on top of a baked potato.

ALTERNATE:
roaster pan

This is a great alternative use of a hard anodized roaster. I prefer finishing this dish in the oven so I don't have to keep an eye on the stove.—Bob

mini food
processor

grill pan

sauté pan

ALTERNATE:
electric skillet

Pork Tenderloin in Spiced Ginger Sauce

¼ cup soy sauce
⅓ cup brown sugar
3 cloves garlic, minced
¼ cup Dijon mustard
1 tablespoon Worcestershire
1 teaspoon fresh gingerroot, minced, or ¼ teaspoon powdered ginger
¼ cup vegetable oil
2 (1-pound) pork tenderloins

Combine all ingredients, except pork, in food processor. Place tenderloins and marinade in a zipper bag in the refrigerator overnight.

Place tenderloins on 500° oven-safe grill pan or roasting pan. Broil 6 inches from heat for 16–18 minutes. Baste often. Slice in ½-inch thick slices to serve. Serves 6–8.

Pork Medallions O'Brien

This is a quick and easy dish that saved me during the busy Christmas shopping season. From the time I started it until we ate was 30 minutes. I love it!
—Barbara Moseley

6 pork loin medallions
Greek seasoning to taste
Salt and pepper to taste
2 teaspoons oil
½ (28-ounce) package O'Brien potatoes

Sprinkle medallions with Greek seasoning and salt and pepper. Brown both sides in oil in 10-inch sauté pan; remove from pan. Add potatoes to pan and toss with any drippings remaining from pork. Place pork medallions on top of potatoes; cover and bake in 350° oven 15–20 minutes, just until potatoes are done. Serves 3–4.

Melinda's Pork Medallions

2 tablespoons margarine or
    butter
1 pound (2 small) pork
    tenderloins, cut into
    ¼-inch slices
½ cup brandy
1 (14-ounce) can chicken
    broth, roasted garlic flavor,
    divided
2 teaspoons Worcestershire

2 teaspoons all-purpose
    seasoning
Salt, black pepper, and
    red pepper to taste
8 small Yukon gold potatoes,
    quartered
1 cup sliced fresh mushrooms
½ cup sliced green onions
2 tablespoons flour

sauté pan

ALTERNATE:
electric skillet

Melt margarine in 12-inch sauté pan or electric skillet on medium-high heat. Add pork slices; cook 3–5 minutes or until browned on both sides. Add brandy to deglaze pan. Remove pork from skillet; set aside.

Reserve ¼ cup chicken broth; add remaining broth, Worcestershire, seasonings, and potatoes to skillet. Bring to a boil. Reduce heat to low; cover and simmer 10 minutes or until potatoes are tender. Stir in mushrooms, onions, and pork mixture. Cover; simmer an additional 5 minutes or until vegetables are tender.

In small bowl, combine flour and reserved ¼ cup chicken broth; blend until smooth. Gradually stir into pork mixture. Cook and stir over medium-high heat until mixture is bubbly and thickened. Makes 4–5 servings.

*When Bob asked Melinda Burnham at Quail Ridge Press what
"fixin' to" meant, she knew he was picking at her southern
colloquialisms. Bob got a big laugh when she teased him,
"Down here, you're the one with the accent."*

kohaishu knife

For this recipe, both a good knife and a mini food chopper are a must.

roaster pan

OPTION:
mini food chopper

Roast Pork Loin with Apples and Vegetables

1 (3- to 4-pound) top loin roast of pork
3 cloves garlic, slivered
Salt and pepper to taste
4 tablespoons olive oil, divided
2 Granny Smith apples, wedged
6 small new potatoes
2 carrots, chunked
1 bulb fennel, quartered

1 red onion, wedged
2 tablespoons butter, melted
1 teaspoon finely chopped fresh rosemary
½ teaspoon finely chopped fresh sage
1 tablespoon finely chopped parsley
1½ cups chicken stock

Preheat oven to 375°. Make small incisions in roast, and insert slivers of garlic. Season roast well; drizzle half the olive oil on top, and place in roaster pan on middle rack. Toss apples and vegetables in a bowl with remaining olive oil, butter, salt, pepper, and combined fresh herbs, reserving 1 tablespoon herbs for later. Spread apples and vegetables around the roast. Pour chicken stock in pan. Roast in a 375° oven for one hour or until internal temperature reads 155°. Serves 6.

An amazing team of professional food stylists backs up Bob, Gwen, Meredith, and Barbara. From left to right, Bob Warden, Tom Estok, Jeri Estok, Nicholas DiCurcio, Gwen McKee, Bonnie DiTomo, Meredith Laurence, Anthony Curado, Barbara Moseley, Lisa Brady, and Carole Haffey.

Taste of the Islands Pork Roast

1 (2-pound) boneless pork loin roast
1 cup firmly packed brown sugar
2 garlic cloves, minced
2 teaspoons ground ginger
1 bay leaf, crumbled
½ teaspoon ground cloves
1 teaspoon salt
½ teaspoon ground pepper
2 tablespoons dark rum

roasting pan

Preheat oven to 375°. Place pork in roasting pan. Roast about 1½ hours. Increase oven temperature to 450°. Mix sugar, garlic, ginger, bay leaf, cloves, salt, pepper, and dark rum in medium bowl until paste forms. Spread spice paste over pork. Continue roasting 8 minutes. Remove pork to platter.

mixing bowl

ISLAND SAUCE:

½ cup chicken stock or canned broth
¼ cup light rum
1 tablespoon all-purpose flour
¼ cup fresh lime juice

Put roasting pan over medium heat on stove. Add chicken stock and light rum; bring to a boil, scraping up any browned bits. Sprinkle flour over stock mixture and stir. Add lime juice, blending in well. Spoon over pork slices. Good over a bed of rice. Serves 6.

electric
stockpot

Taco Muffin Stack

1 (2-pound) pork loin roast
1 medium onion, chopped
1 envelope taco seasoning
   mix
1 (16-ounce) can refried beans
1 (8-ounce) box mild Mexican-
   style processed cheese,
   cubed

12 prepared corn muffins
¾ cup shredded lettuce
¾ cup chopped tomato
¾ cup sour cream
¼ cup chopped fresh
   cilantro (optional)

Place pork in a 3- to 4-quart electric stockpot. Add chopped onion and sprinkle with taco seasoning mix. Top with beans. Cover and cook on SIMMER 2–3 hours.

Remove pork from cooker; place on cutting board. Shred pork using 2 forks. Return pork to cooker, and mix well. Stir in cheese, and allow to melt.

Cut muffins crosswise in half. Place each bottom half on a plate; top with ½ cup pork mixture, about a tablespoon lettuce, and some chopped tomato. Replace muffin tops. Serve with sour cream; sprinkle with cilantro, if desired. Serves 10–12.

Editor's Extra: If you want to make your own muffins, refer to the Cornbread portion of the recipe on page 44. Double the recipe to make 12 muffins, and bake 10–13 minutes.

Pork Chop Swiss Casserole

The juices from the chops and mushroom soup cook down over the vegetables to give them a great flavor!

8 boneless pork loin chops
Butter
Salt and pepper to taste
2 (10¾-ounce) cans cream
  of mushroom soup
3 large baking potatoes,
  peeled and sliced

2 (15½-ounce) cans whole
  green beans, drained
1 large onion, sliced thin
1 (8-ounce) bag shredded
  Swiss cheese
1 (5-ounce) can evaporated
  milk

Brown pork chops in butter; salt and pepper both sides; set aside. Spread a little mushroom soup in the bottom of a large casserole dish with a top lid. Cover bottom of dish with sliced potatoes. Cover potatoes with a layer of green beans and sliced onion. Cover green beans and onions with 4 pork chops. Spoon more soup on top of pork chops and sprinkle half the Swiss cheese over soup. Repeat layers and top all with remaining Swiss cheese. Pour entire can of evaporated milk over casserole. Cover with lid and bake at 350° for 1 hour. Remove top and serve. Serves 8.

cast-iron
casserole

casserole

Tater Chop Casserole

1 (28-ounce) bag frozen
  diced potatoes, onions,
  and peppers, thawed
2 cups shredded Cheddar
  and Monterey Jack cheese
  blend
1 (10¾-ounce) can condensed
  cream of celery soup
1 (8-ounce) container sour
  cream

1 tablespoon Dijon mustard
1 pound boneless, smoked
  pork chops, fully cooked,
  diced
⅔ cup shredded mozzarella
  cheese (or more)
3 slices real bacon, cooked
  and crumbled

Mix potatoes, cheese, soup, sour cream, and mustard in large bowl. Add diced pork chops. Put in greased 3-quart casserole dish. Cook at 350° for 30 minutes; top with mozzarella and bacon bits, and bake an additional 5 minutes until cheese melts. Serves 8.

casserole

casserole with
trivet

ALTERNATE:
casserole with
trivet

sauté pan

ALTERNATE:
electric skillet

Maple-Glazed Pork Chops with Apricot Stuffing

4–6 pork chops
1 cup maple syrup
⅓ cup soy sauce
¼ cup cider vinegar
2 cloves garlic, crushed
2 cups coarse bread crumbs
2 tablespoons chopped
   parsley
½ cup chopped dried
   apricots, rehydrated in warm
   water or chicken stock
1 clove garlic, minced
¾ cup chicken stock
Salt and pepper to taste
1–2 tablespoons oil

Marinate chops in mixture of maple syrup, soy sauce, vinegar, and crushed garlic a few hours or overnight. Reserve marinade and reheat in small saucepan. Combine bread crumbs, parsley, apricots, minced garlic, and stock. Season. Make pocket in each chop and stuff with the bread crumb mixture. Season chops. Heat sauté pan over medium-high heat. Add oil and sauté chops until nicely browned on both sides, basting with the maple glaze. Serves 4–6.

Southern Fried Pork Chops

6 center-cut pork chops
1 cup flour
2 teaspoons Greek seasoning
1 teaspoon Cajun seasoning
½ teaspoon salt
½ teaspoon black pepper
Oil for frying

Place pork chops on wax paper and blot with paper towel. Mix flour and seasonings in small bowl. Sprinkle chops with flour mixture, pressing lightly into the meat; coat both sides of chops. Pour about ½ inch of oil in 12-inch skillet; heat at medium-high until oil is hot. Place chops in hot oil; turn when lightly brown on bottom side. Brown other side and reduce heat; continue to cook about 10 minutes. If more browning is needed, raise heat for a few minutes and turn chops; do not overcook. Serves 6.

skillet

ALTERNATE:
electric skillet

Honey Mustard Pork Chops

2 tablespoons honey
¼ cup Dijon mustard
2 teaspoons red wine vinegar
¼ teaspoon minced garlic
Freshly ground black pepper
 to taste
4 thick pork chops

In small saucepan, heat honey until it liquefies. Add mustard, vinegar, garlic, and pepper; blend thoroughly and set aside to cool slightly. Place pork chops in a one-gallon zipper bag. Pour marinade over chops. Seal bag, very thoroughly squeezing out all air. Squish marinade around inside baggie until chops are completely coated. Let chops sit in marinade in refrigerator overnight.

Remove chops from bag and completely wipe off marinade. Place chops in casserole or baking dish and bake at 375° for 30 minutes. Turn pork chops over and bake another 30 minutes. Serves 4.

casserole

ALTERNATE:
stoneware
baking dish

everyday pan

ALTERNATE:
skillet

One-Pan Tasty Pork Chop Dinner

A fantastic meal!

6 pork chops	**1 cup chopped onion**
1 tablespoon oil	**1 (10¾-ounce) can cream of**
Cajun seasoning to taste	**mushroom soup**
2 (16-ounce) cans sauerkraut,	**1 (4-ounce) can sliced**
drained	**mushrooms, drained**
¼ cup brown sugar	**3 cups hot mashed potatoes**

Preheat oven to 325°. Brown chops on both sides in oil in everyday pan. Season, then remove chops from pan. Drain some fat from pan, then stir in sauerkraut, brown sugar, and onion. Place chops on top of sauerkraut. Spoon mushroom soup over chops, then mushrooms. Cover and bake 1¼ hours.

Spoon the mashed potatoes (or pipe with pastry tube) around edges of casserole, then broil for a few minutes to brown.

Editor's Extra: Use Joe-Tatoes on page 105 for the perfect surround to this great-tasting dish.

The kitchen is the perfect place to stir up romance. Bob's son, Dave, has a kiss for the cook (his wife, Becca).

Casserole Pan Lamb or Pork

Casserole Pan Lamb was something I ate a lot of when I was a kid growing up in Canada. This recipe makes my house smell just like my childhood . . . and drives my appetite crazy! Using shoulder chops makes this a very affordable dish.—Meredith Laurence

1 tablespoon olive oil
8 shoulder chops (about
   3 pounds), trimmed of fat
1 onion, chopped
2 ribs celery, chopped
2 carrots, chopped
3 cloves garlic, minced

6 sprigs fresh thyme
1 bay leaf
4 cups navy beans, cooked
4 cups chicken stock
1 pint cherry tomatoes
Salt and pepper to taste

skillet

ALTERNATE:
electric skillet

Heat skillet over medium-high heat. Add olive oil, and sear chops in batches until nicely browned. Set chops aside. Add onion, celery, and carrots, and cook over medium heat until tender. Add garlic, thyme, and bay leaf, and cook an additional minute. Return chops to pan and add navy beans. Pour in chicken stock and bring mixture to a boil. Reduce heat to a simmer, and cover. Simmer 45–50 minutes, or until lamb is so tender it falls off the bone. (You can also finish this in a 325° oven in about an hour.)

Add cherry tomatoes and season with salt and pepper. Simmer an additional 15–20 minutes. Season again with salt and pepper to taste. Serves 8.

saucepan

Saucepans with lids are so great for sauces and marinades that need refrigerating.

Coffee-Ketch Barbecue Sauce

Use this to marinate or baste chicken, pork, or beef.

1 teaspoon oil	**1 cup ketchup**
½ onion, chopped	**1 teaspoon mustard powder**
1 clove garlic, minced	**½ cup brown sugar**
¼ cup strong coffee	**Salt and pepper to taste**

Heat oil in a small saucepan. Sauté onion and garlic until tender and translucent. Add coffee and bring to a simmer for one minute. Add remaining ingredients and simmer until thickened. Season to taste with salt and pepper.

Cranberry Orange Sauce

Delicious served with pork tenderloin.

1 orange, zest and juice	**1 cinnamon stick**
1 (12-ounce) bag cranberries	**Pinch of nutmeg**
½ cup sugar	**Pinch of salt**

Combine all ingredients in a saucepan and bring just to a simmer. Cool to room temperature. Refrigerate.

Editor's Extra: Believe it or not this recipe requires no other liquid as it makes its own.

saucepan

poultry

It's popular, versatile, and so easy to prepare— chicken is an American favorite! From simple dishes to exotic cuisine, what else lends itself so beautifully to so many kinds of recipes? And poultry goes so well with vegetables, fruits, pastas, and sauces. No matter the method, you can cook chicken in practically every pot and pan cook's essentials makes . . . and that's a lot.

stockpot

ALTERNATE:
pressure cooker

John's Favorite Chicken and Dumplings

While my second son John was living in Paris, the cuisine capital of the world, this is one of the recipes he wrote home for. — Bob Warden

1 whole chicken	**1 green bell pepper, chopped**
1 stalk celery, chopped	**¼ teaspoon crushed**
1 large onion, chopped	**rosemary**
2 large carrots, sliced	**1 clove garlic, minced**
1 bunch fresh parsley,	**½ teaspoon oregano**
chopped, or 1 tablespoon	**1 bay leaf**
dried parsley	**Salt and pepper to taste**

Cut chicken in pieces and simmer in stockpot with water to cover until tender. Remove meat from cooking water (but leave water in pan). Allow meat to cool, then remove from bones. Put bones and skin back into water and continue to simmer about 3–4 more hours. Strain and place back on heat. Add celery, onion, carrots, parsley, pepper, and seasonings. Add chicken meat, cut into bite-sized pieces. Simmer until flavors are well blended, 1–2 hours.

DUMPLINGS:

1 cup biscuit mix	**About ¾ cup milk**

Combine biscuit mix and milk. Drop dough into simmering liquid by large spoonfuls. Cover pan and cook 10 minutes. Uncover and simmer another 10 minutes.

Alternate Method: Just throw everything (except Dumplings) in a pressure cooker and cook on HIGH for one hour. Prepare Dumplings as directed; cook uncovered for 20 minutes.

Lemon, Rosemary, and Garlic Roast Chicken

Nothing beats the smell of a chicken roasting in the oven. I find there's something very satisfying about cooking one as well. This roast chicken uses the garlic that is roasted alongside it to make a delicious gravy. —Meredith Laurence

1 (3½- to 4-pound) roasting chicken
1 lemon, halved
Olive oil
Salt and pepper to taste
3 sprigs fresh rosemary
½ onion
1 head garlic, unpeeled and smashed
1½ cups chicken stock
1 teaspoon finely chopped rosemary
1 tablespoon heavy cream

Place chicken in roaster. Squeeze juice from 1 lemon half all over chicken, including cavity. Drizzle olive oil over outside of chicken. Season chicken inside and out with salt and pepper. Stuff rosemary sprigs, onion, garlic, and squeezed lemon half inside cavity. Pour chicken stock into roaster pan. Roast at 400° until internal temperature reaches 160°, about 45 minutes.

Allow chicken to rest. De-fat the juices at the bottom of the pan. Peel garlic cloves. Purée garlic in a food processor and drizzle in the de-fatted liquid. Add chopped rosemary and cream. Season with remaining lemon juice. Heat gravy, then pour over chicken.

roaster pan

ALTERNATE:
electric roaster

mini food processor

Bob shows off his skill-ets with host Jill Bauer.

mixing bowl

Bowls with lids are so nice for mixing and marinating.

baking pan

Lemon Marinated Chicken

This recipe has been on our menus at my catering business for years and years. Many repeat customers order it for every function they have. The lemon is light and refreshing and the rosemary gives a nice herbed flavor—not too heavy.—Jenny Repko

MARINADE:

1 tablespoon chopped fresh rosemary, or 1 teaspoon dried rosemary leaves
½ teaspoon pepper
2 tablespoons lemon juice
1 tablespoon white wine or water

1 tablespoon oil
2 teaspoons honey
1 teaspoon soy sauce
½ teaspoon Dijon mustard
½ teaspoon lemon peel

In shallow dish, combine all ingredients; mix well.

2 whole chicken breasts (about 1 pound), boned, skinned, and halved

Add chicken to Marinade; turn to coat. Cover; marinate in refrigerator 20–30 minutes. Place marinated chicken in 9-inch square baking pan; broil 4–6 inches from broiler. Cook 8–10 minutes on one side, basting with Marinade. Turn; continue cooking and basting 8–10 minutes longer or until chicken is fork-tender and juices run clear. Serves 4.

Braised Chicken with Sausage Stuffing

4 tablespoons olive oil, divided
1 onion, chopped
½ pound ground Italian sausage with sage
1 Granny Smith apple, diced small
½ cup currants
2 tablespoons chopped parsley
3 cloves garlic, minced
1 teaspoon dried thyme
Salt and pepper to taste
1 large whole chicken
1 cup chicken stock

Heat 2 tablespoons olive oil in pressure cooker; sauté onion. Add sausage and cook through. Turn cooker off. Remove sausage mixture to a bowl, and add apple, parsley, currants, garlic, thyme, salt and pepper. Season chicken inside and out. Stuff sausage mixture into cavity. Truss chicken to secure the opening. Heat remaining 2 tablespoons olive oil in pressure cooker. Brown chicken on all sides. Leave chicken breast side up and add stock. Cook under HIGH pressure 25 minutes. Release pressure manually, remove chicken, and serve with stuffing. Serves 4.

electric pressure cooker

ALTERNATE:
pressure cooker

Divine Chicken Divan

My sister always made this for me because I loved it so much. She wouldn't tell me how she made it—teasing me in a humorous way. Finally, after I got married, she gave me the recipe. It is so easy to make, and now a favorite of my family as well. Thanks, Trena.—Lisa Brady

4 whole boneless chicken breasts
4 (10-ounce) boxes frozen broccoli spears, or 2 large crowns fresh broccoli
¾ pound Velveeta cheese
¾ cup milk
¾ cup mayonnaise or Miracle Whip
Pepper to taste
Onion powder to taste
Paprika to taste

Boil chicken until cooked (will be white all the way through). Drain and place in cold water. Thaw broccoli (or blanch if using fresh). Cut florets into bite-size pieces. Place broccoli in 3-quart casserole. Drain and cut chicken into bite-size pieces; cover all broccoli with it.

In saucepan on low heat, melt cheese and milk; add mayonnaise and seasonings. Pour sauce over chicken. Garnish with paprika. Bake at 350° for ½ hour, or until sauce bubbles. Serve over rice.

casserole

ALTERNATE:
saucepan

everyday pan

ALTERNATE:
electric skillet

The electric skillet cooks entirely away from the heat of the stove. And it keeps food warm so nicely, especially when dinnertime is rarely exact!

Chicken Cacciatore

This is a QVC standard that is seen a lot on air.

3 strips bacon, chopped
1 (3- to 4-pound) chicken, cut into 8 pieces
1 cup all-purpose flour
2 tablespoons salt
1 teaspoon black pepper
1 onion, chopped
1 carrot, finely chopped
2 cloves garlic, minced
8 ounces button mushrooms, quartered

2 teaspoons chopped fresh thyme
½ teaspoon finely chopped fresh rosemary
½ cup red wine
½ cup chicken stock
1 (28-ounce) can chopped tomatoes
1 tablespoon tomato paste
Salt and pepper to taste
Fresh parsley, chopped

Cook chopped bacon in large everyday pan over medium heat, until bacon is almost crispy, and most of the fat has been rendered out. Prepare chicken pieces by dredging in flour, salt, and pepper. Set bacon pieces aside, and drain all but 1–2 tablespoons bacon fat from pan. Over medium-high heat, brown dredged chicken pieces in bacon fat. (Don't overcrowd the pan for this step. If need be, sauté chicken in batches.) When chicken is brown, set aside with bacon, and add onion and carrot to pan. Cook until onion is translucent and slightly brown. Add garlic and continue to cook for one minute. Add mushrooms, thyme, and rosemary; stir well to combine. Cook another 2 minutes or so.

Deglaze pan by adding red wine, and scraping a spatula across bottom to dislodge any bits that may have accumulated there. Bring to a simmer, and let wine reduce by half. Add chicken stock and let this, too, reduce by half. Add tomatoes and tomato paste; stir well and bring mixture to a simmer. Return chicken and bacon to pot and cover with lid.

At this point, you may reduce heat and allow stew to simmer on stovetop 45 minutes, or transfer pot to a 325° oven and cook 1–1½ hours. When chicken is cooked through, remove pan from heat and season to taste with salt and pepper. Garnish with freshly chopped parsley. Serves 4–6.

Moroccan Braised Chicken with Olives and Wild Mushrooms

The flavor of the Mediterranean right in your kitchen.

sauté pan

1–2 tablespoons olive oil
1 whole chicken, cut into
   8 pieces
Salt and freshly ground
   black pepper
1 onion, finely chopped
1 carrot, finely chopped
1 rib celery, finely chopped
1 clove garlic, minced
1 teaspoon crushed or
   ground coriander seed
½ teaspoon ground
   cinnamon
¼ teaspoon cayenne
Pinch of saffron threads
1 lemon, sliced
½ cup green olives, pitted
½ cup white wine
1 cup chicken stock
1 (16-ounce) can chickpeas,
   drained
12 ounces shiitake mushrooms,
   or other types, sliced
3–4 tablespoons chopped
   cilantro
Slivered almonds, toasted

ALTERNATE:
electric skillet

Preheat a large sauté pan over medium-high heat. Add olive oil. Season chicken pieces well with salt and pepper; brown on all sides. Set aside.

Add onion, carrot, and celery to pan; sauté 2–3 minutes. Add garlic, coriander, cinnamon, cayenne, and saffron; continue to sauté for another minute. Add lemon slices and green olives; continue cooking another minute or two. Deglaze pan by adding white wine, simmering until wine has almost completely disappeared. Add chicken stock and bring to a simmer. Return chicken thighs and legs to pan and cover with tight-fitting lid. Reduce heat to very low and braise 10 minutes. Add chicken breasts and wings back to pan along with chickpeas. Cover and continue to simmer gently another 15 minutes. Turn off the heat.

ALTERNATE:
mini food chopper

When finely chopped is what you're after, the mini food chopper is perfect.

Heat a separate sauté pan over medium-high heat. Sauté mushrooms, seasoning with salt and pepper until just tender. Add mushrooms to the braise along with fresh cilantro, and stir until well combined. Serve chicken over couscous and garnish with more cilantro and toasted slivered almonds. Serves 4–6.

Editor's Extra: You may add dried fruit such as apricots or prunes to the dish.

sauté pan

ALTERNATE:
electric skillet

OPTION:
santoku knife

*Makes chopping
veggies and
chicken a breeze.*

Spring Stir-Fry with Chicken, Asparagus, Lemon, and Hazelnuts

1 tablespoon olive oil
1 red pepper, cut into strips
1 bunch asparagus, sliced
   ½ inch thick on the bias
½ pound chicken tenders
1 bunch green onions, sliced
   ¼ inch on bias

1 clove garlic, minced
1 tablespoon lemon zest
½ cup hazelnuts, toasted
   and chopped
Salt and freshly ground
   black pepper

Heat a 9-inch sauté pan or wok over medium-high to high heat or 400° in electric skillet. Add olive oil and stir-fry red pepper and asparagus 2–3 minutes. Add chicken pieces and continue to stir-fry until cooked through. Add green onions and garlic; continue to cook an additional minute. Remove pan from heat (or turn off, if using an electric skillet), and toss in lemon zest and hazelnuts. Season to taste with salt and freshly ground black pepper. Serve with rice or noodles or a green salad. Serves 4.

Bob Warden (far right), at the dinner table with his grandfathers, enjoys good food and fellowship at a holiday family dinner as generations come together.

Chicken Breasts with Tomato Tapenade

4 bone-in, skin-on split chicken breasts
Salt and pepper to taste

1 teaspoon ground turmeric
Pinch of ground cumin

In a heated 12-inch skillet, add enough olive oil to coat the pan. Rub each breast with salt and pepper, turmeric, and cumin. Sear all 4 breasts skin side down until they are deep golden brown. Place pan in a preheated 350° oven and cook about 35 minutes or until internal temperature of chicken is 185°.

TAPENADE:

½ cup plump sun-dried tomatoes
½ cup pitted calamata olives
½ small onion, coarsley chopped

¼ cup roasted pine nuts
½ cup marinated or grilled mushrooms
1 teaspoon fresh garlic

After chicken is in the oven, make Tapenade. Blend sun-dried tomatoes, olives, onion, pine nuts, mushrooms, and garlic to a chunky consistency with food processor or immersion blender.

Put a generous portion of the Tapenade on each breast, and let the chicken sit about 5 minutes prior to serving. If desired, drizzle high quality olive oil on each plate prior to serving, and crumble some goat cheese around the plate to finish it off.

Note: This dish is great served with couscous and wilted spinach.

skillet

ALTERNATE:
everyday pan

food processor

everyday pan

OPTION:
kohaishu knife

Many chefs will tell you their favorite tool in the kitchen is their kohaishu knife.

Photo-Fun Chicken

I made this for a photo shoot for First for Women *magazine. We loved eating the props!—Gwen McKee*

4 boneless, skinless chicken breasts
2 tablespoons olive oil, divided
1 teaspoon Mrs. Dash Table Blend seasoning
1 bell pepper, chopped
1 onion, chopped
3 cloves garlic, minced
1 (16-ounce) can salt-free tomato sauce
1 teaspoon crushed red pepper

Trim all gristle and fat from chicken. Wash and pat dry with paper towels. Heat oil in large everyday pan. Sprinkle chicken on both sides with seasoning; brown on medium-high heat; remove chicken to plate. Heat remaining tablespoon olive oil, and sauté vegetables. Add remaining ingredients; stir and heat about 3 minutes until hot. Return chicken to pan and spoon sauce over. Cover and bake in 350° oven 50 minutes. Serve over whole-wheat toast points, brown rice, or alone. Serves 4.

Note: Good accompaniments include cauliflower, broccoli, or spinach, and a fruit salad, or ripe peeled pears.

Greg Campbell and his daughter Catherine like to help eat the props with Barbara and Cyndi Clark after a Quail Ridge Press photo shoot.

Chicken 'n Peaches

This is a favorite that my grandkids love—they like it over angel hair pasta.
—Gwen McKee

4 chicken breast halves
1 teaspoon Greek seasoning
2 tablespoons butter
1 (16-ounce) can peach
  halves, undrained

2 tablespoons cornstarch
1 cup chicken bouillon
2 tablespoons honey mustard
2 tablespoons brown sugar

electric skillet

Sprinkle chicken breast halves with seasoning. Brown on both sides in electric skillet heated to 370°. Remove from skillet. Lower heat to 220° and add butter. Pour ⅓ cup peach juice into measuring cup; whisk in cornstarch. Add to skillet along with bouillon, and stir well. When it begins to thicken, add mustard, and brown sugar. Return chicken to skillet, cover, and let cook about 15 minutes. Pour peaches and remaining juice from can into skillet, and stir slightly to blend. When heated through, serve chicken, peaches, and sauce over a bed of rice. Serves 4.

ALTERNATE:
buffet pan

Way to Go, Dad, Chicken

Gwen's food photographer in Jackson, Mississippi, Greg Campbell, is a talented young man—a single father who had to learn to prepare quick recipes for his thirteen-year-old daughter when her mother passed away. Greg was going to substitute cornflake crumbs when he was out of cracker crumbs for a recipe Gwen gave him, but all he had was frosted cornflakes, so he decided to give it a try. The results were so good that Catherine declares this her all-time favorite chicken recipe. Way to go, Dad!

4–6 boneless chicken breasts
1 (10¾-ounce) can cream of
  chicken soup
1 (8-ounce) carton sour cream

1 cup crushed frosted
  cornflakes
1 stick butter, melted

everyday pan

In 10-inch everyday pan, boil chicken breasts in water to cover (save the broth for another dish). Tear chicken into small pieces and put back into skillet. Mix soup and sour cream; pour over chicken. Put cornflake crumbs on top; pour melted butter over crumbs. Bake 30 minutes at 350° until bubbly. Serves 4–6.

sauté pan

toaster oven pan

toaster oven

A toaster oven works great for this recipe!

Fantastic Chicken Dijon for Two

Good with a baked potato and steamed broccoli. Light some candles and pour the wine.

½ stick butter
½ teaspoon chopped garlic
2 teaspoons Dijon mustard
¾ cup dry bread crumbs
2 tablespoons shredded
 Parmesan cheese

¼ teaspoon cracked black
 pepper
1 tablespoon minced fresh
 parsley
2 boneless, skinless chicken
 breasts

Melt butter in sauté pan on low heat. Add garlic and simmer 3 minutes; remove from heat and blend in Dijon. Let cool, but do not let it solidify. Whip vigorously until thick. Mix bread crumbs, Parmesan, pepper, and parsley in shallow bowl. Dip chicken in butter mixture until well coated, then in breading mixture, patting to coat heavily. Refrigerate covered for several hours to set. Bake on toaster oven pan at 350° about 12 minutes.

Editor's Extra: Go ahead and double or triple this if you want to impress guests. Bake on a cookie sheet in a regular oven.

Chicken-Asparagus Casserole

2 teaspoons vegetable oil
1 cup seeded and chopped green and/or red bell peppers
1 medium onion, chopped
3 cloves garlic, minced
1 (10¾-ounce) can condensed cream of asparagus soup
1 cup ricotta cheese
1 (8-ounce) package shredded Cheddar cheese, divided

2 eggs
1½ cups chopped cooked chicken
1 (10-ounce) package frozen chopped asparagus, thawed and drained
8 ounces egg noodles, cooked
Black pepper (optional)

Preheat oven to 350°. Grease 3-quart casserole; set aside. Heat oil in small skillet over medium heat. Add bell peppers, onion, and garlic; cook and stir until vegetables are crisp-tender. Mix soup, ricotta cheese, 1 cup Cheddar cheese, and eggs in large bowl until well blended. Add onion mixture, chicken, asparagus, and noodles; mix well. Season with pepper, if desired. Spread mixture evenly in prepared casserole. Top with remaining 1 cup Cheddar cheese. Bake 30 minutes or until center is set and cheese is bubbly. Let stand 5 minutes before serving. Garnish as desired. Serves 12.

casserole
You can use both halves of this double-sided casserole for this dish.

ALTERNATE:
casserole

saucepan

cookie sheet

Surprise Chicken Packets

The taste of Buffalo chicken wings—without the mess.

2 tablespoons red wine
  vinegar
1 tablespoon butter, melted
2 teaspoons hot pepper
  sauce
½ teaspoon celery salt
¼ teaspoon paprika
1 tablespoon Worcestershire
½ cup Buffalo wing sauce
¼ cup crumbled blue
  cheese

1 (12-ounce) package
  precooked chicken strips,
  chopped
1 (8-ounce) can refrigerated
  crescent rolls
¼ cup shredded mozzarella
  cheese
Blue cheese salad dressing
Celery sticks

Combine vinegar, butter, pepper sauce, celery salt, paprika, Worcestershire, and Buffalo wing sauce in 1-quart saucepan and heat thoroughly. Add crumbled blue cheese and chopped chicken, stirring to mix; remove from heat.

Separate crescent rolls into 4 rectangles; place on ungreased cookie sheet. Press each to form a 4x7-inch rectangle, pressing perforations to seal.

With spoon, divide chicken mixture evenly onto center of rectangles. Top each with a tablespoon mozzarella cheese. Fold short sides of dough up over filling, meeting in center; pinch edges to seal, leaving center open. Bake at 375° for 13–17 minutes or until golden brown. Serve with blue cheese dressing and celery sticks. Serves 4.

Editor's Extra: If you end up having any leftover mixture, combine it with a package of cream cheese for an excellent spread on crackers.

"Summersault" Apple-Pecan-Chicken Rollups

In January, of course, this becomes a "wintersault."

½ cup apple juice
½ cup instant brown rice
½ cup finely chopped
  unpeeled apple
¼ cup chopped pecans

3 tablespoons sliced green
  onions
4 boneless, skinless chicken
  breasts (about 1 pound)
1 tablespoon vegetable oil

saucepan

In 1- or 2- quart saucepan, bring apple juice to a boil. Add rice, cover, reduce heat, and simmer 8–10 minutes, or until liquid is absorbed. Stir in apple, pecans, and green onions. Remove from heat. Flatten each chicken breast to about ¼-inch thickness by pounding between two pieces of wax paper. Place ¼ of rice mixture on each chicken breast. Roll up, tucking in edges. Secure with toothpicks.

skillet

Preheat oven to 400°. Heat oil in medium skillet over medium-high heat. Add chicken and cook 4–5 minutes or until lightly browned; place in shallow baking pan. Bake 20–25 minutes or until chicken is no longer pink in center. Makes 4 servings.

Editor's Extra: For this recipe, choose an apple variety that will retain its shape when cooked, such as Granny Smith, Golden Delicious, or Jonathan.

While working on this cookbook at Bob's house, he and Barbara take a break—where else, but in the kitchen.

grill pan

ALTERNATE:
electric skillet

food processor

Grilled Chicken and White Bean Enchiladas

I lived in Tucson for a year and never got over the craving for good Mexican dishes. This one is a family favorite.—Jenny Repko

Mexican-flavored marinade
2 (8-ounce) boneless, skinless chicken breasts
2 tablespoons sour cream
1 (16-ounce) can cannellini beans, rinsed and drained
1 cup grated sharp Cheddar cheese, divided
1 large jalapeño pepper, seeded and chopped
3 large green onions, chopped (about 1 tablespoon)
1 tablespoon chopped fresh cilantro
1 teaspoon ground cumin
1 tablespoon olive oil
6 (8-inch) spinach-flavored flour tortillas
1 (10-ounce) can prepared enchilada sauce

In a shallow dish, pour marinade over chicken. Cover with plastic wrap and refrigerate 30 minutes. Remove chicken from marinade.

In a grill pan, cook chicken, turning once, about 5 minutes per side until cooked through. Cool. Slice into thin strips.

In a food processor, combine the sour cream and cannellini beans. Pulse to combine. Add ½ cup cheese, jalapeño, onions, cilantro, and cumin. Pulse briefly.

Preheat oven to 350°. In a skillet, heat oil over medium-high heat. Cook each tortilla in oil until just beginning to brown, no longer than 1 minute. Place on paper towels. Place several strips of chicken in the center of each tortilla. Top with 2 tablespoons of the bean mixture. Roll tortillas and place seam side down in dish. Spread with enchilada sauce and sprinkle with remaining ½ cup Cheddar cheese. Bake 30 minutes.

Chicken Enchiladas for Twenty

1 pound shredded Pepper
  Jack cheese, divided
1 pound shredded Cheddar
  cheese, divided
3½ pounds chicken breasts,
  cooked and shredded
Salt and pepper to taste

1¾ cups salsa
3 scallions, cut into rings
¼ cup diced jalapeño peppers
20 flour tortillas
1¾ cups black bean dip
3 (17-ounce) bottles enchilada
  sauce

mixing bowl

Reserve some of both cheeses to melt on top of enchiladas. In mixing bowl, toss chicken with seasoning, salsa, Pepper Jack, Cheddar cheese, scallions, and jalapeños. Spread tortillas with black bean dip. Divide chicken mixture among the tortillas. Roll tortilla shells so ends are open. Lay in large roasting pan. Top with enchilada sauce. Top with reserved cheese. Cover with foil. Put roasting pan into 350° oven; heat through for 30 minutes. Remove foil for last 5–10 minutes, until cheese is bubbling. Yields 20 servings.

roasting pan

Chicken Escabèche

6 chicken breasts, cut into
  quarters
3 tablespoons olive oil
1 cup sherry vinegar
2 tablespoons tomato paste
½ cup ketchup
1 teaspoon chopped garlic
1 teaspoon ground cayenne
  pepper
1 tablespoon salt

1 teaspoon pepper
1 cup extra virgin olive oil
1 cup julienne red onion
1 cup julienne red bell pepper
1 cup julienne green bell pepper
1 cup julienne yellow bell
  pepper
3 tablespoons capers
½ cup niçoise olives
2 tomatoes, chopped

pressure cooker

Brown chicken breast quarters in oil in pressure cooker. Whisk together sherry vinegar, tomato paste, ketchup, garlic, cayenne, salt, and pepper. Toss everything into the pressure cooker and cook under HIGH pressure 5 minutes. Yields 6 servings.

Alternate Method: Cook in electric stockpot or roaster for 30–40 minutes.

OPTION:
mandoline

*Save time by using
the mandoline's
julienne insert.*

casserole

mixing bowl

Saucy Chicken Pot Pie

2–3 chicken breasts
½ teaspoon celery salt
1 (10¾-ounce) can cream of chicken soup
1 soup can water
¾ cup seasoning blend (celery, green and red pepper, onion)

1½ cups biscuit mix
1½ cups buttermilk
1 stick butter, melted
¼ teaspoon dried basil
¼ teaspoon poppy seed
½–1 cup chicken broth

Boil chicken breasts in water seasoned with celery salt until tender. Cool and cut into chunks. Combine chicken, soup, water, and seasoning blend, and put into 3-quart casserole. In mixing bowl, combine biscuit mix, buttermilk, melted butter, basil, and poppy seeds; mix well. Spoon over chicken mixture, spreading to edges. Gently pour chicken broth over top. Bake in 400° oven 25–30 minutes, or until golden brown. Let sit 10 minutes before serving. Serves 6–8.

everyday pan

ALTERNATE:
electric skillet

Chinese

I created this dish years ago when my children were small, and they always were excited to hear we were having "Chinese." So that's what this dish has always been called. They still love it.—Gwen McKee

Cajun seasoning to taste
2 boneless chicken breast halves, cut in ¾-inch cubes
2 tablespoons olive oil, divided
1 large onion, coarsely chopped
½ bell pepper, chopped

1 (16-ounce) bag frozen stir-fry vegetables
1 teaspoon minced garlic
4 ounces vermicelli, broken in 1-inch pieces, cooked
1 (8-ounce) can pineapple tidbits
½ cup sweet and sour sauce
1–2 tablespoons soy sauce

Stir-fry seasoned chicken cubes in 1 tablespoon olive oil in everyday pan or electric skillet. Remove to plate. In remaining tablespoon olive oil, stir-fry all vegetables. Add vermicelli, chicken, pineapple, sauces, and additional seasoning to taste. Stir-fry briefly. Serves 6.

Cashew Chicken Stir-Fry

chef's pan

1 tablespoon peanut oil
2 cloves garlic, minced
½ teaspoon dried red
  chile flakes
4 chicken breasts, cut into
  strips
1 red bell pepper, cut into
  very thin strips
¼ cup ketchup

3 tablespoons fish sauce
2 tablespoons white vinegar
2 tablespoons sugar
½ cup chicken stock
1½ tablespoons cornstarch
1 tablespoon water
1 cup cashews, toasted
¼ cup fresh cilantro leaves
Salt and pepper to taste

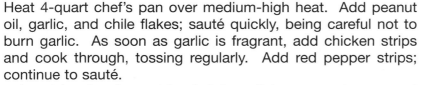

mixing bowl;
whisk

Heat 4-quart chef's pan over medium-high heat. Add peanut oil, garlic, and chile flakes; sauté quickly, being careful not to burn garlic. As soon as garlic is fragrant, add chicken strips and cook through, tossing regularly. Add red pepper strips; continue to sauté.

In mixing bowl, combine ketchup, fish sauce, vinegar, and sugar, and whisk until sugar is dissolved. Add to chef's pan along with chicken stock. Bring mixture to a boil. Dissolve cornstarch in water and whisk into stir-fry. Boil to ensure sauce thickens, then remove pan from heat. Stir in toasted cashews and cilantro leaves. Season to taste with salt and pepper. Serves 4.

sa   sauté pan

ALTERNATE:
electric skillet

*A great alternate
for either of these
recipes.*

lipped skillet

Ruth's Pineapple Chicken

**2 cups cubed chicken
(or pork or beef)
2 tablespoons oil
1 medium green pepper,
sliced
1 small onion, sliced
½ teaspoon salt
1 tablespoon soy sauce**

**¼ cup vinegar
2 tablespoons cornstarch
1 cup cold water
1 chicken bouillon cube
¼ cup brown sugar
1 (20-ounce) can pineapple
chunks, undrained**

Brown chicken (or other meat) in oil in large sauté pan. Add pepper, onion, and salt. Sauté these ingredients, then add soy sauce, vinegar, cornstarch mixed with water, and bouillon cube. Mix well. Add sugar and pineapple. Cook until all ingredients are tender and flavors are blended. Serve with rice. Serves 4.

Far East Chicken

Such an easy last-minute stir-fry.

**4 chicken breast strips
2 tablespoons oil
½ orange bell pepper,
chopped
1 (7-ounce) can mushroom
stems and pieces, drained
3 or 4 broccoli florets,
chopped**

**3 or 4 baby carrots, sliced
½ (11-ounce) can Mandarin
oranges, drained
1 (14-ounce) can Chinese
vegetables, drained
1–2 tablespoons soy sauce
Dash of rice wine vinegar
2 cups Chinese noodles**

Cut chicken strips into bite-size pieces. Brown in oil in large skillet or electric skillet; remove and set aside. Add bell pepper, mushrooms, broccoli, and carrots to skillet and sauté until tender-crisp. Add oranges and vegetables; return chicken to skillet. Add soy sauce and vinegar; toss about and simmer until flavors mingle. Serve over noodles or with noodles on top. Serves 6–8.

Bombay Chicken Wings

These are roasted rather than deep-fried, but you can do them either way.

1½ teaspoons cumin seeds
5½ pounds chicken wings
(about 30)
½ tablespoon minced fresh
ginger
2 teaspoons minced garlic
1 tablespoon ground
coriander
1½ teaspoons kosher salt
½ teaspoon freshly ground
black pepper

1¼ teaspoons cayenne
pepper, divided
¼ teaspoon plus ⅛ teaspoon
paprika, divided
1 cup plain low-fat yogurt
⅓ cup plus 1 teaspoon fresh
lemon juice, divided
About ¼ cup peanut or corn
oil, for basting
2 tablespoons unsalted butter

skillet;
saucepan

mixing bowl

In a small dry skillet, toast cumin seeds over moderate heat until fragrant, about 1 minute. Crush seeds in spice grinder or mortar. Cut wing tips from chicken wings and discard. Pierce wings all over with skewer or knife.

In a large bowl, combine ground cumin seeds, ginger, garlic, coriander, kosher salt, black pepper, 1 teaspoon cayenne, ¼ teaspoon paprika. Stir in yogurt and ⅓ cup lemon juice. Add chicken wings, and stir to coat evenly. Cover and refrigerate for 24 hours, turning wings occasionally. Take wings out of fridge 1 hour before proceeding.

Preheat oven to 450°. Lightly oil wire rack and set it over a large roasting pan. Place wings on rack without touching; reserve marinade.

Using a pastry brush, dab wings lightly with peanut oil, them roast them for 15 minutes. Turn over, baste with reserved marinade, and brush lightly with more oil. Roast about 20 minutes longer, or until cooked through.

In a small saucepan, melt butter with remaining ¼ teaspoon cayenne and ⅛ teaspoon paprika. Stir in remaining 1 teaspoon lemon juice and a pinch of kosher salt, and cook over medium-high heat until hot. Brush spicy butter over roasted chicken wings and serve. Serves 6.

roasting pan;
wire rack

This roaster with lid allows you to take this dish anywhere.

pizza pan

OPTION:
square pan with
bacon press

Chicken Artichoke Pizza

We have really fun lunches at Quail Ridge Press. This was a huge hit with the office staff.

1 prepared pizza crust, or make your own
1 cup Alfredo sauce, more or less
1 (12-ounce) package sliced bacon, cooked and crumbled
10–12 ounces cooked, chopped chicken
1 (14-ounce) can quartered artichoke hearts
1 Roma tomato, diced
1–1½ cups shredded mozzarella cheese

Layer ingredients on top of crust in the order listed. Bake at 375° about 15–20 minutes, or until cheese is browning on top.

Editor's Extra: Adjust amount of Alfredo sauce depending on how much you like.

saucepan

whisk

Use a whisk on gravies—it scares away the lumps!

Bourbon Cream Gravy

The alcohol burns away, but the fragrance stays.

2 tablespoons butter
3 tablespoons flour
1½ cups chicken stock
½ cup bourbon
¼ cup heavy cream
2 tablespoons chopped parsley
Salt and pepper to taste

Heat a medium saucepan over medium-high heat. Add butter and melt. When butter is foamy, add flour and whisk around to combine. Cook, stirring, for 2 minutes. Remove from heat, and whisk in chicken stock and bourbon. Return to heat and bring to a boil. Reduce heat to a simmer, and cook an additional 10 minutes. Remove from heat, add cream and parsley, and season to taste with salt and pepper. Serve with fried chicken. Makes 2 cups.

Note: Also delicious over a steak, mashed potatoes, or rice.

Bryce's Smothered Quail

When my eleven-year-old grandson, Bryce, came home after a successful hunt, he expected Gran to prepare the quail her old-fashioned way. He thought they were wonderful, as did everyone else.—Barbara Moseley

1 cup all-purpose flour	**Oil for frying**
1 teaspoon salt	**1 (14-ounce) can chicken broth**
½ teaspoon black pepper	**Water as needed**
12 dressed quail	

electric skillet

ALTERNATE:
chicken fryer

Combine flour, salt, and pepper in a zipper bag. Add quail and shake well to coat each bird completely. Heat oil, about 1–2 inches, in electric skillet or large chicken fryer with deep sides on medium-high heat. Add birds carefully; do not overcrowd. Brown birds, turning once or twice (do not overcook; just brown). Remove birds from oil to drain.

Pour off excess oil, reserving about ¼ cup and the browned residue in skillet. Add about 3 or 4 tablespoons of the remaining seasoned flour to oil in skillet. Brown flour in oil, scraping the brown particles into the roux, stirring constantly. Brown to light golden color; do not make dark roux for this gravy. Add chicken broth and stir well; add water to make of slightly thin consistency as it will thicken while simmering. Add birds back to gravy, cover, and reduce heat to SIMMER. Simmer about 30 minutes or until breasts are tender. Check water in gravy; add a little at a time if too thick. Serve gravy over cooked rice. Serves 6.

Barbara's grandchildren often request their favorite dishes from Gran, but sometimes Zach and Bailey like to try to make their own recipes.

casserole

OPTION:
santoku knife

Makes chopping veggies and chicken a breeze.

Terrific Turkey Tetrazzini

This dish is said to be named for opera singer Luisa Tetrazzini. It is so popular and delicious, Mama Mia, it will make you want to sing!

2 tablespoons butter
1 onion, finely chopped
2 carrots, diced small
8 ounces mushrooms, sliced
3 cloves garlic, minced
1 teaspoon dried thyme
1 tablespoon flour
2 (10¾-ounce) cans cream of mushroom soup
1 cup milk
3 cups cooked and chopped turkey
1 pound fusilli pasta, cooked
6 ounces frozen sweet peas
½ cup grated Parmesan cheese
1½ cups shredded Cheddar cheese
Salt and pepper to taste
½ cup crumbled Asiago cheese

Preheat oven to 350°. Preheat 4-quart casserole over medium-high heat. Add butter to casserole; sauté onion and carrots until tender. Add mushrooms and cook until tender. Add garlic and thyme and cook an additional minute. Sprinkle in flour and stir well. Cook one minute more. Add soup and milk and bring to a boil. Add turkey, cooked pasta, peas, Parmesan, and Cheddar cheese. Stir well. Season to taste with salt and pepper. Bake in 350° oven 35–45 minutes. For last 5 minutes of cooking, sprinkle crumbled Asiago on top. Serves 8–10.

Editor's Extra: This is how you use up all that leftover turkey after the holidays (and just as good with chicken). If you can say it, you can make it!

There's something so palette pleasing about crispy-on-the-outside, tender-on-the-inside fried seafood. But it's not just for frying—the methods for preparing fish are many and varied: broiled, grilled, stir-fried . . . and fish is so quick to fix. In fact, seafood *should* be cooked quickly. Such a great source of nutrients, the bounty of the sea is truly magnificent. Go fish!

mixing bowls

skillet

ALTERNATE:
lipped skillet

Mike's Coconut Shrimp

My son, Michael, LOVES coconut shrimp. He finally decided that he had to learn to make it himself, not only so that he could have it more often, but so that he could make it to impress the girls he was dating. This is his version.

—Bob Warden

1½ pounds large shrimp, peeled and deveined
½ cup all-purpose flour
½ cup cornstarch
1 tablespoon salt
½ tablespoon ground white pepper

2 tablespoons vegetable oil
1 cup ice water
2 cups shredded coconut
2 tablespoons vegetable oil

Wash shrimp. Dry well on paper towels. Mix together flour, cornstarch, salt, and pepper. Add 2 tablespoons vegetable oil and ice water. Stir to blend. Pour coconut into a shallow pan or bowl. Dip shrimp one at a time into batter, then roll in coconut. Once coated, place each shrimp into a skillet of 350° oil. Sauté shrimp in hot oil until lightly browned, about 5 minutes. Bake fried shrimp in preheated 300° oven another 5 minutes.

DIPPING SAUCE:
½ cup orange marmalade
¼ cup Dijon mustard

¼ cup honey
¼ teaspoon hot pepper sauce

Combine all ingredients in a small bowl. Mix well. Serve shrimp and Dipping Sauce side by side.

Coconut Milk Batter Fried Shrimp

Whenever we show a deep fryer on QVC, the backstage crew always rushes to our set once we are finished to gobble up the leftover food. Coconut shrimp is one of their favorites and disappears quickly.

½ cup coconut milk
¼ cup flour
1 egg
1½ teaspoons curry powder
1½ cups unsweetened shredded coconut

1 pound shrimp (16/20 count), peeled and deveined, tails on
Vegetable oil for frying
1 teaspoon salt
⅛ teaspoon cayenne pepper
1 lime, in wedges

cooling rack; baking sheet

electric deep fryer

In a mixing bowl, combine coconut milk, flour, egg, and curry powder; blend until smooth. Place a cooling rack over a baking sheet. Holding the shrimp by the tail, dip each into batter, shaking off excess. Dredge each shrimp in coconut and allow to dry on cooling rack until all shrimp are coated. May be refrigerated for later at this point.

Heat oil in electric deep fryer to 350°. Fry shrimp in batches. Drain on a paper towels and season with salt and cayenne. Serve with lime wedges and a dipping sauce of your choice.

The Warden family gathers around a spread of the best of the best family recipes every Christmas Eve. Left to right: Michael, Jonathan, Joseph, Becca, Rachel, Becki, and David.

mixing bowls

electric deep
fryer

ALTERNATE:
skillet

"Dressed" Shrimp Po' Boys

A po' boy sandwich is considered "dressed" when you garnish it with pickles, tomatoes, and lettuce.

FRIED SHRIMP:

¾ pound medium shrimp, peeled and deveined
1 egg, beaten
½ cup fine-ground cornmeal
½ cup all-purpose flour

¾ teaspoon salt
¼ teaspoon pepper
⅛ teaspoon cayenne pepper
6 cups vegetable oil

Coat shrimp with egg. Combine cornmeal, flour, salt, pepper, and cayenne together in a large shallow container. Toss about 6 shrimp at a time in the cornmeal mixture to coat well. Set coated shrimp aside while coating the remaining shrimp.

Heat oil in electric deep fryer to 375°. Put about half the shrimp in basket and lower into hot oil. Stir them around so they fry evenly, until golden, about 2 minutes. Transfer Fried Shrimp to paper-towel-lined plate. Return oil to 375°, and fry remaining shrimp.

SANDWICH:

1 long (about 2 feet) baguette, split lengthwise and cut into 4 pieces
½ cup mayonnaise
2 teaspoons fresh lemon juice

Salt and pepper to taste
½ cup minced dill pickles (or slices)
1 tomato, sliced thin
4 green leaf lettuce leaves

Hollow out inside of baguette pieces by removing some of the interior from both top and bottom crusts. Spread mayonnaise liberally inside each hollow, sprinkle with lemon juice, and season. Spread pickles and Fried Shrimp into bottom crusts. Top each with several slices of tomato, a leaf of lettuce, and finally the upper crust. Serves 4.

Fried Butterfly Shrimp with Vegetables

1½ cups all-purpose flour
½ teaspoon Cajun seasoning
½ teaspoon sugar
½ teaspoon salt
1 cup ice water
1 egg, beaten
2 tablespoons oil

2 pounds fresh shrimp, tails intact
1 Vidalia or sweet onion, sliced in ½-inch rings
¾ cup fresh broccoli florets
Oil for frying

Combine flour with Cajun seasoning, sugar, salt, water, egg, and oil until smooth, then set in refrigerator or freezer to chill.

Butterfly shrimp by cutting lengthwise to tail. Dip dry shrimp into batter, and deep-fry in hot oil in electric deep fryer or deep skillet till floating and golden brown, 3–5 minutes.

Dip dry vegetables into batter. Fry in hot oil until golden brown. Drain on paper towels, and serve immediately. Serves 6–8.

electric deep fryer

ALTERNATE:
skillet

Garlic Shrimp with Snow Peas

Quick and easy dinner.

1 tablespoon olive oil
1 tablespoon butter
¾ pound shrimp (16/20 count), peeled and deveined

12–15 snow peas
2 cloves garlic, minced
½ cup chicken or vegetable stock
Salt and pepper to taste

Heat electric skillet to 375°–400°. Add oil and butter. When fats are very hot, add shrimp; sauté 2 minutes. Add snow peas and continue to cook an additional minute. Add garlic and cook 30 seconds. Add stock to gather all the flavors together. Keep the heat high. If the stock evaporates, that's okay. Season to taste with salt and pepper. Serve with rice or polenta.

electric skillet

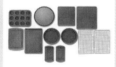

baking pan

ALTERNATE:
casserole

mixing bowl

Angel Hair Pasta and Shrimp Casserole

1 cup half-and-half
1 cup sour cream
½ cup shredded Swiss cheese
⅓ cup ricotta cheese
2 eggs
¼ cup chopped parsley
1 tablespoon crushed dried basil leaves
1 (9-ounce) package refrigerated fresh angel hair pasta, divided

1 (10-ounce) can Ro-Tel tomatoes
1 pound medium shrimp, peeled, deveined, and divided
¾ cup shredded Mexican or pizza blend cheese

Preheat oven to 350°. Butter a 9x13-inch baking pan or 3-quart casserole. Mix together half-and-half, sour cream, Swiss and ricotta cheeses, eggs, parsley, and basil in mixing bowl. Mix with pasta, tomatoes, and shrimp. Spread mixture into prepared pan. Top with Mexican or pizza blend cheese. Bake 30 minutes or until bubbly. Let stand 10 minutes. Serves 6.

Elaine and Bob discuss cookware at the factory.

Easy Grilled Shrimp with Kicky Sauce

This sauce is so good, you'll want to use it as a dip for crackers, chips, and veggies.

KICKY SAUCE:

2 tablespoons chopped fresh parsley
2 tablespoons seasoned bread crumbs
2 tablespoons prepared horseradish

1 cup half-and-half
⅓ cup sour cream
3 tablespoons lemon juice
Big dashes of salt and red pepper

Pulse parsley in mini food processor; add remaining ingredients; blend 30 seconds.

⅔ stick butter
1 teaspoon lemon zest
Juice of half lemon

1 pound large shrimp, peeled, with tails on

Heat electric griddle to 400°. Melt butter in small saucepan with lemon zest and juice. Put shrimp on hot griddle and pour ⅓ lemon-butter mixture over them. Turn shrimp over after a minute or two; pour ⅓ lemon-butter on this side. Remove to serving dish and pour remaining lemon-butter over. Serve with Kicky Sauce on the side. Serves 2–4.

mini food processor

electric griddle

ALTERNATE:
grill pan

saucepan

sauté pan

Shrimp Stroganoff

1 stick butter
½ medium onion, finely
  chopped
½ pound shrimp, peeled
  and deveined
½ cup milk

1 (10¾-ounce) can cream
  of shrimp soup
⅓ cup finely chopped parsley
1 (8-ounce) container sour
  cream
8 ounces fettuccini, cooked

Melt butter in 12-inch sauté pan; add onion and sauté until soft. Add shrimp and continue to sauté until pink. Add milk, soup, and parsley. Heat, but do not boil. Remove from heat and incorporate sour cream. Serve over fettuccini. Serves 6.

Dilled Shrimp and Rice

This is a very easy way to dress up a rice dish. The dill adds a nice light flavor.
—Meredith Laurence

2 tablespoons butter
1 onion, finely chopped
2 cloves garlic, minced
3 cups long-grain rice
6 cups chicken stock

Salt and pepper to taste
2 pounds shrimp, peeled and
  deveined
¼ cup chopped fresh dill
  weed

stockpot

ALTERNATE:
electric
stockpot

Heat 7-quart stockpot over medium-high heat. Add butter, and sauté onion until soft and translucent. Add garlic and rice; sauté an additional 1–2 minutes, stirring to coat rice in butter. Add chicken stock and bring mixture to a simmer. Season with salt and pepper. Cover, and cook rice for 20 minutes.

As soon as rice is tender, fluff with fork and add shrimp and dill; gently stir together well. Cover pan again and let it sit off the heat for 5 minutes. The residual heat should be enough to cook the shrimp. If the shrimp are large, they may require low heat at this point. Be sure shrimp are fully cooked by checking for a bright pink color. Season to taste again with salt and pepper. Serves 6–8.

Crêpes au Poisson

This has become a favorite for my children. They like to serve it when they entertain. —Bob Warden

CRÊPES:

1 cup flour	1 egg yolk
Pinch of salt	1½ cups milk, divided
1 egg	1 tablespoon melted butter

crêpe pan

Sift flour with salt into a medium bowl. Make a well in the center and add egg and egg yolk. Slowly pour in half the milk, stirring constantly, then stir in the melted butter. Beat until smooth. Add remaining milk, cover, and let stand at room temperature at least 30 minutes. The batter will be the consistency of light cream. When cooking, tilt crêpe pan so batter spreads evenly over bottom. When the bottom is golden brown, turn and repeat. Makes 18 Crêpes.

chef's pan

4 tablespoons butter	1 (7½-ounce) can crabmeat, or ¾ cup fresh crabmeat
1–2 cloves minced garlic	
4 tablespoons flour	1 cup fresh bay scallops (optional)
1 cup heavy cream	
1 cup vegetable broth	Salt and freshly ground pepper to taste
1 (4½-ounce) can shrimp, rinsed and drained, or ¾ cup small fresh shrimp	Freshly ground Parmesan cheese for garnish

stoneware baking dish

In a chef's pan or 10-inch skillet, melt butter and brown garlic. Add flour and stir with a wire whisk to create a roux. Add cream and vegetable broth, stirring constantly until slightly thickened. Add shrimp, crabmeat, scallops, if desired, and seasoning.

Place about 2 tablespoons of the seafood mixture in the middle of each Crêpe, then roll, and place in baking dish. Pour remaining mixture over the top. Sprinkle with Parmesan cheese. Bake in a 350° oven approximately 45 minutes.

Editor's Extra: To make homemade vegetable broth, simmer 1 carrot, 1 onion, 1 stick celery with leaves, and 1 small bunch parsley in 2 cups hot water for about an hour. Strain off broth. Makes 2 cups.

**square skillet
with press**

*I like using the
press with very thin
fish fillets, like
tilapia, to keep them
from curling up
during cooking.
—Bob*

Spice-Rubbed Fish
in a Skillet

*Ideal for frozen fish fillets such as tilapia and orange roughy. Quick and tasty
. . . and healthy, too.*

4 (½-inch-thick) fish fillets	**½ teaspoon garlic powder**
½ teaspoon ground cumin	**⅛ teaspoon cayenne**
½ teaspoon curry powder	**2 tablespoons butter**
½ teaspoon ground ginger	**1 tablespoon olive oil**

Rinse fish fillets and pat dry. Mix spices in a custard cup.
Sprinkle, then rub dry spice mixture with fingertips all over each
fillet; put on a sheet of wax paper. Melt butter and oil in a skillet on medium-high. Brown fish quickly on each side for about
1 minute per side. Serve with tartar sauce, sweet and sour
sauce, soy sauce, or all by itself. Serves 4.

skillet

Pan-Fried Halibut for Two

Low on sodium and fat . . . high on flavor.

6 salt-free soda crackers	**½ pound halibut fillets**
¾ teaspoon Mrs. Dash	**¼ cup liquid egg substitute**
Original Blend seasoning	**½ teaspoon light olive oil**
Dash of red pepper	

Crush crackers finely with seasonings. Slice halibut into ½-
inch-thick slices; rinse, then dry on paper towels. Dip fillets into
egg substitute. Heat olive oil in 8-inch skillet. Pat fillets with
crumbs on both sides, and quickly brown in oil, about 2 minutes
per side. If desired, serve with a dab of tartar sauce.

ALTERNATE:
electric skillet

Fish Catch in a Packet

My family loves these. There's something special, almost exciting, about opening your own packet at the table, its steamy aroma welcoming you inside. (Fun for campers who catch their own fish.)—Gwen McKee

baking sheet

4 (4-ounce) halibut or other
  white fish fillets
3 tablespoons Lizano or
  Worcestershire
½ onion, sliced
2 carrots, peeled, thinly sliced

1 (8-ounce) can water
  chestnuts, drained
Black pepper to taste
2 teaspoons snipped parsley
½ stick butter, melted

Preheat oven to 450°. Cut 4 (12x16-inch) strips of heavy-duty foil. Rinse fillets, and pat dry with paper towels. Place 1 fillet on each piece of foil; sprinkle some sauce on each. Divide onion, carrots, and water chestnuts on top of each fillet; season each with black pepper and parsley. Top each with remaining sauce. Fold ends of foil together, and fold ends up tightly. Bake on baking sheet in preheated oven 22 minutes. Offer butter to drizzle over opened packets. Serve with crusty bread and a green or fruit salad. Serves 4.

Mary Beth Roe goes over the talking points of one of Gwen's cookbooks with her as each host does with every guest right before on-air presentations.

pasta pot

grill pan

Sea Bass on Lentils with Tomato and Garlic in Seafood Broth

1 pound lentils
3 cloves garlic, minced
3½ cups diced fresh
  tomatoes
6 basil leaves, slivered
2 tablespoons chopped
  parsley
1 teaspoon salt

1 teaspoon pepper
12 (3-ounce) portions sea bass
¼ cup olive oil
9 cups seafood broth (look in
  gourmet section)
1 bunch parsley, chopped
12 basil sprigs

Using pasta pot with drain lid, cook lentils in salted water until soft but not mushy. Sauté garlic. Drain lentils, then add sautéed garlic, tomatoes, slivered basil leaves, and parsley. Season with salt and pepper. Cover with lid to keep warm.

Brush sea bass with oil; season with salt and pepper. Sear on grill pan. Transfer grill pan to 400° oven to finish, about 20 minutes.

Divide the lentils into 12 serving bowls. Ladle in 6 ounces seafood broth. Top with sea bass. Garnish with chopped parsley and basil sprigs. Yields 12 servings.

Editor's Extra: You can substitute your favorite fleshly fish such as halibut for the sea bass.

Grandma's Kitchen Salmon Patties

These patties were a regular part of our family's menu.—Bob Warden

1 (16-ounce) can salmon, bones removed
1 egg
⅓ cup bread crumbs
½ teaspoon dill weed
½ onion, chopped
Salt and pepper to taste
1–2 tablespoons vegetable oil

Mix salmon, egg, bread crumbs, dill, onion, salt and pepper, and form in patties. In large skillet, fry in vegetable oil on each side until golden brown.

square skillet with press

Margarita Salmon

4 large, thick-cut salmon steaks
1 small red onion, sliced
1 head fresh broccoli, cut into florets
4 yellow squash or small zucchini, sliced
Sliced portobello mushrooms
2 cups margarita mix with tequila
4 medium red-skinned potatoes, unpeeled and sliced
Salt, pepper, and garlic powder to taste
Olive oil (plain or flavored)

Assemble the salmon steaks, onion, broccoli, squash, and mushrooms together in an airtight container. Pour margarita mix over all and seal. Marinate in refrigerator for an hour or longer.

Grease a 9x13-inch baking pan with butter and place salmon steaks, skin side down, in a single layer in pan. Place marinated vegetables on top and around salmon steaks. Layer sliced potatoes on top of salmon steaks and vegetables. Add salt, pepper, and garlic powder to taste over all. Drizzle with olive oil. Cover tightly with foil. Bake in 375° oven about an hour. Remove foil and serve. Salmon should easily separate from skin when lifting from pan. Serves 4.

Editor's Extra: You may also grill marinated salmon steaks and vegetables on a griddle or indoor/outdoor grill. Grill potatoes last and sprinkle with salt, pepper, and garlic powder. Drizzle with olive oil.

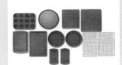

baking pan

ALTERNATE:
electric griddle

pasta pot;
saucepan

everyday pan

Salmon, Capers, and White Wine Cream Sauce over Fettuccine

1 pound fettuccine pasta
1 tablespoon butter
1 shallot, finely chopped
1 clove garlic, minced
3 sprigs fresh thyme
1 cup white wine
2 salmon fillets (about 6 ounces each)

Salt and freshly ground black pepper
2 teaspoons olive oil
1 cup heavy cream
2 tablespoons chopped fresh parsley
2 tablespoons capers, rinsed and lightly chopped

Bring a large pasta pot of salted water to a boil. Cook fettuccine in boiling water until al dente, or it reaches the desired consistency. Drain, using the locking drain lid, then keep the pasta warm.

Preheat oven to 425°. Heat 2-quart saucepan over medium-high heat. Add butter, and lightly sauté shallot and garlic with the fresh thyme sprigs. Add wine, and simmer mixture until wine is reduced by half.

Heat 500° oven-safe everyday pan over high heat. Season both sides of salmon fillets with salt and pepper. Add olive oil to skillet, and place salmon fillets, flesh side down, in the pan. Sear fillets on one side for a couple of minutes, then turn them over and transfer pan to 425° oven to finish cooking, about 20 minutes, or until fish flakes easily with a fork.

Once wine has reduced by half, add heavy cream and continue to simmer until cream has reduced slightly. Season to taste with salt and pepper. Add parsley, reserving a little for a final garnish. Add sauce to fettuccine along with chunks of finished salmon and rinsed, chopped capers. Season once again with salt and freshly ground black pepper. Garnish with remaining parsley.

"If I knew your were coming, I'd have baked a cake." A cake has become the ideal presentation to honor and celebrate people and occasions. In the baking, the trick is to achieve moistness and lightness, both of which require just the right amount of ingredients, just the right time and temperature, and accurate instructions. The result has brought compliments and pride to many a cook.

mixing bowls

cake pans

saucepan

Beautiful Red Velvet Cake

This is a very rich, beautiful cake, and is always a huge success.

2 tablespoons cocoa
2 ounces (4 tablespoons)
   liquid red food coloring
½ cup shortening
1½ cups sugar
2 eggs

1 teaspoon salt
1 teaspoon vanilla extract
1 cup buttermilk
2½ cups all-purpose flour
1½ teaspoons baking soda
1 tablespoon vinegar

Make a paste of the cocoa and red food coloring. Cream shortening, sugar, and eggs. Add salt, vanilla, and buttermilk alternately with flour. Add cocoa paste. Mix soda and vinegar together and fold into cake batter. Pour into 2 greased and floured 9-inch cake pans and bake at 350° for 25 minutes, or until done. Remove from oven; cool layers 10 minutes. Remove from pans and place on wire racks to cool completely.

ICING:

3 tablespoons flour
1 cup milk
1 cup margarine, softened

1 cup sugar
1 teaspoon vanilla

Cook flour and milk on medium heat in saucepan, stirring constantly, until thick; cool completely. Cream together margarine and sugar. Add vanilla; beat the 2 mixtures together with wire whisk attachment until the consistency is that of whipped cream (about 5 minutes). Frost cake.

Apple Cake

3 cups all-purpose flour
2½ cups sugar plus 3
   tablespoons sugar, divided
½ teaspoon salt
3 teaspoons baking soda
1 cup oil

4 large eggs
½ cup orange juice
2½ teaspoons vanilla
6 Granny Smith apples,
   peeled and sliced
2 teaspoons cinnamon

Grease and flour Bundt pan. Preheat oven to 350°. Mix together flour, 2½ cups sugar, salt, and baking soda in a bowl and put aside. In a stand mixer, blend oil, eggs, orange juice, and vanilla. Add flour mixture, and blend well. Toss sliced apples with remaining sugar and cinnamon. Pour ⅓ of batter in bottom of prepared pan, then layer half of apples into pan and repeat until full. Bake 70 minutes or until a toothpick comes out clean when inserted into cake.

bundt pan

mixer

Mini Banana Pecan Upside-Down Cake

3 tablespoons unsalted butter,
   softened, divided
2 tablespoons firmly packed
   brown sugar
2 tablespoons chopped
   pecans, toasted

1 banana, sliced
¼ cup self-rising flour
½ teaspoon ground cardamom
3 tablespoons sugar
1 large egg
¼ teaspoon vanilla

Preheat oven to 350°. Place 2 tablespoons butter into cassoulet; melt butter in oven. Sprinkle brown sugar and pecans over butter. Arrange banana slices over pecans, pressing to fit, if necessary.

   Combine flour and cardamom. Melt remaining tablespoon butter and combine with sugar, egg, and vanilla. Beat in flour mixture to form a batter. Pour batter over banana slices, and bake until a toothpick comes out clean, 20–25 minutes. Invert cake onto plate. Serves 2.

mini cassoulet

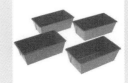

ALTERNATE:
mini loaf pan

mixer

bundt pan

Lemon Poppy Seed Cake

This has been by far the most often baked cake in Warden family history. Little Mike (my youngest son) used to request it by its alternate designation, "poofy seed cake." —Bob Warden

1¼ cups sugar	2 eggs
3 cups all-purpose flour	2 teaspoons lemon extract
2½ teaspoons baking powder	2 teaspoons almond extract
	2 tablespoons poppy seeds
1 teaspoon salt	1 teaspoon grated lemon rind
1 cup butter, softened	1¼ cups milk

Combine ingredients in mixer and mix well. Bake in greased Bundt pan at 350° for 40–45 minutes, till it tests done.

Editor's Extra: I know you've heard that a cake is done when no crumbs are visible when a toothpick inserted in center comes out clean. My opinion . . . I like to see a few moist crumbs, because the cake continues to cook a little after you take it out, and a dry cake is . . . well, dry. So you don't want a lot of raw cake dough on the toothpick, but a few moist crumbs will assure a moist cake.

Bob's daughters-in-law, Abby and Becca stand over a Warden family spread that includes Lemon Poppy Seed Cake (far right).

Pumpkin Roll

¾ cup self-rising flour
2 teaspoons cinnamon
1 teaspoon ginger
½ teaspoon nutmeg
3 eggs
1 cup sugar

⅔ cup canned pumpkin
1 teaspoon lemon juice
¾ cup chopped walnuts or
    pecans
2 tablespoons confectioners'
    sugar, divided

cookie sheet

mixing bowls

Grease a 10x15-inch cookie sheet. In a mixing bowl, stir flour, cinnamon, ginger, and nutmeg together. In another mixing bowl, beat eggs on high about 5 minutes or until thick and lemon-colored. Gradually add sugar and beat until dissolved. Stir in pumpkin and lemon juice. Fold in flour mixture. Spread on cookie sheet and sprinkle with nuts. Bake at 375° for 12–15 minutes. Immediately loosen edges and turn out onto a towel, nuts down, and sprinkle with confectioners' sugar (this will be bottom of cake). Roll warm cake in towel with nuts on outside. Cool.

FILLING:

1 (8-ounce) package cream
    cheese, softened
¼ cup margarine, softened

½ teaspoon vanilla
1 cup confectioners' sugar

Beat cream cheese, margarine, and vanilla until smooth. Add confectioners' sugar. Unroll cooled cake and spread Filling on plain side. Reroll with nuts on the outside. Chill and cut to serve. Serves 10.

mixing bowl

baking pan

mixer

Mockingbird Cake

Not exactly a hummingbird cake, but a grand rendition of an old favorite.

1 (18¼-ounce) package
   spice cake mix
2 eggs, beaten
1¼ cups vegetable oil
1½ teaspoons vanilla extract

1 (20-ounce) can crushed
   pineapple, well drained
1 cup chopped walnuts
1 cup chopped firm ripe
   bananas

Preheat oven to 350°. To spice cake mix, add eggs and oil. Stir with a wooden spoon until ingredients are moistened. Stir in vanilla, pineapple, and walnuts. Stir in bananas. Spoon batter into well-greased 10x15-inch baking pan. Bake 25–30 minutes, or until a wooden pick or cake tester inserted in center comes out clean. Cool in pan 10 minutes before topping with Cream Cheese Frosting.

CREAM CHEESE FROSTING:

2 (8-ounce) packages cream
   cheese, softened
1 stick butter, softened

1 pound confectioners' sugar
2 teaspoons vanilla extract

Combine cream cheese and butter until smooth. Add confectioners' sugar and beat with electric mixer until light and fluffy. Stir in vanilla. Frost cake.

Cornmeal Layer Cake with Lemon Cream

This is one of my very favorite cakes of all time, which is a miracle because there's no chocolate in it! The cornmeal gives the cake a little crunch, which I love. It's perfect for summertime with some strawberries. —Meredith Laurence

mixer

½ pound butter, softened
3 cups granulated sugar
4 eggs
4 teaspoons vanilla extract
4 cups cake flour

⅔ cup cornmeal
2 teaspoons baking soda
½ teaspoon baking powder
½ teaspoon salt
2 cups buttermilk

cake pans

Preheat oven to 350°. Cream butter and sugar together using stainless steel all-in-one mixer or an electric mixer. (This will take about 5 minutes and is a very important step, so don't cut it short.) Add eggs one at a time along with vanilla extract. Blend well.

Combine dry ingredients in a separate bowl. Add dry ingredients and buttermilk alternately to butter mixture. Mix until just combined. Pour batter into 2 greased and floured 9-inch cake pans, and bake in 350° oven 35–45 minutes or until a toothpick inserted in the center of the cake comes out clean. Cool on a cooling rack.

LEMON CREAM:

2 cups heavy cream
½ cup confectioners' sugar

1 teaspoon lemon zest
¼ teaspoon lemon extract

Whip cream and when soft peaks form, add remaining ingredients. Frost cake with Lemon Cream no more than 2 hours before you are ready to serve it.

mixer

cake pans

Raspberry Almond Cake

1 (18¼-ounce) box white
  cake mix
1 (3-ounce) package vanilla
  instant pudding
¾ cup vegetable oil

¼ cup water
4 eggs
1 cup frozen raspberries,
  thawed

Mix all ingredients, and bake in 2 greased 9-inch cake pans at 350° about 30 minutes or until tests done. After 2 minutes, remove cakes from pans and cool on racks.

FROSTING:

1 stick butter, softened
1 (1-pound) box confectioners'
  sugar
½ cup frozen raspberries,
  thawed, drained

2 tablespoons milk
½ teaspoon almond extract
Dash of salt
⅓ cup sliced almonds

Mix all ingredients except almonds together and frost cooled cake. Place sliced almonds around top of cake, or all over it, however you wish to decorate it.

You have to concentrate really hard to frost a cake just right!
Gwen's grandsons, Corey and Nathan, do a really smooth job.

Easy Raspberry Chocolate Cake

There's never any left. So good it's scary.

1 (18¼-ounce) package
  chocolate cake mix
1 (3-ounce) package vanilla
  instant pudding (or
  raspberry Jell-O)
½ cup vegetable oil

4 eggs
1¼ cups water
1 tablespoon raspberry extract
3 tablespoons shortening,
  melted

mixer

Preheat oven to 350°. Mix all but shortening together and pour into Bundt pan that has been painted with the melted shortening. Bake 45–55 minutes. Let rest for 3 minutes; turn over onto cake plate. Frost when cool.

bundt pan

RASPBERRY FROSTING:

4 ounces cream cheese,
  softened
½ stick butter, softened
2 cups confectioners' sugar
1 tablespoon raspberry extract

Dash of salt
1–2 tablespoons heavy cream
1 carton fresh raspberries
Red food coloring (optional)

Mix cream cheese, butter, sugar, extract, salt, and 1 tablespoon cream. Thicken with more sugar or thin with cream to get frosting the right consistency to just barely flow down cake when spooned around top. Add red food coloring if you want it pink. Decorate with raspberries.

bundt pan

saucepan

Chocolate Covered Cherry Cake with White Ganache

Try it . . . you'll like it.   No . . . you'll love it!

1 (18¼-ounce) strawberry
   cake mix
1 (15-ounce) can dark sweet
   pitted cherries in juice
⅓ cup water

⅓ cup vegetable oil
3 eggs
1 (16-ounce) container fudge
   frosting

Mix well the cake mix, cherries with juice, water, oil, and eggs, about 2 minutes. Pour into greased Bundt pan and bake at 350° for 40–45 minutes. Remove cake from oven, cool completely, and frost with canned frosting. Put in refrigerator to chill. Make White Ganache.

WHITE GANACHE:

1 cup heavy whipping
   cream

1 (12-ounce) bag white
   chocolate chips

In small saucepan, heat cream over low heat, stir in white chocolate chips, and stir until completely melted and smooth. Remove from heat and cool about 20 minutes. Drizzle over frosted cake. Return to refrigerator to chill and harden White Ganache. Serves 10–12.

Flourless Chocolate Hazelnut Cake

Sometimes you want to bypass the flour and go straight to the chocolate! That's what you get with this cake. My mother and I are certified chocoholics, and this cake gives us our fix.—Meredith Laurence

double boiler

12 ounces semisweet chocolate, chopped
3 sticks butter
1½ cups cocoa powder, sifted

12 eggs
1½ cups sugar
1 tablespoon vanilla extract
2 cups hazelnuts, finely ground

tube pan

Preheat oven to 325°. Using a double boiler, melt semisweet chocolate and butter together; stir until smooth. (Alternately, you can use a microwave for this purpose, but make sure to stir the chocolate regularly as it melts.) Combine and beat together cocoa powder, eggs, sugar, vanilla, and hazelnuts. Add melted chocolate and whisk to incorporate. Pour batter into greased Bundt pan. If you are using a 4-cup mold, there will be a little extra batter with which you can make mini cakes or cupcakes.

Bake in 325° oven 30–40 minutes or until a toothpick inserted into center of cake comes out clean. Cool in cake pan 10 minutes, then invert onto a plate. Serve with Chocolate Espresso Sauce.

CHOCOLATE ESPRESSO SAUCE:

½ cup heavy cream
½ pound semisweet chocolate
1 tablespoon instant coffee

1 tablespoon water
¼ cup butter
1 teaspoon vanilla extract

Combine all ingredients in chef's pan, heating gently, and stir until smooth.

mixing bowls

cake pans

Chocolate Kahlúa Cake

1½ sticks butter, softened
2¼ cups sugar
4 eggs
2 ounces unsweetened
  chocolate, melted
⅓ cup Kahlúa

2¼ cups sifted cake flour
½ teaspoon baking soda
1 teaspoon cream of tartar
¼ teaspoon salt
¾ cup milk

In mixing bowl, cream butter and sugar; add eggs one at a time. Add chocolate and Kahlúa and beat until blended. Combine flour, soda, cream of tartar, and salt, and add to creamed mixture alternately with milk. Pour batter into 3 lightly greased round cake pans. Bake at 350° for 18–23 minutes. Cool in pans for 10 minutes.

CHOCOLATE KAHLÚA FROSTING:

½ stick butter, softened
1 (8-ounce) package cream
  cheese, softened
1 pound sifted confectioners'
  sugar, divided

3 ounces unsweetened
  chocolate, melted
¼ cup Kahlúa
½ cup chopped pecans,
  toasted, divided

Beat butter and cream cheese. Add 1 cup powdered sugar and chocolate. Beat until smooth. Gradually add remaining confectioners' sugar and Kahlúa; beat until smooth. Stir in most of nuts; frost cake. Sprinkle remaining nuts on top.

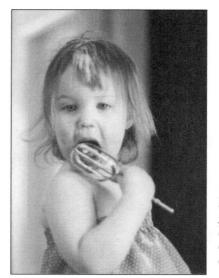

The best part of baking a cake is getting to lick the beaters, as Bob's daughter, Rachel, demonstrates.

Midnight Sunshine Cake

Okay—midnight is chocolate—sunshine is orange. It is truly a delicious combination.

1 (18¼-ounce) box yellow cake mix	⅓ cup vegetable oil
3 eggs	1 square unsweetened chocolate
1¼ cups water	1 teaspoon orange zest

Mix cake mix, eggs, water, and oil in mixer for 3 minutes. Pour half the batter into another bowl. Melt chocolate in microwave, and add to one bowl. Add the orange zest to the other. Drop alternating spoonfuls of each batter into 2 greased and floured 9-inch cake pans. Bake in 350° oven 20–24 minutes. Leave in pans 3 minutes, then turn out onto wire racks to cool.

FROSTING:

Few drops yellow food coloring	2 (16-ounce) containers vanilla butter cream frosting, divided
1 tablespoon freshly squeezed orange juice	1 square unsweetened chocolate

Add a few drops of yellow food coloring and a tablespoon of orange juice to 1 can of vanilla frosting, mixing till smooth. Melt chocolate in microwave, and add to the other can of frosting. Frost the bottom layer and sides with chocolate, then top with orange. Decorate with chocolate chips and candied orange peel, if desired.

mixer

mixing bowls

cake pans

baking pan

mixer

Cup of Coffee
Chocolate Cake

This cake recipe has been in my family about 30 years. It is from my mother's best friend, Masui, a fabulous cook! It is easy to prepare and may be one of the best chocolate cakes you have tasted. The cup of coffee is the secret for bringing out the chocolate flavor!—Jenny Repko

2 cups all-purpose flour	**1 cup oil**
1 teaspoon salt	**1 cup hot coffee**
1 teaspoon baking soda	**1 cup milk**
¾ cup cocoa	**2 eggs, beaten**
2 cups sugar	**1 teaspoon vanilla**

Preheat oven to 350°. Mix together flour, salt, baking soda, cocoa, and sugar. Add in oil, coffee, milk, eggs, and vanilla. Pour into a lightly greased 9x13-inch baking pan, and bake 35–40 minutes. Let cool before icing.

EASY FUDGE ICING:

1 cup butter, softened	**1 teaspoon lemon juice**
½ cup Hershey's cocoa	**2½ cups confectioners' sugar**
1 egg	

Cream butter in mixer; add cocoa, and blend well. Add egg; mix well. Add lemon juice. Beat until smooth. Add confectioners' sugar slowly until consistency is smooth and creamy.

Molten Chocolate Cake

My chocoholic daughter, Janelle, discovered this recipe. We have fun baking it together and fighting over the molten chocolate filling!—Jenny Repko

4 squares semisweet baking
   chocolate
½ cup butter
1 cup powdered sugar
2 eggs

2 egg yolks
6 tablespoons flour
4 tablespoons Cool Whip,
   thawed

Preheat oven to 425°. Butter 4 (¾-cup) mini cassoulets or soufflé dishes. Place on baking sheet. Microwave chocolate and butter in large microwaveable bowl on HIGH 1 minute, or until butter is melted. Stir with wire whisk until chocolate is completely melted. Stir in sugar until well blended. Whisk in eggs and egg yolks. Stir in flour. Divide batter between prepared cassoulets.

Bake 13–14 minutes or until sides are firm but centers are soft. Let stand 1 minute. Carefully run small knife around cakes to loosen. Invert cakes onto dessert dishes. Top with 1 tablespoon whipped topping and serve immediately.

mini cassoulets
*Perfect for both
recipes.*

Jesse's Favorite Warm Chocolate Cakelets

5 ounces semisweet
   chocolate
5 ounces sweet butter
3 eggs

3 egg yolks
⅔ cup sugar
½ cup flour

Melt chocolate and butter in chocolate treat maker. Set aside. Froth eggs and egg yolks lightly. Add sugar and beat together. Add chocolate mixture and flour. Bake in buttered, floured mini cassoulets at 425° for 11–14 minutes. The center should look moist, and the cake should ooze when cut into. Do not overcook. Release cakelets onto dessert plate. Drizzle with raspberry coulis or top with softened vanilla ice cream. Serve immediately.

**chocolate treat
maker**

mixing bowls

springform pan

mixer

Chocolate Meringue Torte

The surprise meringue filling in the middle makes this a real hit.

BROWNIE CRUST:

1 (18-ounce) box brownie mix	**¼ cup oil**
¼ cup water	**1 large egg**

Heat oven to 350°. In large bowl, combine all ingredients. Beat 50 strokes by hand. Spread in greased (bottom only) spring-form pan. Bake at 350° for 15 minutes or until top is shiny. Remove from oven. Reduce heat to 250°.

MERINGUE:

2 egg whites	**1 cup sugar**
¼ teaspoon cream of tartar	**½ cup chopped pecans**

In small bowl, beat egg whites and cream of tartar at medium speed for one minute until soft peaks form. Gradually add sugar, beating at high speed until stiff glossy peaks form. Spoon Meringue evenly over warm, partially baked Brownie Crust; spread carefully to within ¼ inch of sides. Do not allow Meringue to touch sides of pan. Sprinkle pecans over Meringue. Bake at 250° for 50–60 minutes or until Meringue is dry and firm. When Crust and Meringue have baked 25 minutes, begin preparation of Kahlúa Almond Mousse.

KAHLÚA ALMOND MOUSSE:

1 (6-ounce) package	**1 tablespoon Kahlúa**
semisweet chocolate chips	**½ teaspoon almond extract**
3 tablespoons coffee	**1 cup heavy cream**

In medium saucepan over low heat, melt chocolate chips with coffee, stirring occasionally. Remove from heat. Add Kahlúa and almond extract; stir until slightly thickened. Cool 20 minutes.

In large bowl, beat heavy cream until stiff peaks form. Fold cooled chocolate mixture into whipped cream. Spoon and spread over Meringue. Refrigerate 2 hours. Store in refrigerator.

Chocolate Swirl Cheesecake

Everyone should know how to make a cheesecake. Once you've made one, you can make any cheesecake your heart desires.

30 Oreo cookies
2 pounds cream cheese, room temperature
1⅓ cups sugar
1½ teaspoons vanilla extract
4 eggs
2 ounces semisweet chocolate, melted

springform pan

mixer

Crush Oreo cookies, including creme filling, and press into a nonstick springform pan. Refrigerate.

Using the paddle on your mixer on low speed, or regular beaters on a hand mixer on low speed, blend cream cheese until there are no more lumps. You want to be careful not to incorporate too much air needlessly, as air in a cheesecake leads to cracks in the surface. When all lumps in cream cheese are gone, add sugar and vanilla extract. Blend just to incorporate. Add eggs and continue to blend, but don't overbeat. Again, you want to avoid incorporating air needlessly. Remove 1 cup batter, and stir into melted chocolate; set aside.

Pour plain batter over Oreo crust. Drizzle chocolate batter into plain batter in a zigzag motion. Then, drag the blunt edge of a butter knife through the batters to form a marbled effect. Wrap bottom of pan in aluminum foil to create a completely waterproof seal. Place pan in a larger baking pan and pour water in the larger pan until it comes halfway up the sides of the springform pan. Bake at 325° for one hour. At this point, center of cheesecake should still be jiggly. Turn oven off, and leave cheesecake in oven for another ½–1 hour. Remove cake from oven and let cool to room temperature before refrigerating. Refrigerate at least 8 hours before serving.

springform pan

food processor

My Favorite Cheesecake

Kathy Peifer, my assistant at my catering business, brought this cake in one day and we adopted it permanently as one of our house desserts. Always a hit!—Jenny Repko

GRAHAM CRACKER CRUST:
½ cup butter, melted

¼ cup sugar

2 cups graham cracker crumbs

Mix with a fork and press into springform pan.

4 (8-ounce) packages cream cheese, softened

4 eggs

1¼ cups sugar, divided

1 teaspoon vanilla flavoring

1 cup sour cream

1 teaspoon lemon juice

Preheat oven to 350°. Beat softened cream cheese and eggs in food processor on high for several minutes. Add 1 cup sugar and vanilla. Pour mixture into crust in springform pan. Bake for 70 minutes, or until set in center. Cool 20 minutes. Combine sour cream, lemon juice, and remaining ¼ cup sugar, and spread on top of cooled cheesecake. Refrigerate at least 4 hours before serving.

Fabulous Amaretto Cheesecake

Lisa Flynt, Quail Ridge Press's marketing director, makes this for many occasions to rave reviews.

springform pan

GRAHAM CRACKER CRUST:

1¾ cups graham cracker
  crumbs
¼ cup chopped nuts

½ teaspoon cinnamon
½ cup butter, melted

Combine and press on bottom and sides of 9-inch springform pan.

AMARETTO FILLING:

3 (8-ounce) packages cream
  cheese, softened
1 cup sugar
¼ teaspoon salt
4 eggs

⅓ cup amaretto
1½ teaspoons vanilla extract
1½ teaspoons almond extract
1 (16-ounce) container sour
  cream

mixer

Preheat oven to 350°. Mix cream cheese, sugar, and salt. Combine eggs, amaretto, and flavorings, and blend into cream cheese mixture. Blend in sour cream. Pour onto crust. Bake at 350° for 35–40 minutes. Crack oven door. Cool in oven.

Lisa Flynt and her son Jack, shown here at Legoland in California, love to try new foods when they travel, and try to make their favorites when they get home.

baking pan

chocolate
treat maker

mixer

muffin pan

Outrageous Coconut Bon Bons

Just watch people's expressions when they bite into one of these! Outrageous!

1 (18¼-ounce) white cake mix
½ teaspoon coconut extract
½ teaspoon almond extract
½ cup grated coconut

1 (16-ounce) can cream cheese frosting
1¼ (1-pound) packages white or chocolate candy coating

Make cake in 9x13-inch baking pan according to package directions, adding coconut and almond extracts. Cool, then crumble into a big bowl. Pour flaked coconut over cake crumbles and mix well with hands; add frosting and mix thoroughly. Form into balls, put on cookie sheets, and refrigerate at least a couple of hours or overnight.

Melt chocolate in electric treat maker. Dip each ball into chocolate, and place on wax paper until firm.

Quick Cocoa Mayo Cupcakes

⅞ cup unsifted all-purpose flour
½ cup sugar
¼ cup cocoa
¾ teaspoon baking soda

¾ teaspoon baking powder
Dash of salt
½ cup mayonnaise
½ cup water
1 teaspoon vanilla

Combine dry ingredients in mixer bowl. Add remaining ingredients; beat 2 minutes at medium speed. Pour into 6 greased regular muffin tins. Bake at 375° for 30–35 minutes. Cool completely before frosting with your favorite frosting.

Editor's Extra: If you use low-fat mayonnaise, add a tablespoon of liquid egg substitute.

Chocolate Cream Cheese Cupcakes

Moist, chocolate, creamy . . . dee-licious!

1 (8-ounce) package cream
  cheese, softened
½ cup sugar
1 egg, beaten
½ (12-ounce) package
  chocolate chips
1½ cups all-purpose flour
1 cup sugar

¼ cup cocoa
1 teaspoon baking soda
½ teaspoon salt
¾ cup water
½ cup oil
1 tablespoon vinegar
1 teaspoon vanilla

mixing bowls

muffin pan

Preheat oven to 350°. In a small bowl, beat cream cheese, sugar, and egg. Stir in chocolate chips and set aside for topping.

In a large bowl, sift flour, sugar, cocoa, baking soda, and salt. Add water, oil, vinegar, and vanilla, stirring until well blended and smooth. Fill muffin pans ⅓ full of cocoa mixture. Top with 1 tablespoon cream cheese mixture. Bake about 20 minutes, or until toothpick inserted in center comes out clean. Makes 18.

Editor's Extra: Paper liners make cupcakes easier to handle, so that is always an option when making muffins.

Even Bob's grandkids get into Grandma and Grandpa's recipes. Little Brookie likes cupcakes.

mixer

muffin pan

Easy Black Forest Cupcakes

There's a red surprise inside! And what's prettier in the dessert world than red, white, and chocolate?

1 (18¼-ounce) chocolate
  cake mix
1¼ cups water
⅓ cup vegetable oil

3 eggs
1 (21-ounce) can cherry pie
  filling
1 (16-ounce) can vanilla frosting

Combine cake mix, water, oil, and eggs in mixer bowl. Mix well. Spoon batter (about ¼ cup) into muffin cups. Spoon rounded teaspoon of pie filling onto center of each cupcake. Set remaining pie filling aside.

Bake in 350° oven 20–25 minutes or until toothpick inserted in center comes out clean. Remove to wire rack to cool. Frost cupcakes. With reserved cherry pie filling, put one cherry on top of as many cupcakes as you have cherries. Yields 2 dozen cupcakes.

mixing bowl

muffin pan

Fresh Apple Cupcakes

Muffins are so inviting for guests to pick up, so take-able and keep-able, too. These are exceptionally good.

4 cups finely chopped apples
2 cups sugar
½ cup oil
1 cup chopped pecans
2 eggs, well beaten
2 teaspoons vanilla extract

2 cups all-purpose flour
2 teaspoons baking soda
½ teaspoon cinnamon
1 teaspoon salt
1 (16-ounce) can cream
  cheese frosting

Preheat oven to 350°. Mix apples and sugar in a large mixing bowl. Add oil, pecans, eggs, and vanilla; mix well. Add flour, baking soda, cinnamon, and salt, and stir until well mixed. Fill muffin pans ⅔ full. Bake 20–25 minutes, or till tests done. Allow to cool, then frost with cream cheese frosting.

cookies and candies

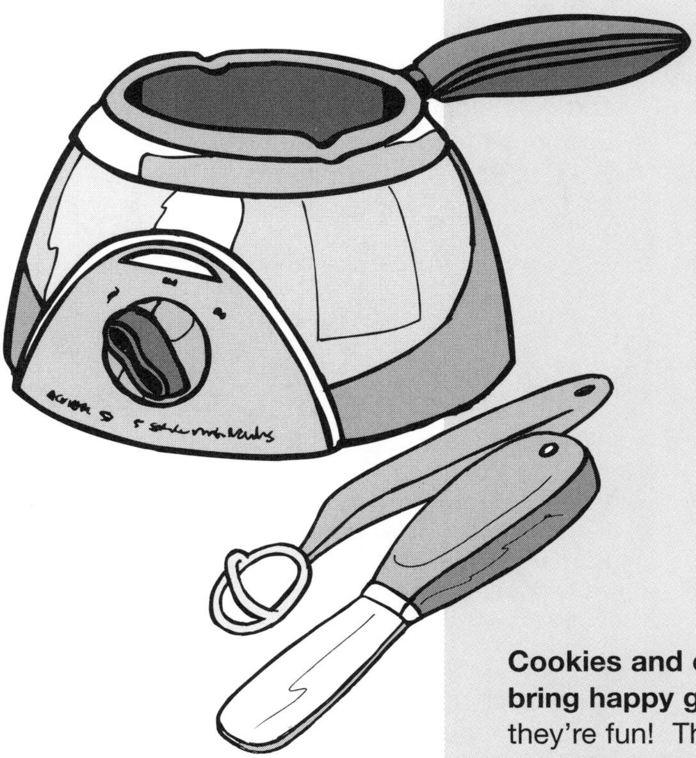

Cookies and candies bring happy grins— they're fun! They are so easy to share, take along, and eat anywhere with no utensils required. Whether you are warmly welcoming a new neighbor, packing some extra love into a lunch, or just brightening up a rainy day for the kids, they are the ideal sweet treat.

double boiler

mini muffin pan

Perfect for both recipes.

Nutty Chocolate Cups

4 squares semisweet
  chocolate
2 sticks butter
1 cup self-rising flour

1½ cups sugar
2 cups chopped pecans
1 teaspoon vanilla
4 eggs, beaten

Melt chocolate and butter in double boiler. Remove from heat and add flour, sugar, pecans, and vanilla; mix eggs in well. Spoon batter into paper-lined mini muffin pan, about ⅔ full. Bake at 350° for 30 minutes. These will rise while baking, but fall to produce a chewy texture. Makes 48 mini muffins.

Chocolate-Cherry Brownie Kiss Cups

1 roll refrigerated sugar
  cookie dough, softened
1 small jar maraschino
  cherries, drained, chopped
  (reserve 3 tablespoons juice)

36 chocolate Hershey's Kisses,
  unwrapped

In mixer bowl, mix cookie dough with cherries and 3 table-spoons cherry juice. Spoon heaping teaspoon of dough into each mini muffin cup (line with paper liners, if desired). Bake at 350° until lightly browned, 8–10 minutes. Take out of oven and top each with a Kiss, pressing down into cookie. Cool until chocolate sets, about 2 hours.

mixer

Chocolate Chip Macadamia Nut Bars with Shortbread Crust

mini food processor

CRUST:

1 cup all-purpose flour
¼ cup sugar

1 stick chilled unsalted butter, cut into 8 pieces

Preheat oven to 350°. Blend flour and sugar in processor. Add butter; pulse on and off until mixture resembles coarse crumbs. Transfer mixture to 9-inch-square baking pan. Press onto bottom and ¾ inch up sides of dish. Bake until Crust is golden brown on edges, about 15 minutes. Prepare Filling.

baking pan

FILLING:

1 cup sugar
½ cup all-purpose flour
2 large eggs
½ stick unsalted butter, melted, cooled

1 teaspoon vanilla extract
1 cup miniature semisweet chocolate chips
1 cup coarsely chopped macadamia nuts

Whisk sugar, flour, eggs, butter, and vanilla in large bowl. Stir in chocolate chips and nuts.

Pour Filling into warm Crust. Bake until filling is golden brown and tester inserted into center comes out with moist crumbs attached, about 50 minutes. Cool completely on rack. Can be prepared a day ahead. Store in airtight container at room temperature. Makes 16 squares.

mixing bowl

springform pan

mixer

Brown Sugar Shortbread Wedges

2 sticks unsalted butter, softened
1 cup packed light brown sugar

2 cups all-purpose flour
¼ teaspoon salt
1 tablespoon sugar
1 teaspoon ground cinnamon

Preheat oven to 325°. Butter a 9-inch springform pan. With mixer, beat butter until light and fluffy. Add brown sugar and beat well. Using rubber spatula, mix in flour and salt. Press dough into prepared pan. Combine sugar and cinnamon in small bowl; sprinkle over dough. Cut into 12 wedges. Prick each wedge several times with toothpick.

Bake about 1 hour, until brown and firm at edges, but still slightly soft in center. Allow to cool completely in pan on rack before removing pan sides. Re-cut cookies into wedges. Makes 12.

baking pan

Grandma King's Soft Gingerbread

½ cup shortening
2 tablespoons sugar
1 egg
1 cup dark sorghum molasses
1 cup boiling water

2¼ cups sifted all-purpose flour
1 teaspoon baking soda
1 teaspoon salt
1 teaspoon ginger
1 teaspoon cinnamon

Cream shortening and sugar in mixing bowl. Add egg, molasses, and water. Sift together flour, baking soda, salt, ginger, and cinnamon. Add to sorghum mixture. Bake in a greased 9-inch-square baking pan at 325° for 45–50 minutes.

Chocolate-Peanut Butter Cookie Bars

2 (18-ounce) packages
  Pillsbury Refrigerated
  Chocolate Chip Cookies
  with Walnuts
3 cups powdered sugar
1 teaspoon vanilla
1½ cups peanut butter

2 tablespoons butter or
  margarine, softened
¼ cup water
1 cup semisweet chocolate
  chips, melted
Peanuts (optional)

Spread both packages of cookie dough on bottom of an ungreased 9x13-inch baking pan, and press with fingertips to form a crust. Bake at 350° about 20 minutes or until golden brown. Cool 15 minutes.

In mixer bowl, combine powdered sugar, vanilla, peanut butter, butter, and water; mix well. (If necessary, add additional water, 1 teaspoon at a time up to 1 tablespoon, until mixture is smooth.) Drop spoonfuls of mixture over baked cookie crust; spread evenly to cover crust.

Spread melted chocolate chips over peanut butter mixture. If desired, decoratively swirl chocolate with fork or decorate with peanuts. Refrigerate 1 hour or until chocolate is set. Makes 24 bars.

baking pan

mixer

OPTION:
chocolate treat maker

Keeps chocolate perfectly melted for whenever you're ready to use it.

baking pan

chocolate treat
maker

*Sometimes you feel
like you need more
than one of these,
especially if you're
having a fondue
party.*

Beautiful Raspberry Chocolate Bars

This serves a lot of people . . . deliciously!

1 (18-ounce) package dark
   chocolate cake mix
⅓ cup butter, softened
1 egg, beaten
1¼ cups raspberry preserves
1 (12-ounce) package white
   chocolate chips

1 (8-ounce) package cream
   cheese, softened
¼ cup milk
½ cup chocolate chips
2 tablespoons butter

Preheat oven to 350°. In mixer bowl, combine cake mix, butter, and egg, and blend well for 2 minutes. Press into a nonstick 15x10x1-inch baking pan. Bake about 10 minutes until crust looks a little dry. Cool about 10 minutes; spread preserves over top. Put aside to cool completely.

Melt white chips in chocolate treat maker; stir. In another bowl, beat cream cheese with milk until smooth. Add melted white chips and stir until smooth. Pour over preserves, then spread carefully.

Melt chocolate chips in chocolate treat maker or microwave bowl for 1 minute (or more), and stir until melted. Stir in butter. Drizzle over white topping. Refrigerate at least 1 hour before cutting into bars. Serve chilled.

Chocolate Sprinkled Blonde Brownies

They are SO GOOD they need no other introduction.

saucepan

⅔ cup butter
2 cups packed light brown
  sugar
2 eggs
2 teaspoons vanilla extract
2 cups all-purpose flour
1 teaspoon baking powder

¼ teaspoon baking soda
1 teaspoon salt
1 cup chopped walnuts
  (optional)
1 cup mini semisweet
  chocolate chips

Melt butter in medium saucepan. Add sugar and mix well. Cool. Add eggs and vanilla; blend well. Add remaining ingredients except chocolate chips. Put into a greased 9x13-inch pan. Sprinkle with chocolate chips, and bake at 350° for 20–25 minutes. Cool and cut into bars.

baking pan

One-Pan Easy Cookie Bars

This is the greatest dessert . . . and so easy. Technique pans are perfect for this recipe because you can melt the butter on the stovetop, layer ingredients, and bake all in the same pan! It makes a lot, but nice to have enough to let guests take some home (my mom brings her own container). The ingredient amounts are perfect for decreasing by ⅓ or ⅔ to suit the amount you need.— Lisa Brady

3 sticks butter or margarine
4½ cups graham cracker
  crumbs
3 (14-ounce) cans
  condensed milk

18 ounces semisweet
  chocolate morsels
9 ounces flaked coconut
3 cups chopped nuts

casserole

Preheat oven to 350°. In a large casserole dish, melt butter. Sprinkle crumbs over butter. Pour milk evenly over crumbs. Layer morsels, coconut, then nuts over all. Press gently. Bake 25–30 minutes.

mixing bowl

cookie sheet

saucepan

cookie sheets

Merry Munchies

½ cup butter, softened
1½ cups brown sugar
1 egg
1 teaspoon vanilla
1½ cups all-purpose flour

1½ teaspoons baking powder
¼ teaspoon salt
1 cup white raisins
1 cup chopped walnuts

Preheat oven to 350°.   Combine butter, brown sugar, egg, and vanilla in mixing bowl. Beat until light and fluffy. Stir in flour, baking powder, and salt. Mix well. Stir in raisins and walnuts. Drop by rounded teaspoonfuls onto nonstick cookie sheet. Bake in upper third of oven 10–12 minutes. Makes 3 dozen.

Aunt JoAnn's Favorite Hat Cookies

(aka Trilbys)

This is another of Grandmother's recipes. They have enormous sentimental appeal.—Bob Warden

⅓ pound dates (or other dried fruit), ground or chopped fine
1⅓ cups sugar, divided
⅓ cup water
¾ cup shortening, or ¾ cup butter, softened

¼ teaspoon salt
½ cup sour milk (or buttermilk)
6 drops almond extract
1 egg
2 cups all-purpose flour
½ teaspoon baking soda
2 cups rolled oats

Cook dates, ⅓ cup sugar, and water in a 2-quart saucepan until mushy; set aside to cool. Cream together shortening or butter, salt, and remaining 1 cup sugar. Mix milk, almond extract, and egg together; add to butter-sugar mixture. Mix together; add flour, soda, and oats. Mixture should be heavy enough to roll. Roll out very thin, then cut into rounds; fill with date mixture, and cover with another round. Bake on cookie sheets at 450° for 12 minutes. These cookies keep quite well. Hide them in a covered tin.

Crispy No Nut-Sense Cookies

I know several people who can't eat nuts or simply don't like them. But most people who eat my cookies want nuts. These cookies have somewhat of a nutty taste, and a definite crunch, so they satisfy everybody! — Gwen McKee

mixer

2 sticks butter, softened
¾ cup sugar
¾ cup dark brown sugar
2 large eggs
2 cups all-purpose flour
1¼ teaspoons baking soda
½ teaspoon salt

1½ teaspoons vanilla
½ teaspoon butter extract
1 (8-ounce) package English
**   Toffee Bits**
1 (10-ounce) package mini
**   M & M's or holiday bits**

cookie sheets

Preheat oven to 375°. Cream butter and sugars. Add eggs, mixing well. Sift flour, soda, and salt together. Gradually add flour mixture to butter mixture while mixer is running until mixed well. Add vanilla and butter extract. Mix in candy bits (save a few for decoration, if desired) only until blended through. Drop teaspoonfuls of batter onto greased cookie sheets, using a small bowl of water to dip your finger into each time you push the batter off the spoon. Bake 9–11 minutes until browned nicely. If desired, put a few more colorful candies immediately on top of some of the cookies before they begin to cool. Let sit on cookie sheet 2 minutes, then remove immediately to brown or parchment paper. Store in a big tin or cookie jar. Makes about 5 dozen.

mixer

cookie sheet;
wire rack

Nutritious Poppin' Fresh Cookies

Crunchy and delicious. I always double the recipe because they don't last long. My favorite cookie recipe of all time. —Jenny Repko

2¼ cups all-purpose flour, divided
2 cups firmly packed brown sugar
1 teaspoon baking soda
1 teaspoon salt
1 cup margarine or butter, softened

2 teaspoons vanilla
2 eggs
2 cups quick cooking oats
1 (6-ounce) package (1 cup) semisweet chocolate chips
½ cup chopped nuts or sunflower seeds

OPTIONAL INGREDIENTS:
(Stir one of the following into the dough, if desired.)

1 cup peanut butter
1 cup wheat germ

1 cup flaked coconut
1 cup nonfat dry milk

Preheat oven to 350°. In mixer, combine 1¼ cups flour, brown sugar, soda, salt, margarine or butter, vanilla, and eggs. Beat at medium speed until well blended, about 1–2 minutes. By hand, stir in remaining flour, oats, chocolate chips, and sunflower seeds. Add one Optional Ingredient, if desired. Drop dough by rounded teaspoons 2 inches apart onto ungreased cookie sheet. Bake 10–15 minutes, or until golden brown. Cool for one minute, then remove from cookie sheet to wire rack. Makes 6–7 dozen cookies.

Chewie Fudge Cookies

¼ cup butter or margarine, softened
2 (3-ounce) packages cream cheese, softened
1 (14-ounce) can sweetened condensed milk
1 egg
1½ cups all-purpose flour

1 (15.9-ounce) package fudge double chocolate brownie mix
1 cup coarsely chopped pecans
1 (3.5-ounce) can flaked coconut
1 (12-ounce) package semisweet chocolate chips, divided

cookie sheets

Heat oven to 375°. Grease cookie sheets. In large mixer bowl, combine margarine and cream cheese; beat until smooth. Add condensed milk and egg; blend well. Lightly spoon flour into measuring cup; level off. Add flour and brownie mix to egg mixture and mix well. Stir in pecans, coconut, and ½ the chocolate chips. Drop by heaping tablespoonfuls 1 inch apart onto greased cookie sheets.

Bake at 375° for 9–12 minutes or until set. Cool one minute; remove from cookie sheets. Cool completely. Heat remaining chocolate chips in chocolate treat maker. Dip cookie tops in melted chocolate, then place on wax paper to dry. Makes about 4 dozen cookies.

mixer

chocolate treat maker

Gwen's grandson, Harrison, enjoys helping make cookies.

mixer

cookie sheets

saucepan

Peanut Butter and Chocolate Chapeaus

2 cups all-purpose flour
2 teaspoons vanilla

1 cup butter, softened
½ cup sugar

In mixer bowl, combine all and mix well. Drop by teaspoon onto cookie sheets. Flatten to ¼ inch with a glass that has been greased on bottom, then dipped in sugar for each cookie. Bake at 325° for 16–20 minutes until lightly browned on bottom. Spread warm cookies with Topping. Swirl with Chocolate Glaze. Let stand until glaze is set. Makes 5 dozen cookies.

TOPPING:
⅓ cup firmly packed brown sugar

¼ cup butter, softened
⅓ cup peanut butter

Cream all ingredients together until light and fluffy.

CHOCOLATE GLAZE:
½ cup semisweet chocolate chips

2 tablespoons milk
⅓ cup sifted powdered sugar

Melt chocolate pieces with milk in a saucepan over low heat, stirring constantly. Remove from heat. Add powdered sugar, and stir until smooth.

Chocolate Almond Toffee Cookies

1 stick unsalted butter, softened
1 cup plus 2 tablespoons sugar
1 large egg
1 tablespoon rum
1 teaspoon vanilla extract

1 cup all-purpose flour
½ cup unsweetened cocoa
½ teaspoon baking soda
¼ teaspoon salt
1½ cups crushed Heath bars
½ cup chopped almonds

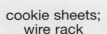

mixer

Preheat oven to 350°. Mix butter and sugar in large mixer bowl until fluffy. Add egg, rum, and vanilla; beat again. Sift flour, cocoa, baking soda, and salt; stir into butter mixture. Mix in crushed Heath bars and chopped almonds.

Drop batter onto large ungreased cookie sheets, spacing 2 inches apart. Bake about 11 minutes. Let cookies cool on sheets 1 minute. Transfer cookies to wire rack and cool completely. Makes 36.

cookie sheets;
wire rack

School House Cookies

Packed with a boost of energy!

½ cup butter, softened
¾ cup brown sugar
1 egg
1½ teaspoons vanilla or almond extract
1 cup self-rising flour

¼ cup all-purpose flour, mixed with ¼ cup oatmeal
¾ cup oatmeal
¾ cup raisins
¾ cup chopped walnuts

mixing bowl

Preheat oven to 375°. In mixing bowl, cream together butter, brown sugar, egg, and extract. Mix flour with oatmeal/flour mixture, and add to creamed mixture. Stir in oatmeal, raisins, and chopped nuts. Spoon ¼-cup portions onto cookie sheet; flatten slightly. Bake 10–12 minutes.

cookie sheet

mixing bowls

cookie sheet;
wire rack

Sugar Cookie Hearts

My birthday is on Valentine's Day and I love hosting a birthday/Valentine's Day dinner for my friends. I always make these heart-shaped cookies for an additional dessert, thus completing the Valentine's Day theme.—Jenny Repko

2 sticks unsalted butter, softened	1 teaspoon salt
1 cup sugar	½ teaspoon baking soda
2 eggs	1 cup sifted confectioners' sugar
1 tablespoon vanilla	2 tablespoons milk
3 cups all-purpose flour	Multicolored nonpareils

Beat butter and sugar until light and fluffy. Blend in eggs and vanilla; mix well. Stir together flour, salt, and baking soda; mix into sugar mixture until well blended. Chill 2 hours.

Preheat oven to 360°. Divide dough into quarters. Roll out one quarter on lightly floured surface to ⅛-inch thickness. Cut into heart shapes with 2-inch cutter; place on ungreased cookie sheet. Repeat with remaining dough. Bake 5–8 minutes or until cookies are barely browned at the edges. Cool on wire rack.

Mix together confectioners' sugar and milk until smooth. Spread on cookies; sprinkle with nonpareils. Makes approximately 6 dozen cookies.

mixing bowl

cookie sheets

Gagy's Sugar Cookies

My grandmother "Gagy" started her Christmas baking the day after Thanksgiving. She and my aunt would bake for weeks making an amazing assortment of cookies to give to family. We always had coffee tins filled with her beautiful and tasty cookies. This basic recipe was one of my personal favorites growing up.—Jenny Repko

1 cup butter	1 teaspoon vanilla
2 cups sugar	3½ cups self-rising flour (approximately)
3 eggs	

Cream together butter, sugar, eggs, and vanilla. Slowly stir in flour until a soft dough is formed. Chill dough overnight.

Preheat oven to 400°. Roll dough into a very thin layer, and cut out cookies. Place on ungreased cookie sheets. Sprinkle with sugar. Bake 4–5 minutes or until light golden brown.

Mrs. Smith's Pralines

A family aquaintance, Mrs. Smith, made these pralines. They are heavenly!
—Bob Warden

3 cups brown sugar
¼ teaspoon salt
1 cup milk or cream

1–2 tablespoons butter
1 teaspoon vanilla
1 cup walnut halves

Dissolve sugar, salt, and cream in a 3-quart saucepan with lid; stir constantly until boiling. Cover; cook about 3 minutes, until steam has washed down any crystals from the sides of the pan. Uncover and cook slowly, without stirring, to the soft-ball stage, 238°. Remove candy from heat; add butter and vanilla. Cool to 110°. Beat until smooth and creamy. Add nuts. Drop candy from a spoon onto a buttered surface or wax paper; allow to cool.

saucepan

Meatball Candy

Since 1984, we've made this candy every Christmas. My children love to make it as well as eat it, having as much fun with the process as the result.
—Bob Warden

1–2 large Hershey's semisweet
chocolate bars
1 (16-ounce) container Cool
Whip, defrosted but kept
chilled

Cocoa powder or powdered
sugar

Melt Hershey's bars slowly in chocolate treat maker. Mix the chocolate and Cool Whip with an electric mixer. Refrigerate about 3 hours.

Form mixture into small balls, and roll in cocoa powder or powdered sugar. Allow to cool and harden.

chocolate treat maker

mixer

mixing bowl

saucepan

baking pan

Every Warden's Favorite Chocolate Fudge

I think this is the best fudge recipe I have ever tasted (as well as the most fattening).—Bob Warden

1 (12-ounce) package
  chocolate chips (semisweet
  or milk)
½ pound butter, cut into
  small pieces

4 cups sugar
1½ cups evaporated milk
20 large marshmallows

Place chocolate in large bowl. Set aside. In a large, heavy saucepan, place butter, sugar, evaporated milk, and marshmallows; bring to a boil and cook 5–8 minutes (the fudge is very soft, but the longer you cook it, the firmer it will be). Pour sugar mixture into bowl with chocolate, and beat well for about one minute. Set aside to cool slightly, then pour into a buttered 9x13-inch pan and refrigerate.

When chilled, cut into squares with a knife that has been dipped in hot water, and wrap each individual piece in plastic wrap or place in candy cups. Keep covered (to prevent drying) and refrigerate.

ROCKY ROAD VERSION:
1–2 cups mini marshmallows,
  or 10–15 large marshmallows,
  cut in fourths

2 cups chopped nuts

Before starting fudge, place marshmallows in a shallow pan. Put these in freezer. Prepare fudge. After cooling slightly, add frozen marshmallows and nuts. Refrigerate, cool, and cut as above.

White Chocolate Fudge with Macadamia Nuts and Dark Chocolate Chunks

1 (7-ounce) jar marshmallow crème
1½ cups sugar
⅔ cup evaporated milk
½ stick unsalted butter
¼ teaspoon salt

3 cups white chocolate chips
1 teaspoon vanilla extract
1 cup macadamia nuts, rough chopped
1 cup dark chocolate chunks

Combine marshmallow crème, sugar, evaporated milk, butter, and salt together in 4-quart saucepan. Bring to a boil and cook, stirring, 5 minutes. Remove pan from heat and stir in white chocolate, until melted and smooth. Add vanilla extract and nuts; stir and pour into a nonstick 7x11-inch baking pan. Once in the pan, sprinkle dark chocolate chunks over top and press into bark. Chill in refrigerator until firm. Cut into squares and serve.

Editor's Extra: For a tasty variation, use milk chocolate chips and/or semisweet chocolate chips with pecans.

saucepan

baking pan

Haystacks

These make a great treat for school and church functions, and are a fun project to do with children.

2 cups semisweet chocolate chips
2 cups butterscotch chips

12 ounces peanuts or cashews
5 (5-ounce) cans chow mein noodles

Melt chips in chocolate treat maker on LOW heat or in microwave in bursts of 10 seconds, stirring between each. Stir in nuts and noodles. Drop by teaspoonfuls onto wax paper-lined nonstick cookie sheets. Cool, and store covered in the refrigerator.

VERSION TWO:

1 package butterscotch chips
1 cup salted peanuts or cashews

2 cups chow mein noodles
1 cup miniature marshmallows (optional)

Prepare as above.

chocolate treat maker

cookie sheets

mixing bowls

mini muffin pan

chocolate treat
maker

cookie sheet

Strawberry Hidden Kisses

Kids' favorites for sure!

1 stick butter, melted
1 (18¼-ounce) box
strawberry cake mix
1 egg, beaten

36 white, strawberry swirl or
chocolate Hershey's Kisses,
unwrapped

Pour melted butter in bowl with cake mix and egg; mix well. Line mini muffin pans with paper liners, if desired. Spoon a heaping teaspoon of dough into each. Bake at 350° until lightly browned, 8–10 minutes. Take out of oven and top each with a Kiss, pressing down into cookie. Cool until chocolate sets, about 2 hours.

Holiday Peppermint Bark

Fun to put in Christmas cellophane bags, tie with ribbons, and put into a Christmas cup as "happies" for your office friends. Fellow office worker Holly Hardy brought each of us one at Quail Ridge Press last year and everybody loved it!—Gwen McKee

2 bags white chocolate
cooking discs

1 bag peppermint brickle

Melt white chocolate in chocolate treat maker. Add crushed peppermint, and stir to incorporate. Pour onto wax paper on a cookie sheet. Refrigerate until it hardens. Break into bite-size pieces.

Editor's Extra: Around the holidays, stores sell white chocolate cooking discs and peppermint brickle. You can substitute white chocolate almond bark, and crush your own peppermint candies or sticks. The formula is 2 to 1.

pies and other desserts

Desserts are like magic!
Take homemade ice cream
. . . put a few simple
ingredients into a handy
ice cream maker and they
are magically transformed
into a luscious dessert!
Homemade ice cream,
fresh fruit pies, yummy
bread puddings, tarts,
crisps, cobblers . . . what
is more tempting than a
gorgeous dessert? More
often than not, it's usually
the showstopper.

mixing bowls

muffin pan;
cookie sheet

Nostalgic Mincemeat Pies

Mincemeat pies remind me of my mother. Every year at Christmas, she would make batches and batches of mincemeat pies, and send them with me to every lesson I had as a gift for my teacher. I don't think any of my teachers actually received the whole gift intended by my mother! My piano teacher absolutely lived for these treats every year. — Meredith Laurence

18 ounces mincemeat pie filling
½ cup walnuts, chopped
½ cup brown sugar

1 cup peeled and diced apple
¼ cup brandy
1 tablespoon lemon juice

Combine mincemeat pie filling, walnuts, sugar, apple, brandy, and lemon juice in mixing bowl. Cover and let mixture sit overnight in the refrigerator.

PASTRY:
½ cup oil
¼ cup milk

2 cups all-purpose flour
1 teaspoon salt

Combine oil and milk in bowl. Gradually add flour to form dough. Roll out to desired thickness. Cut out round top and bottom circles to fit muffin cups. Place Pastry bottoms in muffin tins so they come up sides. Fill with filling and top with Pastry top. Don't overfill muffin tins. Place a cookie sheet under muffin tins to catch any drips of filling. Vent tops with a knife and bake at 400° for 25–30 minutes or until golden brown. Makes 12.

Brown Sugar Custard Pie

1 deep-dish 9-inch pie crust
1 cup packed brown sugar
3 tablespoons all-purpose
 flour
3 eggs

1 egg yolk
1 teaspoon vanilla or almond
 extract
3 tablespoons butter, melted
1½ cups buttermilk

Bake pie crust in preheated 400° oven about 12 minutes, until slightly browned. Remove from oven and allow to cool. Reduce temperature to 350°.

Combine sugar and flour in food processor. Add eggs, yolk and vanilla or almond extract; process until blended. Combine with butter and buttermilk until just blended. Pour into cooled crust.

Bake at 350° about 45 minutes, until filling is almost set in center but still jiggles slightly. Bring to room temperature, then refrigerate at least 2 hours before serving. Yields 6–8 servings.

food processor

Canadian Butter Tarts

You can take the girl out of Canada, but you can't take Canada out of the girl. I don't know why these haven't crossed the border. Perhaps because they have about 10,000 calories a piece! They are part of my childhood.
—Meredith Laurence

2 eggs
1½ cups brown sugar
½ cup corn syrup
3 tablespoons butter, melted
1 cup currants or raisins

½ cup chopped walnuts
2 teaspoons vinegar
Pinch of salt
½ teaspoon vanilla extract
Pastry Shells

Preheat oven to 350°. Beat eggs well. Add sugar, syrup, and melted butter, and beat again. Add currants, walnuts, vinegar, salt, and vanilla extract, and mix vigorously. Place circles of uncooked Pastry Shells (part of Delicious Cream Puffs recipe, page 247) into muffin cups. Fill shells ⅔ full, and bake until the pastry is light brown, about 20 minutes. (For juicier tarts, cook 15–17 minutes.) Makes 12.

mixing bowl

muffin pan

pie pan

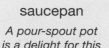

saucepan

A pour-spout pot is a delight for this recipe.

Red Light Raspberry Pie

Stop! You'll want to eat the whole thing.

CRUST:

1 cup all-purpose flour
1 stick unsalted lite butter, softened

¾ cup chopped pecans
¼ cup powdered sugar

Preheat oven to 400°. Mix Crust ingredients and press into 9-inch pie pan. Bake 12–15 minutes until lightly browned. Cool.

FILLING:

1 cup sugar or Splenda
2 tablespoons cornstarch
1 cup water
1 (3-ounce) box raspberry gelatin, minus 1 tablespoon
1 (8-ounce) package fat-free cream cheese, softened

⅔ cup powdered sugar
1 pint fresh raspberries, or 12 ounces frozen, thawed and drained
1 (8-ounce) carton fat-free whipped topping

Combine first 3 ingredients in 3-quart saucepan; cook until thick. Remove from heat and stir in gelatin. Cool. Thoroughly mix cream cheese and powdered sugar in a bowl. Spread cream cheese mixture on Crust. Put raspberries on cream cheese; pour gelatin mixture over berries. Refrigerate until firm. Serve with whipped topping. Serves 8.

Eric Theiss is always surprised when cook's essentials sells out AGAIN!

Kiss Me Chocolate Pie

You are hereby forewarned.

1¼ cups chocolate wafer
  crumbs, divided
½ stick butter, softened
1 (12-ounce) package milk
  chocolate chips
¼ cup milk

1 (8-ounce) package cream
  cheese
¼ teaspoon vanilla extract
1 (12-ounce) carton frozen
  whipped topping, thawed

pie pan

Mix crumbs (reserve a few for topping) and butter, and press into a 9-inch pie pan. Bake in 375° oven 5 minutes; cool.

Melt chocolate with milk over hot water in double boiler. When melted, add cream cheese, stirring until melted; add vanilla. Remove from heat and allow to cool slightly before folding in whipped topping. Pour into cooled crust and garnish with remaining wafer crumbs. Refrigerate until firm. Serves 6–8.

double boiler

Creamy Chocolate-y Peanut Butter Pie

This is a rave-getting dessert that's make-ahead easy.

1 chocolate graham cracker
  pie crust
1 egg white
2 tablespoons butter, softened
1 (8-ounce) package cream
  cheese, softened
½ cup creamy peanut butter
¾ cup powdered sugar
1½ teaspoons vanilla

1 (12-ounce) container frozen
  whipped topping, thawed
¼ cup sliced almonds,
  lightly toasted
¼ cup chocolate syrup
  (optional)
¼ cup caramel syrup
  (optional)

mixer

Preheat oven to 375°. Brush pie crust with egg white and bake 5 minutes. Cool. Beat butter, cream cheese, peanut butter, powdered sugar, and vanilla with mixer until smooth. Blend in whipped topping. Spoon onto cooked crust. Sprinkle toasted almonds over top; freeze about 15 minutes. Drizzle with chocolate or caramel syrup, or both, if desired. Refrigerate until set, preferably a couple of hours.

saucepan

mixer

chocolate treat
maker

Chocolate-Peanut Butter Parfait Pie

As pretty as it is delicious.

1 shortbread (or graham cracker) pie crust

CHOCOLATE GANACHE:

1¼ cups Hershey's special dark chips or semisweet chocolate chips	**½ cup whipping cream** **2 tablespoons butter**

In a heavy 1-quart saucepan, mix all ingredients. Cook over low heat, stirring constantly, until chips are melted. Remove from heat; stir until smooth. Reserve ¼ cup mixture for drizzle; set remaining mixture in freezer to cool.

PARFAIT FILLING:

1¼ cups milk	**3 tablespoons butter**
1 (8-ounce) container whipped cream cheese	**1 (12-ounce) bag peanut butter chips**
1 (4-serving) box white chocolate instant pudding	

In mixer bowl, beat milk, cream cheese, and pudding on high speed about 3 minutes or until smooth and thickened. Set aside.

In small microwaveable bowl, microwave butter and peanut butter chips on HIGH 45 seconds. Stir; if necessary, continue to microwave in 10-second increments, stirring after each, until chips are melted and mixture is smooth. (The chocolate treat maker is great for this.) On low speed, gradually beat peanut butter mixture into pudding mixture until combined; beat on high speed until Parfait Filling is smooth and fluffy. Refrigerate until needed.

TOPPING:

1 (8-ounce) container frozen whipped topping, thawed	**1 cup toffee bits**

To assemble pie, spread cooled Chocolate Ganache mixture evenly in bottom of pie crust. Refrigerate for 30 minutes. Carefully spoon and spread Parfait Filling over Chocolate Ganache layer. Pile whipped topping over Parfait Filling. Refrigerate until set, 3–4 hours.

To serve, microwave reserved Chocolate Ganache mixture on HIGH 15–20 seconds or until of drizzling consistency. Drizzle over top of pie. Sprinkle with toffee bits. Refrigerate. Cut into wedges to serve. Serves 8–10.

Easy Apple Dumplings

1 (6-count) can jumbo-size
  crescent rolls
1 (15-ounce) can sliced apples
  (or pears or peaches),
  drained, or sliced fresh fruit

2 teaspoons cinnamon
½ cup brown sugar
1 (12-ounce) can ginger ale
1 stick butter, melted

Separate crescent roll dough into 6 triangles. Take 2 or 3 slices of fruit and wrap in 1 triangle of dough. Tuck ends under and place seam side down in 4-quart electric stockpot. Sprinkle each with cinnamon and brown sugar. Cook at 375° for 20 minutes or until light brown. Pour ginger ale in electric stockpot over dumplings. Pour melted butter over top. Cover and cook 3 hours on the high end of SIMMER. Keep on low end of SIMMER to keep warm while serving. Serves 6.

electric
stockpot

Maple Whiskey Apples

If you happen to have an abundance of apples in the fall, this is a great way to turn them into a dessert. It can stand alone or be served as a sauce over cake, ice cream, or just use your spoon!

16 Gala apples
½ cup butter
2 cups water
2 cups whiskey
1 cup maple syrup

2 cups brown sugar
6 cloves
2 teaspoons ground cinnamon
2 teaspoons vanilla extract

Core, seed, and quarter apples. Place all ingredients into an 8-quart, nonstick pressure cooker. Cook under LOW pressure for 10 minutes. Release pressure manually. Remove apples and sauce, and serve over ice cream, with puff pastry circles, or however desired.

Alternate Method: To make in a Dutch oven or electric stockpot, cook for 30 minutes.

pressure cooker

ALTERNATE:
dutch oven

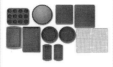

baking pan

saucepan

mixing bowl

Mom's Apple Cobbler Rolls

This wonderful buttery, apple-y, cinnamon-y smell invites you to the kitchen to have a taste.

1 stick margarine
2 cups sugar
2 cups water
½ cup shortening

1½ cups self-rising flour
⅓ cup milk
2 cups chopped apples
1 teaspoon cinnamon (optional)

Preheat oven to 350°. Melt margarine in a 9x13-inch baking dish in oven. In 2-quart saucepan, heat sugar and water until sugar melts.

In a mixing bowl, cut shortening into flour with knives or pastry cutter until particles are like crumbs. Add milk and stir only until dough leaves sides of bowl. Turn out on lightly floured board or pastry cloth. Knead until smooth. Roll out into a large rectangle, spread chopped apples evenly over dough, sprinkle with cinnamon, if desired, and roll up like a jellyroll. Moisten edges and seal. Cut in slices; place in baking dish with margarine. Pour sugar syrup over rolls and bake 55–60 minutes at 350°. This may seem like too much liquid, but don't worry, the rolls will absorb all of it.

A young Bob Warden goes right to the source. The best tasting food always comes directly from the garden or orchard.

No-Bake Cherry Cobbler Ooo La La

1 (8-count) can crescent rolls
½ stick butter
½ cup sugar
1 (21-ounce) can cherry pie filling

1 (16-ounce) can pitted dark sweet cherries, undrained
1¼ cups water
½ teaspoon almond extract

cookie sheet

Bake crescent rolls on cookie sheet per package directions. When cool, cut or break pieces.

Place all ingredients except rolls into 6-quart electric stockpot on 270° till butter is melted. Drop in roll pieces and stir well. Return to bubbling, then cover and cook on low end of SIMMER ½ hour or longer. Serve over ice cream, or with whipped topping or a dollop of sour cream, but delicious all by itself. Serves 8.

electric stockpot

Perfect for both recipes.

Cinnamon Roll Peach Cobbler

An easy cobbler, this one is a variation on good friend Nancy Seale's Crockpot Peach Cobbler recipe but smaller and quicker!—Gwen McKee

1 (7.3-ounce) can cinnamon rolls
½ stick butter

2 (15-ounce) cans sliced peaches

Bake rolls according to package directions; let cool completely. Meanwhile, melt butter with icing packet from rolls in 6-quart electric stockpot at 225°. Add peaches. When peaches are hot and rolls are cool, break up the rolls into the peaches, cover (have all holes closed on lid), and cook about 10 minutes, then turn to low end of SIMMER for up to 4 hours. Serve over vanilla ice cream. Great for a party or buffet, as it stays warm and yummy. Smells divine!

baking pan

saucepan

Easy Peachy Orange Cobbler

A great combination of flavors that has the added bonus of being EASY.

1 (29-ounce) can sliced
  peaches
1 (8-ounce) can crushed
  pineapple

1 (18¼-ounce) package
  orange supreme cake mix
½ stick butter

Pour peaches and pineapple, with juices, into a lightly greased 9x13-inch baking pan. Sprinkle dry cake mix over top, and fold into fruit until completely moistened. Dot with butter, and bake in 350° oven 35–40 minutes.

VANILLA SAUCE:

⅓ cup sugar
3 teaspoons flour
½ stick butter
½–1 cup milk

1 teaspoon vanilla
Dash of salt
Dash of nutmeg

Heat sugar, flour, butter, and ½ cup milk in small saucepan over medium heat, stirring constantly, until thickened to your liking (add up to ½ cup more milk, if desired). Add vanilla, salt, and nutmeg. Whisk together. Serve warm over cobbler.

Gingerbread Cobbler

1 (14-ounce) package
  gingerbread mix
1 (15-ounce) can sliced
  peaches or pears, drained

½ cup toffee bits
¼ stick butter, melted
1 (8-ounce) container frozen
  whipped topping, thawed

Preheat oven to 325°. Prepare gingerbread batter according to package directions. Place fruit in a greased loaf pan. Pour batter over fruit. Sprinkle toffee bits over batter. Drizzle butter over batter. Bake about 40 minutes or until middle is set. Serve warm with whipped topping.

loaf pan

Cherry-Apple Crisp

I made this for a birthday celebration in our office at Quail Ridge Press. It was a hit with everyone, especially the birthday girl who loves cherries.
—Melinda Burnham

1 (16-ounce) can apple slices,
  drained
1 (16-ounce) can tart pie
  cherries, packed in water,
  drained
1 (16-ounce) can dark sweet
  pitted cherries in heavy
  syrup, drained
1 cup firmly packed dark
  brown sugar

2 teaspoons vanilla
2 teaspoons cinnamon
½ cup chopped walnuts
1 (14-ounce) box plain
  granola cereal
1 stick butter or margarine,
  melted
1 (12-ounce) container frozen
  whipped topping, thawed

Mix fruit, brown sugar, vanilla, cinnamon, and walnuts. Spread in 9x13-inch baking pan or large casserole dish. Cover with granola and drizzle with melted butter or margarine. Bake in 350° oven for 30 minutes or until bubbly. Serve with whipped topping.

baking pan

ALTERNATE:
stoneware
baking dish

electric
saucepan

OPTION:
mandoline

*The mandoline
slicer makes it easy
to slice apples
quickly.*

Carrot and Apple Bake

**1 pound carrots, scraped
  and sliced**
½ teaspoon salt
½ cup water
**4 Granny Smith apples,
  peeled and sliced**

2 tablespoons flour
¼ cup sugar
¼ cup orange juice

In 3-quart electric saucepan, boil carrots in salted water until just tender; drain. Layer half the carrots and apple slices. Mix flour and sugar and sprinkle half over carrots and apples. Repeat layers, then drizzle with orange juice. Cook at 350° for 30–35 minutes.

Pear Tarte Tatin

This is another of my favorite desserts, and easier to make in a skillet than a cake pan, since the skillet can go directly on a flame. Legend has it that this recipe came out of a mistake by two French sisters (whose last name was Tatin). They forgot to put the pastry on the bottom of the pie and created a whole new dessert. I love it when mistakes turn out to be the best thing that could have happened!—Meredith Laurence

6 tablespoons butter
5 pears, peeled and quartered
8 tablespoons sugar

1 (9-inch) pastry circle
Whipped topping

Melt butter in 500° oven-safe 9-inch skillet. Arrange pears in a circle in same skillet, placing extra pieces on top in no particular order. Remember to pack them tightly as they will shrink while they cook. Sprinkle sugar over pears and cook over medium-high heat, swirling pears around carefully, until sugar starts to brown, 15–20 minutes. Be careful to avoid burning. Allow to cool.

Preheat oven to 400°. Fit pastry crust over pears and tuck edges down around sides of pears, inside pan. Vent pastry with a knife. Bake in preheated oven 30 minutes, or until pastry is nicely browned. Allow to cool slightly. Drain any liquid that may be in the pan. When you are ready to invert the tart onto a serving plate, heat it briefly on the stovetop. Serve with whipped topping.

skillet

Peachy Turnovers

1½ tablespoons cornstarch
1 cup sugar
1 teaspoon cinnamon

1 (29-ounce) can sliced
   peaches, undrained
2 teaspoons lemon juice

Combine cornstarch with sugar and cinnamon in a 2½-quart saucepan. Add peaches with juice and lemon juice. Cook over medium heat until thickened. Cool.

PASTRY:

1 cup plus 2 tablespoons
   shortening
3 cups flour
1 egg, beaten
7 tablespoons ice water

1 teaspoon salt
1 teaspoon vinegar
Oil for frying
Powdered sugar (optional)

Cut shortening into flour. Combine egg, water, salt, and vinegar in a 4-cup measure. Pour into flour mixture and blend till mixed. Pinch 1½-inch-round pieces of dough and roll out on floured board. Cut out, using a saucer as a guide. Put 1 tablespoon peach mixture on dough. Wet edges of dough with iced water. Fold dough over peach mixture and seal by pressing a floured fork around edges.

Fry in 1–2 inches of oil in deep fryer or electric skillet on highest setting. Cook until golden brown, turning once. Drain on paper towels. Sprinkle with powdered sugar, or glaze with a mixture of powdered sugar and water, if desired. Makes 24 turnovers.

saucepan

electric deep
fryer

ALTERNATE:
electric skillet

electric
stockpot

mixing bowl

Bits-O-Brickle
Kettle Dessert

**6 medium-size crisp tart
  apples
1 teaspoon ground cinnamon
½ cup quick-cooking
  rolled oats
⅓ cup packed brown sugar**

**½ cup all-purpose flour
½ cup cold butter, cut into
  small pieces
½ cup chopped walnuts
½ cup toffee bits
Ice cream (optional)**

Lightly coat 4-quart electric stockpot with oil. Peel apples, if
desired, and cut into ½-inch-thick slices. Mix apples with cinnamon to coat. Place in cooker.

In mixing bowl, mix oats, brown sugar, flour, and butter with
pastry blender or fork until crumbly. Stir in walnuts and toffee
bits. Sprinkle crumb mixture evenly over apples. Cover; cook
on SIMMER 2½–3 hours. Serve with ice cream, if desired.

Variation: May substitute fresh peaches or pears for apples.

*While all kids
enjoyed eating,
Bob's daughter,
Rebecca, wasn't
always enthusiastic
about cooking.*

Delicious Cream Puffs

These are great on a dessert buffet table with simple cookies and mints. I made these for a rehearsal dinner at my house . . . I had to keep refilling the tray!—Gwen McKee

PASTRY SHELLS:

1 cup water
½ cup butter

1 cup flour
4 eggs

In saucepan, heat water and butter to a rolling boil, then stir in flour. Over low heat, stir vigorously for about a minute. Mixture will form into a ball. Remove from heat. Beat in eggs, all at once, until smooth. (You can do this by hand, or in a mixer on low speed.) Drop dough by tablespoonfuls onto ungreased cookie sheet. Bake at 370° for 28 minutes, until puffed and golden. Cool; cut off tops and pull out any filaments of dough. Makes about 32 mini puffs.

CREAM FILLING:

1 (3-ounce) package vanilla
  or chocolate instant
  pudding mix
1 cup milk

1 pint heavy whipping cream
Confectioners' sugar for
  garnish

Combine pudding mix with milk by blending with a mixer on low speed about 2 minutes. Add whipping cream and beat another 2 minutes on medium speed until soft peaks form.

Fill Pastry Shells with Cream Filling. Replace tops on the shells. Dust with confectioners' sugar and refrigerate until served.

VARIATION:
LEMON CURD FILLING:

3 eggs
1 cup sugar

½ stick butter
Juice and zest of 2 lemons

In a double boiler, beat eggs slightly, then cook with remaining ingredients till mixture thickens.

Editor's Extra: A helpful trick is to put the pudding or filling into a zipper bag and cut a small hole in the bottom corner to make a pastry bag. This allows you to distribute the filling into the Pastry Shells with little effort.

saucepan

cookie sheet

mixer

double boiler

roasting pan

Chocolate Trifle

Easy and delicious best describe this trifle, and kids absolutely love it. My nieces and nephews request this creation at family gatherings. — Jenny Repko

1 (18¼-ounce) package chocolate cake mix
1 (3-ounce) package chocolate instant pudding, prepared per directions

2 (16-ounce) cans whipped cream
6 regular Heath bars

Cook cake in 10x14-inch roasting pan according to package directions. Allow to cool. Cut cake into 1-inch squares. Place one layer of cake in a clear serving bowl. Spoon a layer of chocolate pudding over cake squares. Add a layer of whipped cream. Crumble Heath bars, and sprinkle over whipped cream. Repeat layers until the top of the bowl is reached. Keep chilled until served.

Even though Jenny caters for hundreds at a time at her business, she's most at home in her own kitchen cooking up fun meals and desserts.

Swamp Thing

This fun dessert—a variation of my Louisiana Swamp—can be changed to suit different tastes, because you can swap ingredients to have an entirely different flavor! Or mix them up and do some of each. A crowd pleaser, it's delicious all the way to the bottom of the swamp!—Gwen McKee

SWAMP CAKE:
1 (18¼-ounce) white (or coconut or chocolate) cake mix

3 large eggs
1¼ cups water
⅓ cup vegetable oil

Mix all ingredients well; pour into greased large roasting pan or 12x17-inch jellyroll pan. Bake in preheated 325° oven 22–24 minutes, or until cake begins to leave sides of pan.

SWAMP FILLING:
3 (7-ounce) jars marshmallow crème

1 cup flaked coconut, or
1 cup chopped pecans

As soon as cake comes out of oven, dollop marshmallow crème all over top without spreading—it will ooze its way over the cake. Sprinkle coconut or nuts on top, or do half and half, or both!

SWAMP TOPPING:
1 (12-ounce) package white (or chocolate) chips
1 tablespoon butter
1 (16-ounce) can white (or cream cheese or chocolate) frosting

¼ cup water
1 teaspoon almond extract
Strawberries for garnish (optional)

Melt chips and butter in 1-quart saucepan over medium-low heat. Add remaining ingredients and stir till smooth. Pour over filling, but without connecting ribbons, so coconut (or nuts) and marshmallows peep through. Pretty to surround the swamp with a field of strawberries. Now wallow in! Serves a bunch.

roasting pan

ALTERNATE:
jellyroll pan

mixing bowls

toaster oven
baking pan

ALTERNATE:
cake pan

A Bite of Something Sweet

Is it cake, or brownies, or candy? Whatever you want to call it, this fun recipe is a delight when you want just a little bite of something sweet. Great to serve with a cup of coffee or tea, or just plain milk! I also like to make it in a round cake pan and cut into wedges; sprinkle powdered sugar under and on top of it, and add a few cut strawberries alongside. It keeps in the frig, so it's a great make-ahead dessert. —Gwen McKee

1 square semisweet chocolate
¼ cup butter
½ cup sugar
¼ cup flour
1 egg, beaten
Chopped nuts (optional)

In medium bowl, melt chocolate and butter in microwave. Stir sugar and flour into chocolate, then add beaten egg. Stir in a few chopped nuts, if you like. Pour into a greased 7x11-inch toaster oven baking pan. Bake 13–15 minutes at 350°. Cool. Spread Cream Filling over top, and refrigerate about 10 minutes to firm, then drizzle or spread with Chocolate Topping.

CREAM FILLING:
2 tablespoons butter, softened
¼ teaspoon vanilla extract
¼ teaspoon almond extract
1 cup powdered sugar
2 tablespoons cream or milk

Mix all together until creamy.

Variation: Good to substitute amaretto or crème de menthe for extracts, and a little food coloring to match the occasion.

CHOCOLATE TOPPING:
2 squares semisweet
  chocolate
2 tablespoons butter

Melt chocolate and butter in microwave; stir well.

Raisin Bread Chocolate Chip Pudding

This elevates bread pudding to new heights.

IRISH CREAM SAUCE:

⅔ cup milk
1⅓ cups whipping cream
⅔ vanilla bean, split
  lengthwise

4 egg yolks
½ cup sugar
¼ cup Irish cream liqueur

In a 2-quart saucepan, scald milk and cream with vanilla bean. Cream yolks and sugar, and gradually add to scalded mixture. Stir over low heat until sauce is thickened, 5–6 minutes. Do not allow sauce to boil. Remove vanilla bean; stir in liqueur; chill. Serve chilled sauce over warm bread pudding.

saucepan

1 loaf raisin bread, ends and
  crusts removed, cubed
4 eggs, beaten
½ cup brown sugar
1½ cups milk
½ cup heavy whipping cream
⅓ cup Irish cream liqueur

¼ cup dark rum
½ teaspoon vanilla or
  almond extract
1 tablespoon orange zest
½ cup semisweet chocolate
  chips
½ cup raisins

mixing bowls

Put raisin bread in large bowl. In another bowl, cream eggs and sugar. Mix in milk, cream, liqueur, rum, vanilla or almond extract, zest, chocolate chips, and raisins, mixing thoroughly. Pour combined mixture over bread cubes, and mix well. Cover and refrigerate for 30 minutes.

Preheat oven to 350°. Pour bread mixture into a greased 9-inch springform pan; wrap outside with foil. Bake 45–50 minutes, or until center is set. Cool slightly, then remove sides. Serve bread pudding warm, drizzled with chilled Irish Cream Sauce.

springform pan

saucepan

blender

Trinidad Coconut Pudding

This is a dessert that hails from my father's childhood. He grew up in Trinidad and my grandmother made this dessert all the time. —Meredith Laurence

1½ tablespoons unflavored gelatin
½ cup water
2 cups shredded or grated coconut
1 cup hot water
2 (5-ounce) cans evaporated milk

1 (14-ounce) can sweetened condensed milk
1 teaspoon vanilla
Stewed cherries
Toasted shredded coconut

In small saucepan, sprinkle gelatin into ½ cup water, then dissolve over medium heat. Combine coconut and 1 cup hot water in blender. Process about a minute. Pour through a strainer lined with cheesecloth and squeeze out all the liquid. (This is your coconut milk and should yield about a cup of liquid.) Combine coconut milk, evaporated milk, and condensed milk in a mixing bowl. Whisk in vanilla, and slowly add gelatin, whisking while you do so. Pour mixture into molds, and chill in refrigerator until set. Serve with stewed cherries or other stewed fruit and toasted coconut. Serves 8.

Light-As-A-Feather Banana Pudding

Along with all of the other recipes and tips that my mother-in-law Dale Hardy has shared with me, this recipe continues to be an all-time favorite every time I make it. — Holly Hardy

1 pint whipping cream
1 (14-ounce) can sweetened
   condensed milk
1½ cups cold water

1 (3-ounce) package vanilla
   instant pudding
5 small bananas, sliced
1 (12-ounce) box vanilla wafers

First prepare whipping cream by mixing in electric mixer for about 5 minutes on high speed. Next, in a separate large bowl, thoroughly mix milk and water; whisk in pudding mix. Fold in prepared whipping cream. Then layer the pudding, bananas, and wafers in large casserole dish. Serves 8–10.

mixer

mixing bowl;
whisk

Pineapple Bread Pudding

My grandmother declares this an absolute must if you are serving ham for dinner. It complements the meat beautifully. Nice to make ahead, too.
                    —Jenny Repko

¾ cup sugar
¼ cup brown sugar
½ cup butter or margarine
4 eggs

6 slices bread, torn into pieces
1 (20-ounce) can crushed
   pineapple
Cinnamon for sprinkling

Preheat oven to 350°. Mix ingredients in order given above. Put in baking dish. Sprinkle cinnamon on top. Bake for 45 minutes. Serve warm.

stoneware
baking dish

Bowls and casseroles are just what you need for both recipes.

mixing bowls

saucepan

Raspberry Soufflé with Lemon Sauce

This is a fat-free dessert, but can also be sugar-free if you use sugar-free jam. There aren't too many desserts around that can say that!

Butter and sugar (for greasing and dusting molds)
6 ounces seedless raspberry jam
5 egg whites
Pinch of salt

Preheat oven to 350°. Prepare 8 soufflé molds by lightly buttering insides and dusting with sugar for a crunchy exterior. Place jam in a large bowl and break apart any lumps with a fork or whisk. In a separate mixing bowl, whisk egg whites to soft-peak stage, adding salt as you go. Fold whites carefully into jam in batches until jam is evenly distributed. Transfer batter carefully to prepared soufflé molds, piling the mixture high; bake at 350° for 10 minutes or so, until their tops are lightly browned.

LEMON SAUCE:

1 cup water
½ cup sugar
1 tablespoon cornstarch
Pinch of salt
1 tablespoon butter
1 teaspoon lemon zest
2 tablespoons lemon juice
1 lemon peel for garnish
1 pint raspberries for garnish

Bring 1 cup water to a boil in saucepan. Whisk in sugar, cornstarch, and salt, whisking constantly. Simmer until sauce thickens. Remove saucepan from heat, and stir in butter, lemon zest, and lemon juice. Serve warm. Pour sauce over raspberry soufflé, or on an accompanying plate, or serve separately in a small pitcher. Garnish with twisted lemon peel and fresh raspberries.

Molten Chocolate Soufflé

I love making soufflés, mostly because everyone is so impressed since they think soufflés are difficult to make. In reality, they're easy as pie . . . EASIER than pie! Use high-quality chocolate for best results.—*Meredith Laurence*

¼ cup unsalted butter
6 tablespoons all-purpose
  flour
1 cup milk
1½ ounces semisweet or
  bittersweet chocolate
2½ tablespoons cocoa
  powder, divided

1 teaspoon vanilla extract
4 egg yolks, beaten
5 egg whites
6 tablespoons sugar
Pinch of salt
8 (1-inch) squares semisweet
  or bittersweet chocolate
Powdered sugar

saucepan

mixer

Prepare 8 (8-ounce) soufflé molds by buttering insides and wrapping parchment paper or foil collars around them. Preheat a medium saucepan over medium-high heat. Add butter and melt until frothy. Add flour and cook over medium heat, whisking with butter, 2–3 minutes. Remove roux from heat and add milk, whisking vigorously. Bring this mixture back to a boil to thicken.

Melt 1½ ounces chocolate in double boiler or in a bowl over steaming water. Add melted chocolate to saucepan (off the heat), and stir in cocoa powder, vanilla extract, and egg yolks. Mix well and let cool slightly.

Preheat oven to 400°. In a mixer bowl, beat egg whites to soft-peak stage, adding sugar and salt at the end. Fold whites into chocolate base, carefully, and in batches. Transfer batter carefully to soufflé molds, spooning mixture around each 1-inch piece of chocolate. Place molds in a water bath and bake in a 400° oven 30–40 minutes. Dust with powdered sugar immediately and serve. Serves 8.

mini cassoulets

mixing bowls

Use for both recipes.

roasting pan

Use for both recipes.

double boiler

Jeri's Crème Brûlée

You can create unique flavors for this dish with some experimenting. Try rosemary sprigs, lavender, or orange zest instead of vanilla. Make it yours.

—*Jeri Estok*

3 cups heavy cream
½ cup granulated sugar
⅛ teaspoon salt

1 vanilla bean (cut lengthwise),
**   or 1 teaspoon vanilla extract**
9 large egg yolks

Combine cream, sugar, salt, and vanilla in a saucepot. Bring cream mixture to a boil over medium heat. Remove from heat and let steep for 10 minutes. Place egg yolks into stainless steel bowl and whisk. Slowly whisk in warm cream mixture. Pour new mixture into individual mini cassoulet pans.

Preheat oven to 300°. Using a large roasting pan, create a water bath by putting the cassoulet pans into the pan and filling halfway up with warm water. Bake in water bath 25–30 minutes or until there is no jiggle left to the mixture. Remove from water bath and cool in refrigerator until cold. Sprinkle tops with granulated sugar and torch with a butane torch until golden brown.

Chocolate Crème Brûlée

1¼ cups heavy cream
1 vanilla bean
4 ounces dark chocolate,
**   chopped**

4 egg yolks
5 tablespoons sugar, divided

Heat cream and vanilla bean in a double boiler over simmering water 10–15 minutes. Remove vanilla bean and discard, then add chocolate.

Preheat oven to 300°. In a mixing bowl, whisk together egg yolks and 1 tablespoon sugar. Gradually add chocolate mixture, continuously whisking. Place mixture over simmering water until it thickens and coats the back of a spoon, 6–8 minutes. Pour into 4 (4-ounce) custard cups. Place in a baking pan, and add enough warm water to come halfway up the sides of the cups. Bake at 300° for 1 hour or until the custard is set. Remove from water bath and allow to cool, covered, in refrigerator. When cool, sprinkle 1 tablespoon sugar over each, and caramelize the top with a crème brûlée torch. Serves 4.

Espresso Sorbet

When I worked at a restaurant in San Francisco, one of the standard and very popular desserts there was an espresso granita. This is my version of that dessert. —Meredith Laurence

3 tablespoons instant espresso powder
¾ cup sugar
3½ cups water

1 teaspoon vanilla extract
Whipped cream, sweetened, for garnish

Dissolve espresso powder and sugar in water, heating if necessary, but be sure mixture is very well chilled before proceeding with recipe. Add vanilla, and freeze in ice cream maker until set. Serve in a wine glass or champagne flute and garnish with sweetened whipped cream. Serves 4–6.

ice cream maker

Perfect for both recipes.

Cranberry Sorbet

2 cups cranberries
¼ cup orange juice
1 tablespoon orange zest
½ cup water

2½ cups water
1 cup sugar
1 tablespoon lemon juice

Combine first 4 ingredients in a saucepan and cook until berries pop. For a smooth sorbet, push mixture through a strainer at this stage. Otherwise, mash lightly with a fork. Add remaining 3 ingredients and cook, stirring regularly, until mixture is syrupy. Chill very well, then freeze in ice cream maker.

saucepan

ice cream maker

Perfect for all recipes on this page.

blender

Apple Cider Sorbet

2 cups apple cider
1 cup orange juice
¾ cup water

3 tablespoons lemon juice
2–4 tablespoons sugar, to taste

Combine all ingredients, adding sugar to taste. Pour into ice cream maker and freeze.

Blueberry Swirl Frozen Yogurt

2 cups blueberries
¼ cup sugar

1½ cups low-fat vanilla yogurt
2 tablespoons orange juice

Purée blueberries and sugar together in a blender. Pour vanilla yogurt and orange juice into the ice cream maker and start to freeze. After a few minutes, once the vanilla yogurt starts to freeze, pour in blueberry purée, and continue to freeze until set.

Honey Frozen Yogurt

1 quart plain yogurt
1 cup honey

Chopped hazelnuts or pecans (optional)

Combine yogurt and honey in ice cream maker and freeze. Garnish with chopped nuts, if desired.

Raspberry Ice Cream

**1 (10-ounce) package
sweetened frozen
raspberries, partially thawed**

1 cup heavy cream

Crush raspberries slightly with a hammer or other heavy object. Combine heavy cream and raspberries in an ice cream maker and freeze.

ice cream
maker

*Perfect for first two
recipes on this
page.*

Peanut Butter Ice Cream

**2 eggs
½ cup sugar
½ cup chunky peanut butter**

**1½ cups heavy cream
1½ cups milk**

In mixer, lightly beat eggs and sugar together until light and fluffy. Add chunky peanut butter and beat until smooth (except for the peanut chunks). Mix in cream and milk, and blend well. Freeze according to instructions for ice cream maker.

mixer

Holly's Ice Cream Dessert

**12 ice cream sandwiches
1 (12-ounce) jar caramel
topping
1 (16-ounce) container frozen
whipped topping, thawed**

**Optional toppings: milk
chocolate shavings, chopped
nuts, caramel, and/or
chocolate topping**

Place ice cream sandwiches flat side down inside a large baking dish. Pour caramel topping evenly over sandwiches. Spread whipped topping evenly across the caramel. To finish it off, you can add whatever topping you want (I like chocolate shavings). Pour horizontal lines of chocolate and/or caramel topping on top. Then use a knife to make slits through the lines to give it the marbled look. Freeze till time to serve. Serves about 10.

Editor's Extra: Use a vegetable peeler on a chocolate bar to make shavings.

stoneware
baking dish

Orange Royale

This recipe is fit for a queen (or king). Perfect for a hot summer day, garden party, shower, or reception. I have served it at all of the above. Now we can have those wonderful creamsicles we all loved as a child!—Bobbi Cappelli

mixing bowl

baking pan

RASPBERRY SHRUB:

1 quart red raspberries
1 pint ginger ale
1 pint water
¾ cup sugar
Juice of 2 lemons

Put berries in a large bowl and mash to a pulp. Bring water to a boil, then add sugar and lemon juice. Pour over berries. Allow to cool, then press through a colander.

2 (12-ounce) Entenmann's
   Butter Pound Cakes, each
   cut lengthwise into 6 slices
¾ cup Raspberry Shrub
½ gallon plus 1 quart Edy's
   Orange Vanilla Swirl
   Sherbet, softened at room
   temperature for 10 minutes,
   divided
2 (11-ounce) cans Mandarin
   oranges, divided, drained
½ cup Grand Marnier
1 (8-ounce) container frozen
   whipped topping, thawed
1 pint fresh raspberries

Place 6 slices pound cake on the bottom of a 9x13-inch baking pan. Drizzle Raspberry Shrub over pound cake slices. Spread ½ gallon of orange sherbet over the pound cake layer. Top with 1 can Mandarin orange slices, then layer another 6 thin slices of pound cake over orange slices. Press down to level the ice cream layer. Drizzle Grand Marnier over the second layer of pound cake. Top with quart of orange sherbet, then swirl on the whipped topping. Place in freezer overnight to freeze.

Remove from freezer 10–15 minutes prior to serving. Top with fresh raspberries and additional Mandarin oranges. Cut into squares and serve in pretty bowls or glass plates. Drizzle with additional Raspberry Shrub. Serves 20.

Editor's Extra: A shrub is a refreshing drink made from berries or other fresh fruit and served over ice. In Colonial days, it was usually spiked with liquor.

extra help

Remember how many teaspoons are in a tablespoon? Know how much spaghetti to boil for six people? How about cook times for your pressure cooker? When you're in the kitchen, you can always use a little extra help. Here it is.

Pressure Cooker Chart

DISH	REGULAR COOK TIME	PRESSURE COOK TIME
Beef Stock	several hours	60 minutes
Chicken Stock	several hours	30 minutes
Fish Stock	2–3 hours	15 minutes
Vegetable Stock	1–2 hours	10 minutes
Turkey Vegetable Soup	1 hour	12 minutes
Minestrone	1½ hours	20 minutes
Potato Soup	30 minutes	5 minutes
Beef Stew	1–1½ hours	16–20 minutes
Beef Chili	½ hour	16 minutes
Chicken Gumbo	1 hour	9 minutes
Artichokes		6–8 minutes
Asparagus		1½–2 minutes
Broccoli		2–3 minutes
Carrots		4–5 minutes
Corn on the Cob		3–4 minutes
Eggplant		2–3 minutes
Green Beans		2–3 minutes
Sweet Potatoes		4–6 minutes
Zucchini		1 minute
Pot Roast	2–2½ hours	60 minutes
BBQ Spareribs	30–45 minutes	12 minutes
Coq au Vin	45 minutes	9 minutes
Chicken Cacciatore	60 minutes	9 Minutes

Convection Cooking

A convection oven is one that has elements that heat the air, but also a fan that circulates that hot air. This creates more energy, and cooks foods faster and more evenly, giving you crispy exteriors, juicy interiors, and great browning.

Simply reduce the temperature 25° from what your recipe calls for, and expect the foods to be done in less time. For instance, cookies that take eight minutes might be done in six minutes. (Remember to use baking pans with low sides, to take advantage of the convection benefit.)

Equivalents

Apple: 1 medium = 1 cup chopped

Banana: 1 medium = 1/3 cup

Berries: 1 pint = 1 3/4 cups

Bread: 1 slice = 1/2 cup soft crumbs = 1/4 cup fine, dry crumbs

Broth, beef or chicken: 1 cup = 1 bouillon cube dissolved in 1 cup boiling water

Butter: 1 stick = 1/4 pound = 1/2 cup

Cabbage: 2 pounds = 9 cups shredded or 5 cups cooked

Cheese, grated: 1 pound = 4 cups; 8 ounces = 2 cups

Chicken: 1 large boned breast = 2 cups cooked meat

Crabmeat, fresh: 1 pound = 3 cups

Chocolate: 1 square or 1 ounce = 2 tablespoons grated

Coconut: 3 1/2-ounce can = 1 1/3 cups

Cool Whip: 8 ounces = 3 cups

Crackers, saltine: 23 = 1 cup crushed

Crackers, graham: 15 = 1 cup crushed

Cream, heavy: 1 cup = 2–2 1/2 cups whipped

Egg whites: 8–10 = 1 cup

Eggs: 4–5 = 1 cup

Evaporated milk: 5 1/3-ounce can = 2/3 cup; 13-ounce can = 1 1/4 cups

Flour: 1 pound = 4 1/2 cups

Flour, self-rising: 1 cup = 1 cup all-purpose + 1 1/2 teaspoons baking powder + 1/2 teaspoon salt

Garlic powder: 1/8 teaspoon = 1 average clove

Ginger root: 1 teaspoon = 3/4 teaspoon ground

Herbs, fresh: 1 tablespoon = 1 teaspoon dried

Lemon: 1 medium = 3 tablespoons juice

Marshmallows: 1/4 pound = 16 large; 1/2 cup mini = 4 large

Mushrooms: 1/4 pound fresh = 1 cup sliced

Mustard, dry: 1 teaspoon = 1 tablespoon prepared

Noodles: 1 pound = 7 cups cooked

Nuts, chopped: 1/4 pound = 1 cup

Onion: 1 medium = 3/4–1 cup chopped = 2 tablespoons dried chopped (flakes)

Orange: 3–4 medium = 1 cup juice

Pecans: 1 pound shelled = 4 cups

Potatoes: 1 pound = 3 medium

Rice: 1 cup = 3 cups cooked

Spaghetti: 1 pound uncooked = 5 cups cooked

Spinach, fresh: 2 cups chopped = 1 (10-ounce) package frozen chopped

Sugar, brown: 1 pound = 2 1/2 cups

Sugar, powdered: 1 pound = 3 1/2 cups

Sugar, white: 1 pound = 2 1/4 cups

Vanilla wafers: 22 = 1 cup fine crumbs

Whole milk: 1 cup = 1/2 cup evaporated + 1/2 cup water

Substitutions

1 slice cooked **bacon** = 1 tablespoon bacon bits

1 cup **buttermilk** = 1 cup plain yogurt; or 1 tablespoon lemon juice or vinegar + plain milk to make 1 cup

1 cup sifted **cake flour** = $7/8$ cup sifted all-purpose flour

1 ounce **unsweetened chocolate** = 3 tablespoons cocoa + 1 tablespoon butter or margarine

1 ounce **semisweet chocolate** = 3 tablespoons cocoa + 1 tablespoon butter or margarine + 3 tablespoons sugar

1 tablespoon **cornstarch** = 2 tablespoons flour (for thickening)

1 cup **heavy cream** (for cooking, not whipping) = $1/3$ cup butter + $3/4$ cup milk

1 cup **sour cream** = $1/3$ cup milk + $1/3$ cup butter; or 1 cup plain yogurt

1 cup **tartar sauce** = 6 tablespoons mayonnaise or salad dressing + 2 tablespoons pickle relish

1 cup **tomato juice** = $1/2$ cup tomato sauce + $1/2$ cup water

1 cup **vegetable oil** = $1/2$ pound (2 sticks) butter

1 cup **whipping cream**, whipped = 6–8 ounces Cool Whip

1 cup **whole milk** = $1/2$ cup evaporated milk + $1/2$ cup water

Measurements

3 teaspoons = 1 tablespoon

1 tablespoon = $1/2$ fluid ounce

2 tablespoons = $1/8$ cup

3 tablespoons = 1 jigger

4 tablespoons = $1/4$ cup

8 tablespoons = $1/2$ cup or 4 ounces

12 tablespoons = $3/4$ cup

16 tablespoons = 1 cup

$3/8$ cup = $1/4$ cup + 2 tablespoons

$5/8$ cup = $1/2$ cup + 2 tablespoons

$7/8$ cup = $3/4$ cup + 2 tablespoons

$1/2$ cup = 4 fluid ounces

1 cup = $1/2$ pint or 8 fluid ounces

2 cups = 1 pint or 16 fluid ounces

1 pint, liquid = 2 cups or 16 fluid ounces

1 quart, liquid = 2 pints or 4 cups

1 gallon, liquid = 4 quarts or 8 pints or 16 cups

Pan Sizes for Baking

4 cups will fit into
- 8-inch round cake pan
- 9-inch round pie pan
- 9-inch pie pan
- 4 x 8 x 2¾-inch loaf pan (small)

5 cups will fit into
- 7 x 11 x 1¾-inch pan
- 10-inch pie pan

6 cups will fit into
- 8 x 8 x 2-inch square pan
- 10 x 10 x 2-inch casserole
- 5 x 9 x 3¼-inch loaf pan (large)

8 cups will fit into
- 9 x 9 x 2¼-inch casserole
- 7½ x 11¾ x 2-inch pan

12 cups will fit into
- 8½ x 13½ x 2½-inch glass dish
- 9 x 13 x 2-inch pan

Greasing Bakeware

Although the nonstick surface of cook's essentials bakeware is excellent, it is always a good idea to grease your pans before using them. Be sure to use butter or vegetable oil or shortening, however, rather than a commercial spray. Sprays actually make cook's essentials pans less nonstick and can create a sticky build-up on your bakeware. Butter, on the other hand, contributes to browning and adds great flavor to your finished products.

Oven-to-Crockpot

15–30 minutes (oven) = 1½–2½ hours on HIGH or 4–6 hours on LOW

35–45 minutes (oven) = 2–3 hours on HIGH or 6–8 hours on LOW

50 minutes–3 hours (oven) = 4–5 hours on HIGH or 8–10 hours on LOW

Square Skillet with Press

One of our favorite pans is the skillet with the press. A lot of foods cook better under the press. Here are some of our favorite techniques.

Frying bacon: Simply place slices of bacon in the accompanying skillet and place the press on top. Turn stove to medium heat and allow to cook for approximately 10 minutes. You do not need to turn the bacon. It will eventually cook evenly on both sides. When the bacon is done to your desired crispness, hold the press with your off hand and pour off the excess grease. You will be left with perfectly crisp bacon with most of the fat rendered away.

Grilled sandwiches with cheese: Here is how to apply the press to make evenly browned grilled cheese sandwiches with molten cheese inside. Assemble your sandwich with your favorite cheese and add any other desired ingredients such as bacon or ham. Butter both outsides of the bread and place the sandwiches in accompanying skillet. Turn the stove to medium heat, and grill until evenly browned on one side, turn over with a spatula, then place the press on top of the sandwiches. In just a couple of minutes, the second side will be brown and the press will have helped melt the cheese for perfectly hot, evenly browned sandwiches.

Homemade hamburgers: Hate the way homemade hamburgers shrivel up into round balls? Use the press to keep them perfectly shaped. Simply form the hamburgers into the shape and size you desire; place them in accompanying skillet with the press on top. Cook until brown on one side, then flip them over, put the press back on top, and finish cooking on the second side. When cooked to your desired doneness, hold the press with your off hand and pour off the excess grease. Voila! Perfectly shaped and sized hamburgers.

Pork, chicken, beef, and veal cutlets: Want perfectly browned thinly sliced meats that never curl up? Use the press. Preheat your accompanying skillet to medium heat. You may use oil if you desire. Add your breaded or un-breaded cutlets and place the press on top. Quickly brown on the down side, then flip over and replace the press. No more curl.

product index

Wondering what to cook it in? Which pot fits the dish? Here are our suggestions for pots, pans, and utensils we like to use; however, we encourage you to find other solutions. Mix and match the very best recipes in the very best equipment. This index serves as your guide.

This product index allows you to search for recipes that use many of your cook's essentials products; however it does not include all of the products included in this book. Please refer to the recipe index on page 271 for a compete listing of the recipes.

This product index allows you to search for recipes that use many of your cook's essentials products; however it does not include all of the products included in this book. Please refer to the recipe index on page 271 for a compete listing of the recipes.

This product index allows you to search for recipes that use many of your cook's essentials products; however it does not include all of the products included in this book. Please refer to the recipe index on page 271 for a compete listing of the recipes.

recipe index

Where can you find the best recipes? They're all right here! You'll find them listed alphabetically by title, by category, and by main ingredients.

About the Authors

Cookbook editors Gwen McKee and Barbara Moseley have been best friends for over thirty years. Having met on the golf course, they now live four houses apart . . . on a golf course in Brandon, Mississippi. They developed the BEST OF THE BEST STATE COOKBOOK SERIES in 1982, and in 2004, after completing BEST OF THE BEST COOKBOOKS from every state, they were finally able to say, "We did it!" Now they have started over with brand new cookbooks from states they first finished. Suffice to say, they love what they do. They celebrate ten years with QVC in 2007, a relationship they treasure. "We feel so much a part of the QVC family, and love sharing cherished recipes with QVC viewers."

Bob Warden has over thirty-five years experience as a chef, restaurateur, hotel executive, housewares designer, and cooking show host. When Bob first started at QVC, he appeared only once a month or so for the first six months. Within a year he was averaging over forty appearances a month. Meredith Laurence joined his team five years ago and took up about a third of the load. Last year Jenny Repko and Lisa Brady joined the team when he started Technique. The team now averages over seventy-five appearances a month with all of the cook's essentials and Technique products.

Bob and his associates, Eric Theiss and Meredith Laurence, work with the QVC merchant team to design all of the cook's essentials and Technique products, which are only available on QVC. He, his on-air team, and the food stylists who work behind the scenes are delighted to share the BEST OF THE BEST of their favorite family and professional recipes.

Good cookin' and big hugs from Bob and Gwen.